STUDY GUIDE

WFT

Corporations, Partnerships, Estates & Trusts

2000 Edition

William H. Hoffman, Jr.
J.D., Ph.D., C.P.A.
University of Houston

James E. Smith
Ph.D., C.P.A.
College of William and Mary

Eugene Willis
Ph.D., C.P.A.
University of Illinois at Urbana

William A. Raabe
Ph.D., C.P.A.
Samford University

David M. Maloney
Ph.D., C.P.A.
University of Virginia

Prepared by
Paul O'Brien
Governors State University

South-Western College Publishing
an International Thomson Publishing company ITP®

Cincinnati • Albany • Boston • Detroit • Johannesburg • London • Madrid • Melbourne • Mexico City
New York • Pacific Grove • San Francisco • Scottsdale • Singapore • Tokyo • Toronto

Accounting Team Director: Richard K. Lindgren
Acquisitions Editor: Maureen Riopelle
Developmental Editor: Esther Craig
Production Editor: Rebecca Glaab
Marketing Manager: Jennifer Codner
Manufacturing Coordinator: Doug Wilke

Copyright © 2000
by SOUTH-WESTERN COLLEGE PUBLISHING
Cincinnati, Ohio

ALL RIGHTS RESERVED
The text of this publication, or any part thereof, may not be reproduced or transmitted in any form or by any means, electronic or mechanical, including photocopying, recording, storage in an information retrieval system, or otherwise, without prior written permission of the publisher.

ISBN: 0-324-01260-8

1 2 3 4 5 6 7 GP 5 4 3 2 1 0 9

Printed in the United States of America

I(T)P®

International Thomson Publishing
South-Western College Publishing is an ITP Company.
The ITP trademark is used under license.

Contents

Chapter 1	Understanding and Working with the Federal Tax Law	1-1
Chapter 2	Corporations: Introduction, Operating Rules and Related Corporations	2-1
Chapter 3	Corporations: Organization and Capital Structure	3-1
Chapter 4	Corporations: Earnings & Profits and Dividend Distributions	4-1
Chapter 5	Corporations: Redemptions and Liquidations	5-1
Chapter 6	Alternative Minimum Tax and Certain Penalty Taxes Imposed on Corporations	6-1
Chapter 7	Corporations: Reorganizations	7-1
Chapter 8	Consolidated Tax Returns	8-1
Chapter 9	Taxation of International Transactions	9-1
Chapter 10	Partnerships: Formation, Operations, and Basis	10-1
Chapter 11	Partnerships: Distributions, Transfer of Interests, and Terminations	11-1
Chapter 12	S Corporations	12-1
Chapter 13	Comparative Forms of Doing Business	13-1
Chapter 14	Exempt Entities	14-1
Chapter 15	Multistate Corporate Taxation	15-1
Chapter 16	Tax Administration and Practice	16-1
Chapter 17	The Federal Gift and Estate Taxes	17-1
Chapter 18	Family Tax Planning	18-1
Chapter 19	Income Taxation of Trusts and Estates	19-1

To the Student

This Study Guide has been designed to be used as a supplement to the 2000 Annual Edition of *West's Federal Taxation: Corporations, Partnerships, Estates, and Trusts*. The purpose of this Study Guide is to aid you in mastering the textbook material, not to replace it.

Each Study Guide chapter contains:

- A list describing the Learning Objectives.

- A list of Key Terms discussed in the text chapter.

- A review, in outline form, of major points covered in the text.

- Test questions and solutions.

In addition, flowcharts describing the application of particular Code sections appear in various chapters. Problems covering corporate, partnership and S corporation tax return preparation have been inserted at the end of Chapters 3, 11, and 12 respectively.

Though no study technique is equally effective for all students, I suggest that you first review the list of Key Terms, read the textbook chapter, then review the Outline in the Study Guide.

My thanks to Marge Kessler for her assistance in updating this Study Guide.

Paul O'Brien
March, 1999

CHAPTER 1

UNDERSTANDING AND WORKING WITH THE FEDERAL TAX LAW

LEARNING OBJECTIVES

After completing Chapter 1, you should be able to:

1. Realize the importance of revenue needs as an objective of Federal tax law.

2. Appreciate the influence of economic, social, equity, and political considerations on the development of the tax law.

3. Understand how the IRS, as the protector of the revenue, has affected tax law.

4. Recognize the role of the courts in interpreting and shaping tax law.

5. Identify tax law sources -- statutory, administrative, and judicial.

6. Locate tax law sources.

7. Assess the validity and weight of tax law sources.

8. Make use of various tax planning procedures.

9. Have an awareness of computer-assisted tax research.

KEY TERMS

Acquiescence	Determination letters	Revenue neutral
Arm's length concept	Indexation	Revenue Procedures
Business purposes concept	Letter rulings	Revenue Rulings
Certiorari	Nonacquiescence	Tax benefit rule
Continuity of interest concept	Proposed Regulations	Temporary Regulations
		Wherewithal to pay

OUTLINE

I. THE WHYS OF THE TAX LAW

    A. Revenue Needs
1. The major objective of the Federal tax law is raising revenue to absorb the cost of government operations.
2. In recent years, budget deficit considerations have emphasized the concept of revenue neutrality.
3. Revenue neutrality neither reduces nor increases the deficit, the net revenue raised remains the same.

    B. Economic Considerations
1. Control of the economy
   a. capital outlays for business property is
      1. encouraged through shorter asset lives and accelerated methods of depreciation.
      2. discouraged through longer asset lives and slower methods of depreciation.
   b. spending is promoted by lower tax rates.
2. Encouragement of certain activities
   a. technological progress is encouraged by favorable tax provisions concerning the treatment of
      1. research and development expenditures.
      2. inventors and patents.
   b. a healthy environment is encouraged through amortization of pollution control facilities.
   c. low income rental housing is encouraged through tax credits.
   d. exports are encouraged through foreign sales corporations.
3. Encouragement of certain industries
   a. farmers are allowed elections to
      1. expense certain soil and water conservation expenditures.
      2. defer gain recognition on crop insurance proceeds.
   b. extractors of gas, oil and some minerals are allowed to use percentage depletion and may expense rather than capitalize some exploration costs.
4. Encouragement of small business
   a. ordinary loss treatment allowed on certain small business corporation's stock encourages investments.
   b. the S corporation election allow the corporation to pass through profits and losses to shareholders without a corporate level income tax.
   c. provisions for corporate reorganizations allow corporations to combine without adverse tax consequences.

C. Social Considerations
   1. Nontaxability of some employer sponsored insurance coverage encourages private sector financial support for employees and their families in the event of an employee's illness, injury, or death.
   2. Deferred taxability of private retirement plans encourages saving to supplement social security benefits in post-employment years.
   3. Qualified charitable contribution deductions encourages private sector support for socially desirable programs.
   4. Child and dependent care tax credits encourages taxpayers to work.
   5. Educational credits and student loan interest deductions encourage higher educational achievements.

D. Equity Considerations
   1. To alleviate the effect of multiple taxation
      a. deductions are allowed for state and local income taxes.
      b. credits or deductions are allowed for foreign income taxes paid.
      c. corporations are allowed a deduction for certain dividends received.
   2. The wherewithal to pay concept allows deferral of gain recognition in specific situations where a taxpayer's economic positions has not significantly changed.
   3. To mitigate the effect of annual accounting periods
      a. provisions allow the carryback and carryover of net operating and capital losses.
      b. gain on installment sales is recognized over the payout period.

E. Political Considerations
   1. Special interest legislation is an inevitable product of our political system; certain groups influence Congress to promote the enactment of laws providing special tax treatment for their particular business or interest.
   2. Political expediency refers to tax provisions developed in response to popular opinion at the time of enactment.
   3. State and local influences on Federal tax law developed in response to disparities in Federal income tax treatment based on state of residence.

F. Influence of the Internal Revenue Service
   1. The IRS as protector of the revenue has been instrumental in securing passage of much legislation designed to close tax loopholes.
   2. Administrative feasibility of the tax laws is aided by provisions which place taxpayers on a pay-as-you-go basis, and impose interest and penalties on taxpayers for noncompliance.

G. Influence of the Courts
   1. Judicial concepts relating to tax law serve as guides in applying various tax provisions.

2. Judicial influence on statutory provisions came into being as a result of certain key court decisions.

II. WORKING WITH THE TAX LAW - TAX SOURCES

   A. Statutory Sources of the Tax Law
      1. Origin of the Internal Revenue Code
         a. The Internal Revenue Code of 1939 arranged all Federal tax provisions enacted by Congress prior to that time in a separate part of the Federal statutes.
         b. The Internal Revenue Code of 1954 was a revision of the 1939 Code.
         c. The Internal Revenue Code of 1986 adds to, deletes and amends the 1954 Code.
         d. Statutory amendments to the tax law, such as the Internal Revenue Service Restructuring and Reform Act of 1998, are integrated into the existing Code.
      2. The Legislative Process
         a. tax legislation generally originates in the House of Representatives
            1. considered by the House Ways and Means Committee
            2. if accepted, referred to entire House for a vote
            3. if approved, referred to Senate Finance Committee
            4. if accepted, referred to entire Senate for a vote
            5. if approved, referred to the President
            6. if accepted, the bill becomes law.
         b. tax bills may originate in the Senate as riders to other legislation.
         c. when the House and Senate versions of a bill differ, the Joint Conference Committee attempts to resolve the differences.

   B. Administrative Sources of the Tax Law
      1. Treasury Department Regulations
         a. provide taxpayers with guidance on the meaning and application of the Code.
         b. new Regulations are usually issued in proposed form before finalization to permit comment from taxpayers.
         c. Temporary Regulations are issued when immediate guidance is critical.
         d. Temporary Regulations are simultaneously issued as Proposed Regulations and automatically expire within three years.
         e. Final Regulations are issued as Treasury Decisions.

2. Revenue Rulings and Revenue Procedures
    a. Revenue Rulings provide interpretation of the tax law as it applies to a particular set of circumstances.
    b. Revenue Procedures deal with the internal management practices and procedures of the IRS.
3. Other Administrative Pronouncements
    a. Treasury Decisions are issued to make known Final Regulations, to change existing Regulations, or to announce the Government's position on selected court decisions.
    b. Technical Information Releases are issued to announce the publication of various IRS pronouncements.
    c. Letter rulings are issued, upon a taxpayer's request, to describe how a proposed transaction will be treated for tax purposes.
        1. letter rulings generally apply only to the requesting taxpayer.
        2. the issuance of letter rulings is limited to restricted, preannounced areas.
    d. Technical advice memoranda are issued in response to IRS personnel during audits and give the IRS's determination of an issue.
    e. Determination letters are issued at the request of taxpayers to provide guidance concerning the tax laws applicable to a completed transaction.

C. Judicial Sources of the Tax Law
    1. The judicial process
        a. if no satisfactory settlement has been reached with the IRS, the dispute can be taken to Federal court.
        b. the case is first considered by a court of original jurisdiction.
            1. Federal District Court
            2. U.S. Court of Federal Claims
            3. Tax Court
            4. Small Cases Division of the Tax Court
        c. any appeal is taken to the appropriate appellate court.
            1. Court of Appeals of appropriate jurisdiction
            2. Court of Appeals for the Federal Circuit
            3. Supreme Court
    2. Judicial Decisions
        a. under the doctrine of stare decisis, each case has precedential value for future cases having the same controlling set of facts.
        b. The U.S. Tax Court issues two types of decisions:
            1. Regular decisions involve issues not previously resolved by the Court.

2. Memorandum decisions involve application of already established principles of law.
c. if the IRS loses in a decision, it usually indicates agreement: acquiescence, or disagreement: nonacquiescence.

III. WORKING WITH THE TAX LAW - TAX RESEARCH

A. Identify the Problem
1. Gather all of the facts that might have a bearing on the problem.
2. Refine the problem and determine the tax consequences of each possibility.

B. Locate the Appropriate Tax Law Sources - be sure your information is up to date.

C. Assess the Validity of Tax Law Sources
1. Assess the relevance of the tax law source in light of the facts and circumstances of the problem at hand.
2. Assess the weight of the tax law source in light of the facts and circumstances of the problem at hand.
3. Different sources have varying degrees of authority.

D. Arrive at the Solution or at Alternative Solutions

E. Communicate Tax Research
1. Present a clear statement of the issue.
2. Provide a short review of the factual pattern that raised the issue.
3. Provide a review of the pertinent tax law sources.
4. Describe any assumptions made in arriving at the solution.
5. State the recommended solution and the reasoning to support it.
6. List the references consulted.

IV. WORKING WITH THE TAX LAW - TAX PLANNING

A. The primary purpose of the effective tax planning is to reduce the taxpayer's total tax bill.

B. Minimization of tax payments must
1. Be consistent with the taxpayer's legitimate business goals.
2. Consider the impact of a particular action over time, not just the current year.

C. Tax Avoidance minimizes tax liabilities through legal means; tax evasion implies the use of subterfuge and fraud to minimize taxes.

TEST FOR SELF-EVALUATION

True or False

T F 1. Revenue Procedures are official IRS statements of procedure that either affect the rights or duties of taxpayers or other members of the public, or concern matters that are considered to be matters of public knowledge. (IRS 97 4A-7)

T F 2. Nonacquiescence by the Commissioner of Internal Revenue to an adverse decision in a regular Tax Court case means the Internal Revenue Service will NOT accept the decision and will NOT follow it in cases involving similar facts. (IRS 96 4A-27)

T F 3. A Memorandum Decision is a report of a Tax Court decision thought to be of little value as a precedent because the issue has been decided many times. (IRS 96 4A-28)

T F 4. An income tax case NOT resolved at an appeals conference can proceed to the United States Tax Court WITHOUT the taxpayer paying the disputed tax, but generally, the United States District Court and United States Claims Court hear tax cases ONLY after the tax is paid and a claim for credit or refund is filed by the taxpayer and is rejected by the IRS or the IRS has not acted on the taxpayer's claim within six months from the date of filing the claim for refund. (IRS 95 4A-11)

T F 5. All courts except the Tax Court are bound by legislative regulations. (IRS 95 4A-24)

T F 6. Proposed regulations automatically replace the temporary regulations. (IRS 95 4A-25)

T F 7. Revenue rulings are the published conclusions of the IRS concerning the application of tax law to a specific set of facts. (IRS 95 4A-26)

T F 8. The courts are NOT bound by Treasury Regulations. (IRS 94 4A-27)

T F 9. Decisions of the courts other than the Supreme Court are binding on the Commissioner of Internal Revenue ONLY for the particular taxpayer and for the years litigated. (IRS 94 4A-28)

T F 10. If the Supreme Court determines that various lower courts are deciding a tax issue in an inconsistent manner, it may review a decision and resolve the contradiction. (IRS 94 4A-29)

Fill in the Blanks

1. _____, _____, _____, and _____ play a significant role in the development of Federal tax law.

2. _____, _____ and _____ are examples of political considerations.

3. The courts have influenced and formulated tax law through the two techniques of _____ and _____.

4. If the IRS loses in a Regular decision of the Tax Court, it will indicate _____ or _____ with the result reached by the Court.

5. Appeal to the U.S. Supreme Court is by _____.

6. _____ are issued at the request of taxpayers and provide guidance concerning the application of tax law to completed transactions.

7. Tax reform legislation which does not change net revenues raised is _____.

8. The _____ concept applies to situations in which a taxpayer's economic position has not significantly changed; gain recognition is postponed.

9. _____ is the method whereby one determines the best solution or series of solutions to a particular problem with tax ramifications.

10. _____ is the minimization of tax payments through legal means.

Multiple Choice

_____ 1. Which of the following statements is correct with respect to the small tax case procedures of the United States Tax Court? (IRS 97 4B-67)

    a. The amount in the case must be $5,000 or less for any one tax year or period.
    b. The taxpayer can request small case procedures without any approval from the Tax Court.
    c. Small case procedures require the taxpayer and the IRS to submit briefs presenting their positions on the issues.
    d. The Tax Court decision is final and you CANNOT appeal.

_____ 2. With respect to the small case procedure in the Tax Court, all of the following statements are correct except: (IRS 95 4B-70)

    a. Within 90 days of receiving a statutory notice of deficiency, the taxpayer must pay a filing fee and file a petition form with the Tax Court in Washington, DC.

b. The total disputed deficiency (tax and penalties) for ALL tax years at issue must be $10,000 or less.
c. The decision of the Tax Court CANNOT be appealed to another court and CANNOT be used as a precedent for any other case.
d. The proceedings are conducted in accordance with such rules of evidence and procedures as the Tax Court may prescribe.

_____ 3. With regard to revenue rulings and revenue procedures, all of the following statements are are correct except: (IRS 96 4B-69)

a. A revenue ruling is a published official interpretation of tax law by the IRS that sets forth the conclusion of the IRS on how the tax law is applied to an entire set of facts.
b. Revenue rulings have the force and effect of Treasury Regulations.
c. A revenue procedure is a published official statement of procedure that either affects the rights or duties of taxpayers or other members of the public under the Internal Revenue Code and related statutes and regulations or, if not necessarily affecting the rights and duties of the public, should be a matter of public knowledge.
d. Revenue procedures are directive and NOT mandatory so that a taxpayer has no vested right to the benefit of the procedures when the IRS deviates from its internal rules.

_____ 4. Which of the following statements BEST describes the applicability of a constitutionally valid Internal Revenue Code section on the various courts? (IRS 95 4B-70)

a. Only the Supreme Court is NOT bound to follow the code section. All other courts are bound to the Code section.
b. Only the Tax Court is bound to the Code section, all other courts may waiver from the Code section.
c. Only District, Claims and Appellate Courts are bound by the Code section, the Supreme and Tax Courts may waiver from it.
d. All courts are bound by the Code section.

_____ 5. All of the following statements with respect to classes of regulations are CORRECT except: (IRS 95 4B-71)

a. All regulations are written by the Office of the Chief Counsel, IRS, and approved by the Secretary of the Treasury.
b. Public hearings are NOT held on temporary regulations.
c. Although IRS employees are bound by the regulations, the courts are NOT.
d. Public hearings are NOT held on proposed regulations.

_____ 6. Which of the following is NOT one of the three classes of Treasury Regulations? (IRS 95 4B-72)

   a. Temporary
   b. Judicial
   c. Final
   d. Proposed

_____ 7. Which of the following statements is FALSE? (IRS 95 4B-73)

   a. The Tax Court will issue either a regular report or a memorandum decision depending upon the issues involved and the relative value of the decision being made.
   b. The Commissioner of Internal Revenue does NOT isssue a public acquiescence or nonacquiescence on District or Claims court cases.
   c. Interpretative regulations are issued under the general authority of Internal Revenue Code Section 7805(a) and legislative regulations are issued under the authority of the specific Internal Revenue Code section to which they relate.
   d. The government prints the regular and memorandum Tax Court decisions in bound volumes.

_____ 8. With regard to the small tax case procedures of the United States Tax Court, all of the following statements are correct except: (IRS 94 4B-41)

   a. The amount of tax involved in the case must be $10,000 or less for any one tax year or period.
   b. The taxpayer must request small case procedures and the Tax Court must approve the request.
   c. The taxpayer must pay the tax and file a claim for credit or refund that the IRS rejects.
   d. The Tax Court decision is final and you CANNOT appeal.

_____ 9. With regard to Treasury Regulations, all of the following statements are correct except: (IRS 94 4B-69)

   a. Notices of proposed rulemaking are REQUIRED for proposed regulations and are published in the Federal Register so that interested parties have an opportunity to participate in the rulemaking process.
   b. Until final regulations are issued, temporary regulations have the same force and effect of law as final regulations.
   c. Legislative regulations are those for which the IRS is specifically authorized by the IR Code to provide the details of the meaning and rules for particular Code sections.
   d. Interpretative regulations, which explain the IRS's position on the various sections of the IR Code, are NOT accorded great weight by the courts.

_____ 10. With regard to revenue rulings and revenue procedures, all of the following statements are correct except: (IRS 94 4B-70)

  a. A revenue ruling is a published official interpretation of tax law by the IRS that sets forth the conclusion of the IRS on how the tax law is applied to an entire set of facts.
  b. Revenue rulings have the force and effect of Treasury Regulations.
  c. A revenue procedure is a published official statement of procedure that either affects the rights or duties of taxpayers or other members of the public under the Internal Revenue Code and related statutes and regulations or, if not necessarily affecting the rights and duties of the public, should be a matter of public record.
  d. Revenue procedures are directive and NOT mandatory so that a taxpayer has no vested right to the benefit of the procedures when the IRS deviates from its internal rules.

_____ 11. If a taxpayer with a notice of deficiency wishes his/her case heard by a court before paying the tax, which court would the taxpayer petition? (IRS 94 4B-71)

  a. United States Tax Court
  b. United States Claims Court
  c. United States District Court
  d. United States Court of Appeals

_____ 12. With regard to terminology relating to court decisions, all of the following statements are correct except: (IRS 94 4B-72)

  a. DECISION, the court's formal answer to the principal issue in litigation, has legal sanction and is enforceable by the authority of the court.
  b. DICTUM, a court's statement of opinion on a legal point NOT raised by the facts of the case, is NOT controlling, but may be persuasive to another court deciding the issue dealt with by the dictum.
  c. Acquiescence by the Commissioner of Internal Revenue Service on adverse regular Tax Court decisions, generally means the IRS will follow the Court's decision in cases involving similar facts.
  d. Writ of Certiorari is a petition issued by the lower appellate court to the Supreme Court to hear a case that is NOT subject to obligatory review by the Supreme Court.

SOLUTIONS

True or False

1. T (p. 1-23)
2. T (p. 1-31)
3. T (p. 1-29)
4. T (p. 1-26)
5. F (p. 1-16, 37; no exceptions)
6. F (p. 1-22; temorary regs are simultaneously issued as proposed regs)
7. F (p. 1-22; interpretations not conclusions)
8. T (p. 1-37)
9. T (p. 1-27)
10. T (p. 1-29)

Fill in the Blanks

1. Economic, social, equity and political factors (p. 1-2)
2. Special interest legislation, political expediency, and state and local influences (p. 1-11)
3. Judicial concepts and key decisions (p. 1-14)
4. acquiescence, nonacquiescence (p. 1-31)
5. writ of certiorari (p. 1-28)
6. Determination Letters (p. 1-24)
7. revenue neutral (p. 1-3)
8. wherewithal to pay (p. 1-7)
9. Tax research (p. 1-32)
10. Tax avoidance (p. 1-42)

Multiple Choice

1. d (p. 1-25)
2. b (p. 1-25; $50,000)
3. b (p. 1-22; deal with more restrictive problems)
4. d (p. 1-16)
5. d (p. 1-22)
6. b (p. 1-22)
7. d (p. 1-29, 31, 37)
8. c (p. 1-26)
9. d (p. 1-22, 37)
10. b (p. 1-22)
11. a (p. 1-26)
12. d (p. 1-28, 29)

CHAPTER 2

CORPORATIONS: INTRODUCTION, OPERATING RULES, AND RELATED CORPORATIONS

LEARNING OBJECTIVES

After completing Chapter 2, you should be able to:

1. Summarize the various forms of conducting a business.

2. Compare the taxation of individuals and corporations.

3. Discuss the tax rules unique to corporations.

4. Compute the corporate income tax.

5. Explain the tax rules unique to multiple corporations.

6. Describe the reporting process for corporations.

7. Evaluate corporations for conducting a business.

KEY TERMS

Brother-sister controlled group	Limited liability company	Personal service corporation
C corporation	Limited partnership	Regular corporation
Check-the-box Regulations	Organizational expenditures	Related corporations
Controlled group	Parent-subsidiary controlled group	S corporation
Dividends received deduction	Passive loss	Schedule M-1

OUTLINE

I. TAX TREATMENT OF VARIOUS BUSINESS FORMS

   A. Sole Proprietorships report all business activity on the individual owner's Schedule C, Form 1040.

   B. Partnerships report all of the partnership's business activity on Form 1065 and allocate to each partner their share on Schedule K-1, this information is then transferred to and included in each partner's Form 1040.

   C. S corporations are similar to partnerships, the entity reports its activities on Form 1120S and K-1's are issued to each shareholder and included on their Form 1040.

   D. Regular, C corporations report all business activity on Form 1120. These corporations are taxable entities separate and distinct from their owner, shareholders.

   E. Limited liability companies may be taxed as partnerships. Check-the-box rules permit a domestic entity to elect taxation as a corporation or as a partnership regardless of its corporate or noncorporate characteristics.

II. INCOME TAXATION OF CORPORATIONS

   A. Overview
      1. The gross income of a corporation, including gains and losses from property transactions is determined in much the same manner as it is for individuals.
      2. Business deductions of corporations parallel those of individuals, deductions are allowed for all ordinary and necessary expenses paid or incurred in carrying on a trade or business.

   B. Specific Provisions
      1. Accounting periods and methods
         a. regular corporations may choose a calendar or fiscal tax year.
         b. a Personal Service Corporation must, generally, use a calendar year. A corporation is a PSC if:
            1. the principal activity is the performance of personal services in the fields of: health, law engineering, architecture, accounting, actuarial science, performing arts or consulting;
            2. services are substantially performed by owner-employees;
            3. more than 10% of the value of the corporation's stock is held by owner-employees.

CORPORATIONS: INTRODUCTION, OPERATING RULES, AND RELATED CORPORATIONS 2-3

- c. generally, a regular corporation must use the accrual method of accounting.
- d. the cash method may be used by:
  1. corporations engaged in the trade or business of farming and timber.
  2. corporations having average annual gross receipts of $5 million or less.
  3. qualified PSCs.
  4. S Corporations.

2. Capital gains and losses
   a. net capital gain is fully included in a corporation's taxable income.
   b. capital losses can offset only capital gains.
   c. net capital losses may be carried back 3 years and forward 5 years.
   d. when carried back or forward, all capital losses are treated as short-term.

3. Recapture of depreciation
   a. depreciation recapture for §1245 property is the same for corporations as for individuals.
   b. recapture of 20% of the excess of any amount treated as ordinary income under §1245 over the amount treated as ordinary income under §1250 for corporate sales of depreciable real estate that is §1250 property.

4. Passive losses
   a. closely held C corporations may offset passive losses against active income, but not against portfolio income.
   b. a corporation is closely held if more than 50% of the value of the corporation's outstanding stock is held by 5 or fewer individuals at any time during the tax year.
   c. PSCs cannot offset passive losses against either active income or portfolio income.

5. Charitable contributions
   a. the recipient must be a qualified charitable organization.
   b. an accrual basis corporation may claim the deduction in the year preceding payment if:
      1. the contribution has been authorized by the end of that year, and
      2. the payment is made on or before the 15th day of the 3rd month of the next year.
   c. property contributions
      1. the deduction for long-term capital gain property donated is, generally, fair market value.
      2. the deduction for ordinary income property donated is, generally, limited to its basis.
      3. the flowchart following this chapter outline reviews exceptions for property contributions.

d. a corporate taxpayer's charitable contribution deduction for any one year is limited to 10% of taxable income.
6. Net operating losses may be carried back 2 years and forward 20 years to offset taxable income.
7. Deductions available only to corporations
   a. the dividends received deduction mitigates triple taxation
      1. a corporation may deduct 70, 80 or 100% of the amount of dividends received from domestic corporations.
      2. the percentage of ownership in the payor corporation determines the deductible percentage.
      3. this deduction may be limited by the corporation's taxable income.
   b. organizational expenditures
      1. a corporation may elect to amortize organizational expenditures over a period of 60 months or more.
      2. amortizable expenses include:
         a. legal services incident to organization
         b. necessary accounting services
         c. expenses of temporary directors
         d. expenses of organizational meetings of directors or shareholders
         e. fees paid to the state of incorporation
      3. the expenditures must be incurred before the end of the taxable year in which the corporation begins business.

III. DETERMINING THE CORPORATION INCOME TAX LIABILITY

A. 1998 Corporate Income Tax Rates:

Taxable Income Over---	But Not Over---	Tax Is:	Of the Amount Over---
$ 0	$ 50,000	15%	$ 0
50,000	75,000	7,500 + 25%	50,000
75,000	100,000	13,750 + 34%	75,000
100,000	335,000	22,250 + 39%	100,000
335,000	10,000,000	113,900 + 34%	335,000
10,000,000	15,000,000	3,400,000 + 35%	10,000,000
15,000,000	18,333,333	5,150,000 + 38%	15,000,000
18,333,333	--	35%	0

B. Qualified PSCs are taxed at a flat 35% rate on all taxable income.

C. Corporations are subject to the Alternative Minimum Tax.

D. A controlled group of corporations' taxable income is limited in the tax brackets below 35% to the amount the corporations in the group would have if they were one corporation.

IV. PROCEDURAL MATTERS

A. A corporation, whether or not it has taxable income, must file its return by the 15th day of the 3rd month after the close of its tax year.

B. An automatic extension of six months for filing the corporate return may be requested on Form 7004.

C. Estimated tax payments are required of corporations expecting a tax liability of $500 or more.

V. TAX PLANNING CONSIDERATIONS

A. Tax planning to reduce corporate income taxes should occur before year end.

B. Particular attention should be focused on:
1. Charitable contributions
2. Timing capital gains and losses
3. Net operating losses
4. Dividends received deductions
5. Organizational expenditures
6. Shareholder-employee payment of corporate expense

Section 170-Charitable Contributions

```
┌─────────────────────────────────────┐   No    ┌──────────────────────────────────┐
│ Is recipient a qualified charitable │────────▶│ No deduction allowed for corporate│
│ organization within the meaning of  │         │ or noncorporate taxpayers.        │
│ 170?                                │         └──────────────────────────────────┘
└─────────────────────────────────────┘
              │ Yes
              ▼
┌─────────────────────────────────────┐   No    ┌──────────────────────────────────┐
│ Is the contributor an accrual basis │────────▶│ Deduction is only allowed in the │
│ corporation?                        │         │ year in which the payment is made.│
└─────────────────────────────────────┘         └──────────────────────────────────┘
              │ Yes                                           │
              ▼                                               ▼
┌─────────────────────────────────────┐         ┌──────────────────────────────────┐
│ Deduction may be claimed in the     │         │ Is "ordinary income property"    │
│ year prior to payment if the        │         │ that has appreciated in value    │──No──▶
│ contribution has been authorized by │         │ being donated (i.e. property that│
│ the board of directors by the end   │         │ would not yield long term        │
│ of that year, and is paid on or     │         │ capital gain)?                   │
│ before the 15th day of the third    │         └──────────────────────────────────┘
│ month of the next year.             │                         │ Yes
└─────────────────────────────────────┘                         ▼
                                                  ┌──────────────────────────────────┐
                                          ┌──No───│ Is the distributor a corporate   │
                                          │       │ taxpayer?                        │
                                          ▼       └──────────────────────────────────┘
                              ┌─────────────────────────┐      │ Yes
                              │ Deduction = Adjusted    │      ▼
                              │ Basis of the Property   │    ┌──────────────────────────────────┐
                              │ subject to entity       │    │ Is the property used in a manner │
                              │ limitations             │    │ related to the exempt purpose of │
                              └─────────────────────────┘    │ the donee and used soley for the │
                                                             │ care of the ill, needy, or       │
┌──────────────┐  No   ┌──────────────────────┐              │ infants, or is it used for       │
│ Use deduction│◀──────│ Is the deduction     │              │ reaearch purposes under          │
│ as computed  │       │ greater than (10% x  │              │ specified conditions?            │
│ above        │       │ taxable income)?     │              └──────────────────────────────────┘
└──────────────┘       └──────────────────────┘                           │ Yes
                                   │ Yes                                  ▼
                                   ▼                       ┌──────────────────────────────────┐
               ┌─────────────────────────────────────┐     │ Deduction = Adjusted Basis Plus  │
               │ Deduction is limited to (10% x      │     │ Half of the Appreciation on the  │
               │ taxable income). Excess may be      │     │ Property                         │
               │ carried forward to the five         │     └──────────────────────────────────┘
               │ succeeding tax years. Any carry     │
               │ forward must be added to subsequent │
               │ contributions and will be subject   │
               │ to the 10% limit. In applying the   │
               │ limit, current year's contributions │
               │ must be deducted first, with excess │
               │ deductions from past years deducted │
               │ in order of time.                   │
               └─────────────────────────────────────┘
```

CORPORATIONS: INTRODUCTION, OPERATING RULES, AND RELATED CORPORATIONS

```
                    ┌─────────────────┐   No    ┌─────────────────────┐
  ──────────────────▶│ Is appreciated  │────────▶│ The general rule    │
                    │ long term       │         │ applies:            │
                    │ capital gain    │         │ Deduction = FMV of  │
                    │ property being  │         │ property on date of │
                    │ donated?        │         │ donation            │
                    └────────┬────────┘         └──────────┬──────────┘
                             │ Yes                         │
                             ▼                             │
                    ┌─────────────────┐                    │
                    │ Is              │                    │
                    │ (1) Tangible    │                    │
                    │ personal        │                    │
                    │ property (use   │   No    ┌────────────────────┐
                    │ unrelated to tax│────────▶│ Deduction =        │
                    │ exempt status   │         │ FMV of property    │
                    │ of donee)       │         │ on distribution    │
                    │ Or              │         │ date               │
                    │ (2) Long term   │         └──────────┬─────────┘
                    │ capital gain    │                    │
                    │ property to a   │                    │
                    │ private         │                    │
                    │ foundation      │                    │
                    │ being donated?  │                    │
                    └────────┬────────┘                    │
                             │ Yes                         │
                             │ (either of the above is true)
                             ▼                             ▼
                    ┌─────────────────┐         ┌─────────────────────┐  No   ┌─────────────────┐
                    │ Deduction =     │────────▶│ Is the deduction    │──────▶│ Use deduction as│
                    │ Adjusted Basis  │         │ greater than        │       │ computed above. │
                    │ of the Property │         │ (10% x taxable      │       └─────────────────┘
                    └─────────────────┘         │ income)?            │
                                                └──────────┬──────────┘
                                                           │ Yes
                                                           ▼
                                        ┌───────────────────────────────────────┐
                                        │ Deduction is limited to (10% x        │
                                        │ taxable income). Excess may be        │
                                        │ carried forward to the five           │
                                        │ succeeding tax years. Any carry       │
                                        │ forward must be added to subsequent   │
                                        │ contributions and will be subject to  │
                                        │ the 10% limit. In applying the limit, │
                                        │ current year's contributions must be  │
                                        │ deducted first, with excess           │
                                        │ deductions from past years deducted   │
                                        │ in order of time.                     │
                                        └───────────────────────────────────────┘
```

Section 243 – Dividends Received Deductions

```
┌─────────────────────────────┐
│ Purpose:                    │
│ To Minimize triple taxation │
│ on corporate earnings       │
└─────────────┬───────────────┘
              │
              ▼
┌─────────────────────────────┐   NO    ┌──────────────────────────┐
│ Was the dividend received   ├────────▶│ Deduction NOT allowed    │
│ from a domestic corporation?│         │ §245                     │
└─────────────┬───────────────┘         └──────────────────────────┘
              │ YES
              ▼
┌──────────────────┐  NO  ┌──────────────────────┐  NO  ┌──────────────────┐
│ Is ownership of  ├─────▶│ Is ownership of payor├─────▶│ Is ownership of  │
│ payor less than  │      │ 20% or more and less │      │ payor 80% or     │
│ 20%?             │      │ than 80%?            │      │ more?            │
└────────┬─────────┘      └──────────┬───────────┘      └────────┬─────────┘
         │ YES                       │ YES                       │ YES
         ▼                           ▼                           ▼
┌──────────────────┐      ┌──────────────────────┐      ┌──────────────────────┐
│ Compute deduction│      │ Compute deduction    │      │ Payor is a member of │
│ at 70%           │      │ at 80%               │      │ an affiliated group  │
│                  │      │                      │      │ with recipient       │
└────────┬─────────┘      └──────────┬───────────┘      └────────┬─────────────┘
         │                           │                           │
         │                           │                           ▼
         │                           │                  ┌──────────────────────┐
         │                           │                  │ Deduction is 100% of │
         │                           │                  │ the dividend received│
         │                           │                  └──────────────────────┘
         ▼                           ▼
┌──────────────────────────────────────────────────────┐
│ Compute:                                             │
│ Taxable income of the corporation without regard to  │
│ net operating loss, dividends received deduction,    │
│ and any capital loss carryback to the current year.  │
└─────────────────────┬────────────────────────────────┘
                      │
                      ▼
┌──────────────────────────────────────────┐   YES
│ Does taxable income minus the deduction  ├──────────┐
│ percentage times the dividend received   │          │
│ equal a loss?                            │          │
└─────────────────────┬────────────────────┘          │
                      │ NO                            │
                      ▼                               │
          ┌──────────────────────────┐                │
          │ Is taxable income greater│                │
          │ than dividend received?  │                │
          └──────┬──────────────┬────┘                │
                 │ NO           │ YES                 │
                 ▼              ▼                     ▼
     ┌─────────────────────┐  ┌─────────────────────────┐
     │ Deduction is limited│  │ Deduction is % of       │
     │ to % of taxable     │  │ dividend received       │
     │ income              │  │                         │
     └─────────────────────┘  └─────────────────────────┘
```

TEST FOR SELF-EVALUATION

True or False

T F 1. A professional service organization must be BOTH organized and operated as a corporation to be classified as one. (IRS 97 3A-1)

T F 2. In 1996, CDS, a C corporation, has a net short-term capital gain of $3,000 and a net long-term capital loss of $9,000. The short-term gain offsets some of the long-term loss, leaving a net capital loss of $6,000. CDS treats this $6,000 as a short-term loss when carried back or forward. (IRS 97 3A-15)

T F 3. A corporation will receive an automatic 6-month extension of time for filing its return by submitting an application for extension on Form 7004. The IRS can terminate this extension at any time by mailing a notice of termination to the corporation. (IRS 96 3A-1)

T F 4. Corporation Y, a calendar year corporation, incurred qualifying organizational expenses of $7,000, and started business on January 1, 1995. Corporation Y may elect to deduct the organizational expenses in full in 1995 or treat them as deferred expenses and amortize them over a period of no less than 60 months.
(IRS 96 3A-4)

T F 5. Advertising expenses for the opening of a business of a corporation that has not yet begun its business operations MUST be considered a start-up expense.
(IRS 95 3A-3)

T F 6. In 1993, Rock Corporation incurred a net operating loss and elected to forgo the carryback period. Rock incurred another net operating loss in 1994. Since Rock elected to forgo the carryback period for 1993, it CANNOT carry the 1994 net operating loss back to 1991. (IRS 95 3A-7)

T F 7. Corporation W, a calendar year corporation, incurred organizational expenses of $1,000 and started business on January 1, 1990. It filed its return on March 20, 1991, without an extension. We can automatically amortize some of its organizational expenses in 1990. (IRS 91 3A-4)

T F 8. Generally, the total deduction for dividends received is limited to 70% of the taxable income of a corporation. In figuring this limitation, taxable income is determined without regard to any capital loss carryback to the tax year.
(IRS 90 3A-6)

T F 9. During 1992, a corporation set up a contingent liability on its books to take into account a customer's claim. The claim was NOT settled in 1992. The contingent liability is NOT deductible in determining the corporation's 1992 taxable income but it does REDUCE unappropriated retained earnings and is shown as an adjustment on Schedule M-2 of Form 1120. (IRS 93 3A-7)

T F 10. The component members of a controlled group of corporations are generally limited to one apportionable $50,000 amount and one $25,000 amount (in that order) in each taxable income bracket below 35%. Unless the component members of the controlled group agree to a different allocation, the $50,000 and $25,000 (in that order) amount is to be divided equally among all members.
(IRS 91 3A-11)

T F 11. If a corporation's capital losses from two or more years are carried to the same year, the loss from the earliest year is deducted first. When that loss is completely used up, the loss from the next earliest year is deducted, and so on.
(IRS 91 3A-9)

Fill in the Blanks

1. Corporations are to include the amount of net long-term capital gain in _____ .

2. Corporations may carryback capital losses to the _____ preceding years.

3. Generally charitable contributions of long-term capital gain property are measured at their _____ on the date of their donation.

4. The charitable deduction for "ordinary income property" that has appreciated in value is generally limited to the _____ of the property.

5. For net operating losses of a corporation, the carryback period is _____ years and forward _____ years.

6. A corporation is required to file its tax return on or before the 15th day of the _____ month following the close of its fiscal year.

7. A group of corporations form a _____ if each corporation is a member of either a parent-subsidiary controlled group or a brother-sister controlled group, at least one of the corporations is a _____ of a parent-subsidiary controlled group and the parent corporation is also a member of a _____ .

Multiple Choice

_____ 1. All of the following are considered characteristics of a C corporation except: (IRS 97 3B-21)

   a. Continuity of life.
   b. Free transferability of corporate ownership interests.
   c. Limited liability of shareholders for corporate debts.
   d. A limited number of shareholders.

_____ 2. Rabid Corporation uses a fiscal year ending November 30 and receives an automatic extension of time for filing its tax return for the fiscal year ending November 30, 1996. Including the extension, what is the due date for filing Rabid's tax return (not considering weekends and holidays)? (IRS 97 3B-34)

   a. February 15, 1997
   b. June 30, 1997
   c. July 15, 1997
   d. August 15, 1997

_____ 3. The dividends received deduction (IRS 97 3B-38)

   a. May be claimed by S corporations.
   b. Must exceed the applicable percentage of the recipient shareholder's taxable income.
   c. Is affected by a requirement that the investor corporation must own the investee's stock for a specified minimum holding period.
   d. Is unaffected by the percentage of the investee's stock owned by the investor corporation.

_____ 4. Which of the following statements concerning the charitable contribution deduction by a corporation is CORRECT? (IRS 97 3B-39)

   a. A corporation cannot deduct contributions that exceed 10% of its taxable income.
   b. A corporation can only deduct contributions to charitable organizations if they are made in cash.
   c. A corporation utilizing the accrual basis of accounting must have made the charitable donation by the close of its tax year.
   d. A corporation is not permitted to carry over any charitable contributions that were not deducted in the current year.

_____ 5. With regard to the treatment of capital losses by corporations, other than S corporations, which of the following statements is correct? (IRS 97 3B-40)

a. When a corporation carries a long-term net loss to another tax year, the character is automatically changed to short-term loss.
b. Assuming no capital gains to offset the corporation's capital losses, the maximum deduction is $3,000.
c. A net capital loss may be carried back 3 years and carried forward for up to 15 years.
d. None of the above.

_____ 6. With regard to a controlled corporate group, all of the following statements are CORRECT except: (IRS 97 3B-41)

a. Controlled groups are allowed ONE exemption of up to $40,000 for alternative minimum tax purposes.
b. The controlled group is allowed only ONE set of graduated income tax brackets.
c. The controlled group is allowed a $250,000 accumulated earnings credit for EACH member.
d. The tax benefits of the graduated rate schedule are to be allocated equally among the members of the group unless they all consent to a different apportionment.

_____ 7. The amount required to be paid in estimated tax installments by a corporation is the lesser of 100% of the tax shown on its return for the preceding 12 month tax year (if some tax was reflected), or what percentage of the tax shown on its return for the current year (determined on the basis of actual income or annualized income)? (IRS 97 3B-42)

a. 100 percent
b. 97 percent
c. 95 percent
d. 90 percent

_____ 8. Crock Corporation has a fiscal year beginning September 1 and ending August 31. Crock's estimated tax for the fiscal year beginning September 1, 1996 is $10,000. The first installment of Crock Corporation's estimated tax would be due by: (IRS 97 3B-43)

a. December 1, 1996
b. December 15, 1996
c. January 1, 1997
d. January 15, 1997

CORPORATIONS: INTRODUCTION, OPERATING RULES, AND RELATED CORPORATIONS 2-13

_____ 9. Vagabond Corporation was organized and began active business on January 2, 1996. Vagabond incurred the following expenses in connection with creating the business.

State incorporation fee	2,000
Legal fees for drafting the charter	6,000
Printing costs for stock certificates	1,500
Professional fees for issuance of stock	4,000
Broker's commission on sale of stock	7,000
Expense for temporary directors	5,000
Total	25,000

What is the maximum amount of organizational expense that Vagabond Corporation may deduct on its 1996 income tax return? (IRS 97 3C-58)

a. $2,600
b. $5,100
c. $17,000
d. $25,000

_____ 10. Kappa Corporation owns 20% interest in Sigma Corporation, a domestic corporation. For 1996, Kappa had gross receipts of $390,000, operating expenses of $400,000, and dividend income of $120,000 from Sigma Corporation. The dividends were NOT from debt-financed portfolio stock. What is the amount of Kappa Corporation's dividends received deduction for 1996? (IRS 97 3C-61)

a. $96,000
b. $88,000
c. $84,000
d. $24,000

_____ 11. During 1996, HOOS Corporation had the following income and expenses:

Gross receipts	$700,000
Salaries	300,000
Contributions to qualified charitable organizations	60,000
Capital gains	7,000
Depreciation expense	28,000
Dividend income	60,000
Dividends received deduction	42,000

What is the amount of HOOS Corporation's charitable contribution deduction for 1996? (IRS 97 3C-62)

a. $33,400
b. $43,900
c. $46,900
d. $60,000

_____ 12. During 1996, Glitz, a C corporation, realized a long-term capital gain of $5,000 from the sale of a tract of land, a long-term capital gain of $10,000 from the sale of stock of Meg Corporation, and a long-term capital loss of $23,000 from the sale of U. S. Government securities. What amount of the long-term capital loss may Glitz deduct on its 1996 income tax return? (IRS 97 3C-63)

a. $8,000
b. $15,000
c. $18,000
d. $23,000

_____ 13. For the tax year ended December 31, 1996, Muncie Corporation had gross income of $300,000 and operating expenses of $450,000. Contributions of $2,500 were included in the expenses, Muncie had a net operating loss carryover of $8,000. What is the amount of Muncie Corporation's net operating loss for 1996?
(IRS 97 3C-64)

a. $156,500
b. $152,500
c. $150,000
d. $147,500

_____ 14. For the calendar year 1996, Cincy Cooperation had operating income of $80,000, exclusive of the following capital gains and losses:

Long-term capital gain	$14,000
Short-term capital gain	6,000
Long-term capital loss	(2,000)
Short-term capital loss	(8,000)

What is Cincy's income tax liability for 1996? (IRS 97 3C-66)

a. $22,250
b. $18,850
c. $18,250
d. $15,450

_____ 15. For tax year 1996, Bosse Corporation's books and records reflect the following:

Net income per books	$76,000
Tax-exempt interest	4,000
Excess contributions	2,000
Meal in excess of 50% limitation	8,000
Accrued federal income taxes	18,000

What is the amount of Bosse's taxable income as it would be shown on Schedule M-1 of its corporate income tax return? (IRS 97 3C-68)

a. $92,000
b. $100,000
c. $104,000
d. $108,000

SOLUTIONS

True or False

1. T (p. 2-7)
2. T (p. 2-12)
3. T (p. 2-27)
4. F (p. 2-20; amortize or capitalize, not deductible)
5. T (p. 2-21)
6. F (p. 2-18; the election is made on a year by year basis)
7. F (p. 2-20; the election must be timely made)
8. T (p. 2-18)
9. T (p. 2-29)
10. T (p. 2-23)
11. T (p. 2-12)

Fill in the Blanks

1. ordinary income (p. 2-12)
2. three (p. 2-12)
3. fair market value (p. 2-15)
4. adjusted basis (p. 2-16)
5. two; twenty (p. 2-17)
6. third (p. 2-27)
7. combined group; parent; brother-sister controlled group (p. 2-26)

Multiple Choice

1. d (p. 2-7)
2. d (p. 2-27)
3. c (p. 2-18; process of elimination)
4. a (p. 2-15)
5. a (p. 2-12)
6. c (p. 2-23)
7. a (p. 2-27)
8. b (p. 2-28)
9. a (p. 2-20; (2,000 + 6,000 + 5,000)/60*12)
10. b (80% of taxable income, without dividend received deduction)
11. b ((700,000 + 7,000 + 60,000 - 300,000 - 28,000)*10%)
12. b (limited to capital gain)
13. d (-150,000 + 2,500)
14. b (p. 2-21; 90,000 taxable income)
15. b (p. 2-29; 76,000 - 4,000 + 2,000 + 8,000 + 18,000)

CHAPTER 3

CORPORATIONS: ORGANIZATION AND CAPITAL STRUCTURE

LEARNING OBJECTIVES

After completing Chapter 3, you should be able to:

1. Identify the tax consequences of incorporating a business.

2. Understand the special rules that apply when liabilities are assumed by a corporation.

3. Recognize the basis issues relevant to the shareholder and the corporation.

4. Appreciate the tax aspects of the capital structure of a corporation.

5. Recognize the tax differences between debt and equity investments.

6. Handle the tax treatment of shareholder debt and stock losses.

7. Identify tax planning opportunities associated with organizing and financing a corporation.

KEY TERMS

Assumption of liabilities	Liabilities in excess of basis	Qualified small business stock
Capital contribution	Nonbusiness bad debt	Section 1244 stock
Control	Property	Securities
Investor losses	Qualified small business corporation	Thin capitalization

OUTLINE

I. ORGANIZATION OF AND TRANSFERS TO CONTROLLED CORPORATIONS

    A. In General
1. Normally, gain or loss is recognized on a property transfer.
2. The Code provides exceptions where:
   a. a taxpayer's economic status has not changed, and
   b. the wherewithal to pay is lacking.
3. Section 351 provides nonrecognition of gain or loss when:
   a. property is transferred for
   b. stock, and
   c. the transferors are in control of the transferee corporation.
4. Section 351 is mandatory.

    B. Property Defined
1. The Code specifically excludes services rendered.
2. With the above exception, the definition of property is comprehensive.

    C. Stock Transferred
1. Common and most preferred stocks are included in this definition.
2. Stock rights or warrants are not included in this definition.
3. Any property, other than stock, received in the exchange, by the transferor, is considered boot.
4. All corporate debt constitutes boot.
5. Boot is taxable to the extent of any gain realized.

    D. Control of the Corporation
1. 80% stock ownership
   a. 80% of the total combined voting power, and
   b. 80% of the total number of shares of all other classes of stock.
2. Control immediately after the transfer
   a. may refer to one person or several individuals.
   b. all transfers need not be made simultaneously.
   c. for transfers involving more than one person:
      1. the rights of the persons should be defined, in a written agreement, prior to any transfers.
      2. the transfers should occur close together in time.
      3. Transfers for property and services
         a. persons who transfer property and perform services for stock are considered members of the transferring group, generally, the value of the property must be at least 10% of the value of the service provided.
         b. that person is taxed on the value of stock issued for services.

c. all the stock received by that person is counted to determine whether or not the control requirement is met.

E. Assumption of Liabilities
1. Generally, a corporation's assumption of a liability or acceptance of property subject to a liability does not result in boot to the transferor shareholder.
2. Liabilities assumed by the corporation are treated as boot for determining the shareholder's basis in the stock received.
3. Liabilities in excess of basis cause taxable gain because, without this provision, the stock basis would be negative.

F. Basis Determination
1. Basis of stock to shareholder
    a. basis held in the property transferred, plus
    b. gain recognized on the exchange, minus
    c. boot received, including any liabilities transferred.
2. Basis of property to corporation
    a. transferor's basis, plus
    b. gain recognized by the transferor shareholder.
3. Holding period for shareholder's stock received for
    a. transfer of a capital asset or §1231 property, includes the holding period of the property transferred.
    b. transfer of inventory, begins the day after the exchange.
4. Holding period for corporate property received is the holding period of the transferor shareholder.

II. CAPITAL STRUCTURE OF A CORPORATION

A. Capital Contributions
1. The basis of property received by a corporation from a shareholder is the transferor's basis plus gain recognized by the transferor/shareholder.
2. The basis of property received by a corporation from a nonshareholder is zero.
3. Money received by a corporation from a nonshareholder
    a. reduces the basis of any property acquired with the money during the 12 months following receipt of such contribution.
    b. any excess over the cost of new property reduces the basis of other corporate property in proportion to the relative bases of the properties, in the following order
        1. depreciable property
        2. amortizable property
        3. depletable property

4. all other remaining property.

B. Debt in the Capital Structure
1. Advantages of debt
   a. interest is deductible by the corporation, dividends are not.
   b. shareholders are not taxed on loan repayments.
   c. a stock investment cannot be withdrawn tax-free while the corporation has earnings and profits.
2. Reclassification of debt as equity
   a. a debt instrument having too many features of stock may be treated as a form of stock.
   b. factors to be considered include:
      1. the form of the debt instrument
      2. a definite maturity date and reasonable interest rate
      3. timely payment
      4. subordination to other liabilities
      5. the ratio of debt to equity.

III. INVESTOR LOSSES

A. Stock and security losses
1. for stocks and bonds held as capital assets, capital losses materialize as of the last day of the year in which the stocks or bonds become completely worthless.
2. no deduction is allowed for partial worthlessness.

B. Business versus nonbusiness bad debts
1. business bad debts are deducted as ordinary losses.
2. nonbusiness bad debts are treated as short-term capital losses and limited to noncorporate taxpayers.
3. partial worthlessness can be deducted only for business bad debts.
4. all corporate bad debts qualify as business bad debts.

C. Section 1244 stock
1. §1244 allows ordinary loss treatment for losses on the sale or worthlessness of a small business corporation's stock.
2. the amount of loss deductible in any one year is limited to $50,000 or $100,000 for a jointly filed return.
3. only the original holder of §1244 stock qualifies for ordinary loss treatment.
4. to qualify as §1244 stock
   a. the total stock offered cannot exceed $1 million.
   b. more than 50% of the corporation's gross receipts must be derived from the active conduct of a trade or business.

CORPORATIONS: ORGANIZATION AND CAPITAL STRUCTURE

IV. **GAIN FROM QUALIFIED SMALL BUSINESS STOCK**
   A. Is stock in a C corporation
      1. issued after August 10, 1993, whose aggregate gross assets did not exceed $50 million on August 10, 1993, through the date the stock was issued.
      2. who used at least 80% of its assets in the active conduct of a trade or business.

   B. Noncorporate shareholders may exclude 50% of the gain on a sale or exchange of qualified small business stock.
      1. the taxpayer must have held the stock for more than 5 years.
      2. the taxpayer must have acquired the stock as part of an original issue.

   C. The 50% exclusion can apply to the greater of
      1. $10 million, $5 million for married filing separately, or
      2. 10 times the shareholder's aggregate adjusted basis in the qualified stock disposed of during the year.

V. **TAX PLANNING CONSIDERATIONS**

   A. Working with §351
      1. Does compliance with §351 yield the desired tax result?
      2. Utilizing §351
         a. ensure all parties transferring property receive control.
         b. be sure later transfers of property satisfy the control requirement if gain recognition is to be avoided.

   B. Determine which assets and liabilities should be transferred to the corporation.

   C. The debt to equity ratio of the corporation's capital structure
         a. thin capitalization and potential reclassification,
         b. investor losses and §1244 attributes.

TEST FOR SELF-EVALUATION

True or False

T F 1. Rene transferred money and property to Stable Corporation solely in exchange for stock in Stable. Immediately after the exchange, Rene owned 80% of the total combined voting power of all classes of stock entitled to vote and 51% of all other classes of stock. No gain or loss will be recognized by Rene or Stable.
(IRS 97 3A-12)

T F 2. If an individual transfers mortgaged property to a corporation he or she controls, the individual generally will NOT have to recognize gain as a result of the corporation's assumption of a liability unless the liability is greater than the individual's adjusted basis in the property. (IRS 97 3A-13)

T F 3. Mike transferred money and property to Growth Corporation solely in exchange for stock in Growth. Immediately after the exchange, Mike owned 80% of the total combined voting power of all classes of stock entitled to vote and 51% of all other classes of stock. No gain or loss will be recognized by Mike or Growth.
(IRS 96 3A-2)

T F 4. A corporation does not recognize gain or loss if you transfer property and money to the corporation in exchange for the corporation's stock (including treasury stock). (IRS 96 3A-3)

T F 5. If you acquire an asset in exchange for another asset and your basis for the new asset is figured, in whole or in part, by your basis in the old property, the holding period of the new property begins the day after the date of the exchange.
(IRS 96 3A-5)

T F 6. If the sole shareholder of a corporation receives no additional shares for a contribution of property to the corporation, the basis of the property received by the corporation is the same as it was to the shareholder. (IRS 96 3A-7)

T F 7. In order to protect her investment, Beth, an officer and principal shareholder of Turbo Corporation, guaranteed payment of a bank loan Turbo received. During 1994, Turbo defaulted on the loan and Beth made full payment. Beth is entitled to a business bad debt deduction. (IRS 95 2A-9)

T F 8. Steve transferred his services to a corporation in exchange for 85% of all classes of the corporation's stock. Steve will NOT have to report the fair market value of the stock as taxable compensation. (IRS 95 3A-1)

T F 9. If an individual transfers mortgaged property to a corporation he or she controls, the individual generally will NOT have to recognize gain as a result of the corporation's assumption of a liability unless the liability is greater than the individual's adjusted basis in the property. (IRS 95 3A-2)

T F 10. On January 1, 1994, Mr. Kitars transferred property he had originally acquired on July 1, 1991, to Westco Corporation in a nontaxable exchange for Westco's stock. After the transfer, Mr. Kitars had control of the corporation. On October 1, 1994, Westco Corporation sold the property for a gain. Westco's holding period does NOT include the period it was held by Mr. Kitars. (IRS 95 3A-4)

Fill in the Blanks

1. _____ in a §351 transaction does not result in boot to the transferor shareholder.

2. For _____ of property received from a nonshareholder, the corporation's basis is zero.

3. _____ immediately after §351 exchange requires _____ stock ownership in the transferee corporation.

4. _____ transferred, without taxable gain recognition, would cause the transferor shareholder to have a _____ basis in the stock received.

5. _____ are treated as short-term capital losses of noncorporate taxpayers.

6. Property for purposes of §351 specifically excludes _____.

7. _____ allows ordinary loss treatment on the sale or worthlessness of small business corporation's stock.

8. _____ are long-term debt instruments.

9. _____ situations arise when shareholder debt is high relative to shareholder equity.

Multiple Choice

____ 1. During 1996, Chip and Dale formed a corporation to which Chip transferred a patent right that had a fair market value of $25,000 and a zero adjusted basis. Dale transferred a building that had a fair market value of $100,000 and an adjusted basis to him of $75,000. In return, Chip received 200 shares and Dale 800 shares of the corporation's 1,000 outstanding shares of its only class of stock. As a result of this transaction, Dale should report: (IRS 97 3B-35)

a. Neither a gain or loss.
b. A capital gain of $25,000.
c. A Section 1250 gain of $25,000.
d. An ordinary gain of $25,000.

_____ 2. Laura, an attorney, performed legal services valued at $2,000 for Fine Corporation, a newly formed corporation, in exchange for 1% of the issued and outstanding stock. The fair market value of the shares received was $2,000. Laura would recognize: (IRS 97 3B-36)

a. No income until the stock is sold.
b. $2,000 as ordinary income ratable over 60 months.
c. Compensation of $2,000.
d. A short term capital gain of $2,000.

_____ 3. The basis of stock received in exchange for property transferred to a corporation is the same as the basis of the property transferred with certain adjustments. Which one of the following would NOT decrease the basis of the stock received?
(IRS 97 3B-37)

a. The fair market value of other property received.
b. Any amount treated as a dividend.
c. Any money received.
d. Any loss recognized on the exchange.

_____ 4. During 1996, Dylon transferred land having an adjusted basis of $35,000 and a fair market value of $47,000 to Octopus Corporation. In exchange for the land he received $5,000 cash, equipment having an adjusted basis of $3,000 and a fair market value of $5,000 and 80% of Octopus Corporation's only class of stock outstanding. The stock received by Dylon had a fair market value of $37,000. What is the amount of gain that Dylon will recognize? (IRS 97 3C-54)

a. $0
b. $10,000
c. $12,000
d. $20,000

_____ 5. Mr. Francois transferred an office building to Slim Corporation in exchange for 100% of Slim's only class of outstanding stock and $30,000 in cash. The building had an adjusted basis of $150,000 and a fair market value of $250,000. The building was subject to a mortgage of $120,000 which Slim assumed for a valid business reason. The fair market value of Slim Corporation's stock on the date of the transfer was $100,000. What is the amount of Mr. Francois' recognized gain?
(IRS 97 3C-55)

a. $100,000
b. $70,000
c. $30,000
d. $0

_____ 6. Mr. Naqvi transferred a building having an adjusted basis of $18,500 and a fair market value of $23,000 to Nadir Corporation. In exchange for the building he received $3,000 cash and 90% of Nadir's only class of stock outstanding. The stock received by Mr. Naqvi had a fair market value of $20,000. What is Nadir Corporation's basis in the building received in this exchange? (IRS 97 3C-56)

a. $25,000
b. $21,500
c. $20,000
d. $18,500

_____ 7. Rod, Sydney, and Edgar decided to form Parody Corporation. Rod transferred property with an adjusted basis of $35,000 and a fair market value of $44,000 for 440 shares of stock. Sydney exchanged $33,000 cash for 330 shares of stock. Edgar performed services valued at $33,000 for 330 shares of stock. The fair market value of Parody Corporation's stock is $100 per share. What is Parody's basis in the property received from Rod? (IRS 97 3C-57)

a. $44,000
b. $35,000
c. $9,000
d. $0

_____ 8. Which of the following factors is NOT taken into account when determining if a gain or loss should be recognized on the transfer of property to a corporation in exchange for a controlling interest in stock of the corporation?
(IRS 96 3B-21)
a. Receipt of money in addition to the stock.
b. Fair market value of the property transferred to the corporation.
c. Ownership of at least 80% of the total combined voting power of all stock entitled to vote.
d. Ownership of at least 80% of the total number of shares of all other classes of stock.

_____ 9. During 1995, Randy and Audra formed a corporation to which Randy transferred equipment that had a fair market value of $25,000 and zero adjusted basis. Audra transferred a building that had a fair market value of $100,000 and an adjusted basis to her of $80,000. In return, Randy received 200 shares and Audra received

800 shares of the corporation's outstanding shares of its only class of stock. As a result of this transaction, Audra should report: (IRS 96 3B-22)

a. Neither a gain or loss.
b. A section 1250 gain of $20,000.
c. An ordinary gain of $20,000.
d. A capital gain of $20,000.

_____ 10. In exchange for Thunder Corporation stock, Sydney performed legal services for Thunder valued at $7,000 and paid Thunder $18,000 cash. The stock received by Sydney had a fair market value at the time of the exchange of $25,000. What is the amount of Sydney's recognized gain from this exchange? (IRS 96 3C-46)

a. $25,000
b. $18,000
c. $7,000
d. $0

_____ 11. During 1995, Shelly transferred property having an adjusted basis to her of $20,000 and a fair market value of $27,000 to DLW Corporation. In exchange for the property she received $6,000 cash and 100% of DLW's only class of stock. If the stock received by Shelly had a fair market value of $21,000 at the time of the transfer, what is the amount of her recognized gain? (IRS 96 3C-47)

a. $0
b. $6,000
c. $7,000
d. $21,000

_____ 12. Andrew transferred an office building that had an adjusted basis of $180,000 and a fair market value of $350,000 to Dickens Corporation in exchange for 80% of Dickens' only class of stock. The building was subject to a mortgage of $200,000, which Dickens assumed for valid business reasons. The fair market value of the stock on the date of the transfer was $150,000. What is the amount of Andrew's recognized gain? (IRS 96 3C-48)

a. $0
b. $20,000
c. $170,000
d. $350,000

CORPORATIONS: ORGANIZATION AND CAPITAL STRUCTURE

SOLUTIONS

True or False

1. F (p. 3-5; 80% of all other classes required)
2. T (p. 3-10)
3. F (p. 3-5; 80% of all other classes required)
4. T (p. 3-14)
5. F (p. 3-14; includes the holding period of the asset transferred)
6. F (p. 3-14; additional price paid for shares held)
7. F (p. 3-18; non-business, to protect her investment)
8. F (p. 3-4; he must report FMV of stock as compensation)
9. T (p. 3-10)
10. F (p. 3-14; holding period does carry over)

Fill in the Blanks

1. liabilities assumed (p. 3-9)
2. capital contributions (p. 3-15)
3. control, 80% (p. 3-5)
4. liabilities in excess of basis, negative (p. 3-10)
5. nonbusiness bad debts (p. 3-18)
6. services (p. 3-4)
7. §1244 (p. 3-20)
8. bonds (p. 3-5)
9. thin capitalization (p. 3-16)

Multiple Choice

1. a (p. 3-4; §351 is mandatory)
2. c (p. 3-4; stock for services is compensation)
3. b (p. 3-12; a dividend on the stock would be income to the shareholder)
4. b (p. 3-3; boot received, 5,000 cash + 5,000 FMV of equipment)
5. c (p. 3-3; boot received, 30,000 cash)
6. b (p. 3-12; transferor's basis plus gain recognized, 18,500 + 3,000)
7. a (p. 3-5, 12; fair market of property, control requirement was not met for Section 351)
8. b (p. 3-3; "a" refers to boot, "c" & "d" are control requirements)
9. a (p. 3-4; §351 is mandatory)
10. c (p. 3-4; stock for services is compensation)
11. b (p. 3-3; boot received, 6,000)
12. b (p. 3-10; excess of liabilities over basis, 200,000 - 180,000)

Return Problem

Given the following data, prepare Form 1120, U.S. Corporation Income Tax Return, Form 4562, Depreciation and Amortization and any required schedules.

Name:	ABC Corporation
Address:	123 School Street, Joslin, IL 60838
EIN:	36-6135404
Business Activity:	Manufacture toys for pre-schoolers
Officers:	President, Mary Robert 336-58-5900
	Secretary-Treasurer, Michael Williams 382-31-8401

ABC Corporation was formed on January 2, 1997, by Michael Williams and Mary Robert. Michael and Mary each own ½ of the outstanding common stock; no other class of stock is authorized. Both Michael and Mary are full-time employees of the corporation and each receives a salary of $35,000. Michael handles all paperwork as well as sales and deliveries. Mary designs the toys and supervises production.

ABC rents space for $5,000 per month; the factory and inventory storage areas occupy 85% of this space. The corporation uses the accrual method of accounting and has adopted a calendar year. The specific charge-off method is used for bad debts. Depreciation is calculated under MACRS for both book and tax purposes; no new assets were purchased in 1998. The following amounts represent selected book balances at December 31, 1998.

Gross Sales		$750,000	Machinery	$75,000
Sales returns		2,500	Office equipment	4,500
Raw materials		256,000	Delivery truck	11,000
*Wages:	factory	150,000	Accumulated Depreciation	
	office	15,000	machinery	29,085
Payroll taxes:	factory	15,650	office	1,745
	office	4,225	truck	5,720
Insurance:	factory	10,000	Advertising	5,000
	office	2,000	Telephone	4,800
Heat & electric		16,000	Packaging	7,000
Small tools		1,200	Delivery	2,400
Machinery maintenance		2,200	Dues & subscriptions	725
Materials & supplies		5,000	Office supplies	2,500
Dividends		12,000	Legal & accounting	1,000
Estimated tax payments		15,000	Entertainment	750

*Wages do not include officer salaries.
Portions of the Schedule L, Balance Sheet have been completed for you.

CORPORATIONS: ORGANIZATION AND CAPITAL STRUCTURE 3-13

Form **1120** Department of the Treasury Internal Revenue Service	**U.S. Corporation Income Tax Return** For calendar year 1998 or tax year beginning , ending ▶ Instructions are separate. See page 1 for Paperwork Reduction Act Notice.	OMB No. 1545-0123 **1998**

A Check if a:		Use IRS label. Other- wise, print or type.	Name		B Employer identification number
1	Consolidated return (attach Form 851)				
2	Personal holding co. (attach Sch. PH)		Number, street, & room or suite no.		C Date incorporated
3	Personal service corp. (as defined in Temporary Regs. sec. 1.441-4T— see instructions)		City or town, state, and ZIP code		D Total assets (see page 5 of instructions) $

E Check applicable boxes: (1) ☐ Initial return (2) ☐ Final return (3) ☐ Change of address

Income

1a	Gross receipts/sales _____ **b** Less returns & allowances _____ **c** Bal ▶	1c
2	Cost of goods sold (Schedule A, line 8)	2
3	Gross profit. Subtract line 2 from line 1c	3
4	Dividends (Schedule C, line 19)	4
5	Interest	5
6	Gross rents	6
7	Gross royalties	7
8	Capital gain net income (attach Sch. D (Form 1120))	8
9	Net gain or (loss) from Form 4797, Part II, line 18 (attach Form 4797)	9
10	Other income (see page 6 of instructions–attach schedule)	10
11	**Total income.** Add lines 3 through 10 ▶	11

Deductions

(See instructions for limitations on deductions.)

12	Compensation of officers (Schedule E, line 4)	12
13	Salaries and wages (less employment credits)	13
14	Repairs and maintenance	14
15	Bad debts	15
16	Rents	16
17	Taxes and licenses	17
18	Interest	18
19	Charitable contributions (see page 8 of instructions for 10% limitation)	19
20	Depreciation (attach Form 4562) _____ 20	
21	Less depreciation claimed on Schedule A and elsewhere on return _____ 21a	21b
22	Depletion	22
23	Advertising	23
24	Pension, profit-sharing, etc., plans	24
25	Employee benefit programs	25
26	Other deductions (attach schedule)	26
27	**Total deductions.** Add ln. 12 through 26 ▶	27
28	Taxable income before net operating loss deduction & special deductions. Subtract line 27 from ln. 11	28
29	**Less: a** Net operating loss deduction (see page 9 of instructions) _____ 29a	
	b Special deductions (Schedule C, line 20) _____ 29b	29c

Tax and Payments

30	**Taxable income.** Subtract line 29c from line 28	30
31	**Total tax** (Schedule J, line 12)	31
32	Payments: **a** 1997 overpayment credited to 1998 _____ 32a	
	b 1998 estimated tax payments _____ 32b	
	c Less 1998 refund applied for on Form 4466 _____ 32c ( ) **d** Bal ▶ 32d	
	e Tax deposited with Form 7004 _____ 32e	
	f Credit for tax paid on undistributed capital gains (attach Form 2439) _____ 32f	
	g Credit for Federal tax on fuels (attach Form 4136). See instructions _____ 32g	32h
33	Estimated tax penalty (see page 10 of instructions). Check if Form 2220 is attached ▶ ☐	33
34	**Tax due.** If line 32h is smaller than the total of lines 31 and 33, enter amount owed	34
35	**Overpayment.** If line 32h is larger than the total of lines 31 and 33, enter amount overpaid	35
36	Enter amt. of line 35 you want: **Credited to 1999 est. tax** ▶ _____ **Refunded** ▶	36

Sign Here

Under penalties of perjury, I declare that I have examined this return, including accompanying schedules and statements, and to the best of my knowledge and belief, it is true, correct, and complete. Declaration of preparer (other than taxpayer) is based on all information of which preparer has any knowledge.

▶ _____ _____ _____
  Signature of officer   Date   Title

Paid Preparer's Use Only

Preparer's signature ▶		Date	Check if self-employed ☐	Preparer's social security number
Firm's name (or yours if self-employed) and address ▶			EIN ▶	
			ZIP code ▶	

DAA

Form 1120 (1998) Page 2

Schedule A — Cost of Goods Sold (See page 10 of instructions.)

1	Inventory at beginning of year	1
2	Purchases	2
3	Cost of labor	3
4	Additional section 263A costs (attach schedule)	4
5	Other costs (attach schedule)	5
6	**Total.** Add lines 1 through 5	6
7	Inventory at end of year	7
8	**Cost of goods sold.** Subtract line 7 from line 6. Enter here and on page 1, line 2	8

9a Check all methods used for valuing closing inventory:
  (i) ☐ Cost as described in Regulations section 1.471–3
  (ii) ☐ Lower of cost or market as described in Regulations section 1.471–4
  (iii) ☐ Other (Specify method used and attach explanation.) ▶

b Check if there was a writedown of subnormal goods as described in Regulations section 1.471–2(c) ▶ ☐
c Check if the LIFO inventory method was adopted this tax year for any goods (if checked, attach Form 970) ▶ ☐
d If the LIFO inventory method was used for this tax year, enter percentage (or amounts) of closing inventory computed under LIFO — 9d
e If property is produced or acquired for resale, do the rules of section 263A apply to the corporation? ☐ Yes ☐ No
f Was there any change in determining quantities, cost, or valuations between opening and closing inventory? If "Yes," attach explanation ☐ Yes ☐ No

Schedule C — Dividends and Special Deductions (See page 11 of instructions.)

		(a) Dividends received	(b) %	(c) Special deductions (a) × (b)
1	Dividends from less-than-20%-owned domestic corporations that are subject to the 70% deduction (other than debt-financed stock)		70	
2	Dividends from 20%-or-more-owned domestic corporations that are subject to the 80% deduction (other than debt-financed stock)		80	
3	Dividends on debt-financed stock of domestic & foreign corporations (section 246A)		see instr.	
4	Dividends on certain preferred stock of less-than-20%-owned public utilities		42	
5	Dividends on certain preferred stock of 20%-or-more-owned public utilities		48	
6	Dividends from less-than-20%-owned foreign corporations and certain FSCs that are subject to the 70% deduction		70	
7	Dividends from 20%-or-more-owned foreign corporations and certain FSCs that are subject to the 80% deduction		80	
8	Dividends from wholly owned foreign subsidiaries subject to the 100% deduction (section 245(b))		100	
9	**Total.** Add lines 1 through 8. See page 12 of instructions for limitation			
10	Dividends from domestic corporations received by a small business investment company operating under the Small Business Investment Act of 1958		100	
11	Dividends from certain FSCs that are subject to the 100% deduction (section 245(c)(1))		100	
12	Dividends from affiliated group members subject to the 100% deduction (section 243(a)(3))		100	
13	Other dividends from foreign corporations not included on lines 3, 6, 7, 8, or 11			
14	Income from controlled foreign corporations under subpart F (att. Form(s) 5471)			
15	Foreign dividend gross-up (section 78)			
16	IC-DISC and former DISC dividends not included on lines 1, 2, or 3 (section 246(d))			
17	Other dividends			
18	Deduction for dividends paid on certain preferred stock of public utilities			
19	**Total dividends.** Add lines 1 through 17. Enter here and on line 4, page 1 ▶			
20	**Total special deductions.** Add lines 9, 10, 11, 12, and 18. Enter here and on line 29b, page 1 ▶			

Schedule E — Compensation of Officers (See instructions for line 12, page 1.)

Complete Schedule E only if total receipts (line 1a plus lines 4 through 10 on page 1, Form 1120) are $500,000 or more.

(a) Name of officer	(b) Social security number	(c) Percent of time devoted to business	Percent of corporation stock owned		(f) Amount of compensation
			(d) Common	(e) Preferred	
1		%	%	%	
		%	%	%	
		%	%	%	
		%	%	%	
		%	%	%	

2 Total compensation of officers
3 Compensation of officers claimed on Schedule A and elsewhere on return
4 Subtract line 3 from line 2. Enter the result here and on line 12, page 1

DAA

Form 1120 (1998) Page 3

Schedule J — Tax Computation (See page 13 of instructions.)

1. Check if the corporation is a member of a controlled group (see sections 1561 and 1563) ▶ ☐
   Important: Members of a controlled group, see instructions on page 13.
2a. If the box on line 1 is checked, enter the corporation's share of the $50,000, $25,000, and $9,925,000 taxable income brackets (in that order):
   (1) $ _____ (2) $ _____ (3) $ _____
 b. Enter the corporation's share of: (1) Additional 5% tax (not more than $11,750) $ _____
   (2) Additional 3% tax (not more than $100,000) $ _____
3. Income tax. Check if a qualified personal service corporation under section 448(d)(2) (see page 13) ▶ ☐ | 3 |
4a. Foreign tax credit (attach Form 1118) | 4a |
 b. Possessions tax credit (attach Form 5735) | 4b |
 c. Check: ☐ Nonconventional source fuel credit ☐ QEV credit (att. Form 8834) | 4c |
 d. General business credit. Enter here & check which forms are att.: ☐ 3800
   ☐ 3468 ☐ 5884 ☐ 6478 ☐ 6765 ☐ 8586 ☐ 8830 ☐ 8826
   ☐ 8835 ☐ 8844 ☐ 8845 ☐ 8846 ☐ 8820 ☐ 8847 ☐ 8861 | 4d |
 e. Credit for prior year minimum tax (attach Form 8827) | 4e |
5. **Total credits.** Add lines 4a through 4e | 5 |
6. Subtract line 5 from line 3 | 6 |
7. Personal holding company tax (attach Schedule PH (Form 1120)) | 7 |
8. Recapture taxes. Check if from: ☐ Form 4255 ☐ Form 8611 | 8 |
9. Alternative min. tax (att. Form 4626) | 9 |
10. Add lines 6 through 9 | 10 |
11. Qualified zone academy bond credit (attach Form 8860) | 11 |
12. **Total tax.** Subtract line 11 from line 10. Enter here and on line 31, page 1 | 12 |

Schedule K — Other Information (See page 15 of instructions.)

1. Check method of accounting: a ☐ Cash
   b ☐ Accrual
   c ☐ Other (specify) ▶
2. See page 17 of the instructions and state the:
 a. Business activity code no. **(NEW)** ▶
 b. Business activity ▶
 c. Product or service ▶
3. At the end of the tax year, did the corporation own, directly or indirectly, 50% or more of the voting stock of a domestic corporation? (For rules of attribution, see section 267(c).)
   If "Yes," attach a schedule showing: **(a)** name and identifying number, **(b)** percentage owned, and **(c)** taxable income or (loss) before NOL and special deductions of such corporation for the tax year ending with or within your tax year.
4. Is the corporation a subsidiary in an affiliated group or a parent-subsidiary controlled group?
   If "Yes," enter employer identification number and name of the parent corporation ▶
5. At the end of the tax year, did any individual, partnership, corporation, estate or trust own, directly or indirectly, 50% or more of the corporation's voting stock? (For rules of attribution, see section 267(c).)
   If "Yes," attach a schedule showing name and identifying number. (Do not include any information already entered in **4** above.) Enter percentage owned ▶
6. During this tax year, did the corporation pay dividends (other than stock dividends and distributions in exchange for stock) in excess of the corporation's current and accumulated earnings and profits? (See sections 301 and 316.)
   If "Yes," file Form 5452. If this is a consolidated return, answer here for the parent corporation and on **Form 851**, Affiliations Schedule, for each subsidiary.
7. Was the corporation a U.S. shareholder of any controlled foreign corporation? (See sections 951 and 957.)
   If "Yes," attach Form 5471 for each such corporation. Enter number of Forms 5471 attached ▶
8. At any time during the 1998 calendar yr., did the corporation have an interest in or a signature or other authority over a financial account (such as a bank acct., securities acct., or other financial account) in a foreign country?
   If "Yes," the corporation may have to file Form TD F 90-22.1.
   If "Yes," enter name of foreign country ▶
9. During the tax year, did the corporation receive a distribution from, or was it the grantor of, or transferor to, a foreign trust? If "Yes," the corporation may have to file Form 3520
10. At any time during the tax year, did one foreign person own, directly or indirectly, at least 25% of: **(a)** the total voting power of all classes of stock of the corporation entitled to vote, or **(b)** the total value of all classes of stock of the corporation? If "Yes,"
 a. Enter percentage owned ▶
 b. Enter owner's country ▶
 c. The corporation may have to file Form 5472. Enter number of Forms 5472 attached ▶
11. Check this box if the corporation issued publicly offered debt instruments with original issue discount ▶ ☐
    If so, the corporation may have to file Form 8281.
12. Enter the amount of tax-exempt interest received or accrued during the tax year ▶ $
13. If there were 35 or fewer shareholders at the end of the tax year, enter the number ▶
14. If the corp. has an NOL for the tax year and is electing to forego the carryback period, check here ▶ ☐
15. Enter the available NOL carryover from prior tax years (Do not reduce it by any deduction on line 29a.) ▶ $

Form 1120 (1998)   ABC Corporation   36-6135404   Page 4

Schedule L — Balance Sheets per Books

Assets	Beginning of tax year (a)	(b)	End of tax year (c)	(d)
1 Cash		11,338.		32,408.
2a Trade notes and accounts receivable	23,100.		65,595.	
b Less allowance for bad debts		23,100.		65,595.
3 Inventories		61,621.		46,718.
4 U.S. government obligations				
5 Tax-exempt securities (see instructions)				
6 Other current assets (attach schedule)				
7 Loans to stockholders				
8 Mortgage and real estate loans				
9 Other investments (attach schedule)				
10a Buildings and other depreciable assets	90,500.			
b Less accumulated depreciation	13,561.	76,939.		
11a Depletable assets				
b Less accumulated depletion				
12 Land (net of any amortization)				
13a Intangible assets (amortizable only)				
b Less accumulated amortization				
14 Other assets (attach schedule)				
15 Total assets		172,998.		144,721.
Liabilities and Stockholders' Equity				
16 Accounts payable		48,810.		23,325.
17 Mortgages, notes, bonds payable in less than 1 year				
18 Other current liabilities (attach sch)				
19 Loans from stockholders				
20 Mortgages, notes, bonds payable in 1 year or more				
21 Other liabilities (attach schedule)				
22 Capital stock: a Preferred stock				
b Common stock	100,000.	100,000.	100,000.	100,000.
23 Additional paid-in capital				
24 Retained earnings — Approp				
25 Retained earnings — Unappropriated		24,188.		
26 Adjustments to shareholders' equity				
27 Less cost of treasury stock				
28 Total liabilities and stockholders' equity		172,998.		123,325.

Note: You are not required to complete Schedules M-1 and M-2 below if the total assets on line 15, column (d) of Schedule L are less than $25,000.

Schedule M-1 — Reconciliation of Income (Loss) per Books With Income per Return (see instructions.)

1 Net income (loss) per books		7 Income recorded on books this year not included on this return (itemize):		
2 Federal income tax	14,951.	Tax-exempt interest $ _____ 0.		
3 Excess of capital losses over capital gains		_____		0.
4 Income subject to tax not recorded on books this year:		8 Deductions on this return not charged against book income this year (itemize):		
5 Expenses recorded on books this year not deducted on this return (itemize):		a Depreciation .. $ _____		
a Depreciation ...... $ _____		b Contrib carryover . $ _____		
b Contributions carryover .. $ _____				
c Travel & entertainment .. $ _____				
		9 Add lines 7 and 8		0.
6 Add lines 1 through 5	14,951.	10 Income (line 28, page 1) — line 6 less line 9		14,951.

Schedule M-2 — Analysis of Unappropriated Retained Earnings per Books (Line 25, Schedule L)

1 Balance at beginning of year	24,188.	5 Distributions .... a Cash		
2 Net income (loss) per books		b Stock _____ c Property		
3 Other increases (itemize): _____		6 Other decreases (itemize):		
_____		7 Add lines 5 and 6		
4 Add lines 1, 2, and 3	24,188.	8 Balance at end of year (line 4 less line 7)		24,188.

CPCA0234 12/13/98

CORPORATIONS: ORGANIZATION AND CAPITAL STRUCTURE 3-17

Form 4562
Department of the Treasury
Internal Revenue Service (99)

Depreciation and Amortization
(Including Information on Listed Property)
▶ See separate instructions.   ▶ Attach this form to your return.

OMB No. 1545-0172
1998
Attachment Sequence No. **67**

Name(s) shown on return | Identifying number

Business or activity to which this form relates

Part I — Election To Expense Certain Tangible Property (Section 179) (Note: If you have any "listed property," complete Pt. V before Pt. I.)

1	Maximum dollar limitation. If an enterprise zone business, see page 2 of the instructions	1	$18,500
2	Total cost of section 179 property placed in service. See page 2 of the instructions	2	
3	Threshold cost of section 179 property before reduction in limitation	3	$200,000
4	Reduction in limitation. Subtract line 3 from line 2. If zero or less, enter –0–	4	
5	Dollar limitation for tax year. Subtract line 4 from line 1. If zero or less, enter –0–. If married filing separately, see page 2 of the instructions	5	

(a) Description of property	(b) Cost (business use only)	(c) Elected cost
6		

7	Listed property. Enter amount from line 27	7	
8	Total elected cost of section 179 property. Add amounts in column (c), lines 6 and 7	8	
9	Tentative deduction. Enter the smaller of line 5 or line 8	9	
10	Carryover of disallowed deduction from 1997. See page 3 of the instructions	10	
11	Business income limitation. Enter the smaller of business income (not less than zero) or line 5 (see instructions)	11	
12	Section 179 expense deduction. Add lines 9 and 10, but do not enter more than line 11	12	
13	Carryover of disallowed deduction to 1999. Add lines 9 and 10, less line 12 ▶	13	

Note: Do not use Part II or Part III below for listed property (automobiles, certain other vehicles, cellular telephones, certain computers, or property used for entertainment, recreation, or amusement). Instead, use Part V for listed property.

Part II — MACRS Depreciation For Assets Placed in Service ONLY During Your 1998 Tax Year (Do Not Include Listed Property.)

Section A—General Asset Account Election

14 If you are making the election under section 168(i)(4) to group any assets placed in service during the tax year into one or more general asset accounts, check this box. See page 3 of the instructions ▶ ☐

Section B—General Depreciation System (GDS) (See page 3 of the instructions.)

(a) Classification of property	(b) Month and year placed in service	(c) Basis for depreciation (business/investment use only—see instructions)	(d) Recovery period	(e) Convention	(f) Method	(g) Depreciation deduction
15a 3-year property						
b 5-year property						
c 7-year property						
d 10-year property						
e 15-year property						
f 20-year property						
g 25-year property			25 yrs.		S/L	
h Residential rental property			27.5 yrs.	MM	S/L	
			27.5 yrs.	MM	S/L	
i Nonresidential real property			39 yrs.	MM	S/L	
				MM	S/L	

Section C—Alternative Depreciation System (ADS) (See page 5 of the instructions.)

16a Class life					S/L	
b 12-year			12 yrs.		S/L	
c 40-year			40 yrs.	MM	S/L	

Part III — Other Depreciation (Do Not Include Listed Property.) (See page 6 of the instructions.)

17	GDS and ADS deductions for assets placed in service in tax years beginning before 1998	17	
18	Property subject to section 168(f)(1) election	18	
19	ACRS and other depreciation	19	

Part IV — Summary (See page 6 of the instructions.)

20	Listed property. Enter amount from line 26	20	
21	**Total.** Add deductions on line 12, lines 15 and 16 in column (g), and lines 17 through 20. Enter here and on the appropriate lines of your return. Partnerships and S corporations—see instructions	21	
22	For assets shown above and placed in service during the current year, enter the portion of the basis attributable to section 263A costs	22	

For Paperwork Reduction Act Notice, see the separate instructions.

Form **4562** (1998)

DAA

Form 4562 (1998)   Page 2

Part V   Listed Property–Automobiles, Certain Other Vehicles, Cellular Telephones, Certain Computers, and Property Used for Entertainment, Recreation, or Amusement

Note: For any vehicle for which you are using the standard mileage rate or deducting lease expense, complete **only** 23a, 23b, columns (a) through (c) of Section A, all of Section B, and Section C if applicable.

Section A–Depreciation and Other Information (Caution: See page 8 of the instructions for limits for passenger automobiles.)

23a   Do you have evidence to support the busn./invest. use claimed?   ☐ Yes   ☐ No   23b   If "Yes," is the evidence written?   ☐ Yes   ☐ No

(a) Type of prop. (list vehicles first)	(b) Date placed in service	(c) Busn./invest. use percentage	(d) Cost or other basis	(e) Basis for depreciation (business/investment use only)	(f) Recovery period	(g) Method/ Convention	(h) Depreciation deduction	(i) Elected section 179 cost

24   Property used more than 50% in a qualified business use (See page 7 of the instructions.):

| | | % | | | | | | |
| | | % | | | | | | |

25   Property used 50% or less in a qualified business use (See page 7 of the instructions.):

| | | % | | | | S/L– | | |
| | | % | | | | S/L– | | |

26   Add amounts in column (h). Enter the total here and on line 20, page 1   **26**

27   Add amounts in column (i). Enter the total here and on line 7, page 1   **27**

Section B–Information on Use of Vehicles

Complete this section for vehicles used by a sole proprietor, partner, or other "more than 5% owner," or related person.

If you provided vehicles to your employees, first answer the questions in Section C to see if you meet an exception to completing this section for those vehicles.

	(a) Vehicle 1	(b) Vehicle 2	(c) Vehicle 3	(d) Vehicle 4	(e) Vehicle 5	(f) Vehicle 6
28 Total business/investment miles driven during the year (DO NOT include commuting miles)						
29 Total commuting miles driven during the year						
30 Total other personal (noncommuting) miles driven						
31 Total miles driven during the year. Add lines 28 through 30						

	Yes	No	Yes	No	Yes	No	Yes	No	Yes	No	Yes	No
32 Was the vehicle available for personal use during off–duty hours?												
33 Was the vehicle used primarily by a more than 5% owner or related person?												
34 Is another vehicle available for personal use?												

Section C–Questions for Employers Who Provide Vehicles for Use by Their Employees

Answer these questions to determine if you meet an exception to completing Section B for vehicles used by employees who **are not** more than 5% owners or related persons.

	Yes	No
35 Do you maintain a written policy statement that prohibits all personal use of vehicles, including commuting, by your employees?		
36 Do you maintain a written policy statement that prohibits personal use of vehicles, except commuting, by your employees? See page 9 of the instructions for vehicles used by corporate officers, directors, or 1% or more owners		
37 Do you treat all use of vehicles by employees as personal use?		
38 Do you provide more than five vehicles to your employees, obtain information from your employees about the use of the vehicles, and retain the information received?		
39 Do you meet the requirements concerning qualified automobile demonstration use? See page 9 of the instructions		

Note: If your answer to 35, 36, 37, 38, or 39 is "Yes," you need not complete Section B for the covered vehicles.

Part VI   **Amortization**

(a) Description of costs	(b) Date amortization begins	(c) Amortizable amount	(d) Code section	(e) Amortization period or percentage	(f) Amortization for this year

40   Amortization of costs that begins during your 1998 tax year:

| | | | | | |
| | | | | | |

41   Amortization of costs that began before 1998   **41**

42   **Total.** Enter here and on "Other Deductions" or "Other Expenses" line of your return   **42**

DAA

CORPORATIONS: ORGANIZATION AND CAPITAL STRUCTURE 3-19

Form 1120 — U.S. Corporation Income Tax Return 1998

Department of the Treasury Internal Revenue Service
► Instructions are separate. See instructions for Paperwork Reduction Act Notice.
IRS use only — Do not write or staple in this space.

For calendar year 1998 or tax year beginning , 1998, ending , 19

OMB No. 1545-0123

A Check if a:
1. Consolidated return (attach Form 851)
2. Personal holding co (attach Sch PH)
3. Personal service corp (as defined in Temp Regs Sec 1.441-4T — see instructions)

Use IRS label. Otherwise, please print or type.

Name: **ABC Corporation**
Number, Street, and Room or Suite Number: **123 School Street**
City or Town: **Joslin** State: **IL** ZIP Code: **60838**

B Employer ID Number: **36-6135404**
C Date Incorporated: **01/02/97**
D Total Assets: **$198,720.**

E Check applicable boxes: (1) Initial return (2) Final return (3) Change of address

Income

1a	Gross receipts or sales . 750,000. **b** Less returns & allowances . 2,500. **c** Balance	1c	747,500.
2	Cost of goods sold (Schedule A, line 8)	2	572,920.
3	Gross profit. Subtract line 2 from line 1c	3	174,580.
4	Dividends (Schedule C, line 19)	4	
5	Interest	5	
6	Gross rents	6	
7	Gross royalties	7	
8	Capital gain net income (attach Schedule D (Form 1120))	8	
9	Net gain or (loss) from Form 4797, Part II, line 18 (attach Form 4797)	9	
10	Other income (see instructions — attach schedule)	10	
11	**Total income.** Add lines 3 through 10	11	174,580.

Deductions (See instructions for limitations on deductions)

12	Compensation of officers (Schedule E, line 4)	12	35,000.
13	Salaries and wages (less employment credits)	13	15,000.
14	Repairs and maintenance	14	
15	Bad debts	15	
16	Rents	16	9,000.
17	Taxes and licenses	17	4,225.
18	Interest	18	
19	Charitable contributions (see instructions for 10% limitation)	19	
20	Depreciation (attach Form 4562) . . . 20 22,989.		
21	Less depreciation claimed on Schedule A and elsewhere on return . . 21a 18,367.	21b	4,622.
22	Depletion	22	
23	Advertising	23	5,000.
24	Pension, profit-sharing, etc, plans	24	
25	Employee benefit programs	25	
26	Other deductions (attach schedule)	26	23,200.
27	**Total deductions.** Add lines 12 through 26	27	96,047.
28	Taxable income before net operating loss deduction and special deductions. Subtract line 27 from line 11	28	78,533.
29	Less: **a** Net operating loss deduction (see instructions) . . . 29a		
	b Special deductions (Schedule C, line 20) . . . 29b	29c	

Tax and Payments

30	**Taxable income.** Subtract line 29c from line 28	30	78,533.
31	Total tax (Schedule J, line 12)	31	14,951.
32	Payments: **a** 1997 overpayment credited to 1998 . . . 32a 0.		
	b 1998 estimated tax payments . . . 32b 15,000.		
	c Less 1998 refund applied for on Form 4466 . . 32c **d** Bal ► 32d 15,000.		
	e Tax deposited with Form 7004 . . . 32e		
	f Credit for tax paid on undistributed capital gains (attach Form 2439) . . . 32f		
	g Credit for federal tax on fuels (attach Form 4136). See instructions . . . 32g	32h	15,000.
33	Estimated tax penalty (see instructions). Check if Form 2220 is attached ► ☐	33	
34	Tax due. If line 32h is smaller than the total of lines 31 and 33, enter amount owed	34	
35	Overpayment. If line 32h is larger than the total of lines 31 and 33, enter amount overpaid	35	49.
36	Enter amount of line 35 you want: Credited to 1999 estimated tax ► . . . Refunded ►	36	49.

Sign Here

Under penalties of perjury, I declare that I have examined this return, including accompanying schedules and statements, and to the best of my knowledge and belief, it is true, correct, and complete. Declaration of preparer (other than taxpayer) is based on all information of which preparer has any knowledge.

► Signature of Officer   Date   ► Title

Paid Preparer's Use Only

Preparer's Signature ►
Firm's Name (or yours if self-employed) and Address ► **Self Prepared**
Date
Check if self-employed ☐
Preparer's Social Security Number ►
EIN ►
ZIP Code ►

BAA CPCA0212 11/16/98

Form 1120 (1998) ABC Corporation   36-6135404   Page 2

Schedule A — Cost of Goods Sold (see instructions.)

1	Inventory at beginning of year	61,621.
2	Purchases	256,000.
3	Cost of labor	185,000.
4	Additional Section 263A costs (attach schedule)	
5	Other costs (attach schedule)...See Other Costs Statement	117,017.
6	**Total.** Add lines 1 through 5	619,638.
7	Inventory at end of year	46,718.
8	**Cost of goods sold.** Subtract line 7 from line 6. Enter here and on page 1, line 2	572,920.

9a Check all methods used for valuing closing inventory:
  (i) ☐ Cost as described in Regulations Section 1.471-3
  (ii) ☐ Lower of cost or market as described in Regulations Section 1.471-4
  (iii) ☐ Other (specify method used and attach explanation.) ▶ _____

b Check if there was a writedown of subnormal goods as described in Regulations Section 1.471-2(c) .... ▶ ☐
c Check if the LIFO inventory method was adopted this tax year for any goods (if checked, attach Form 970) ...... ▶ ☐
d If the LIFO inventory method was used for this tax year, enter percentage (or amounts) of closing inventory computed under LIFO 9d
e If property is produced or acquired for resale, do the rules of Section 263A apply to the corporation? ...... ☐ Yes ☐ No
f Was there any change in determining quantities, cost, or valuations between opening and closing inventory? If 'Yes,' attach explanation .... ☐ Yes ☐ No

Schedule C — Dividends and Special Deductions (see instructions.)

		(a) Dividends received	(b) Percentage	(c) Special deductions (a) x (b)
1	Dividends from less-than-20%-owned domestic corporations that are subject to the 70% deduction (other than debt-financed stock)		70	
2	Dividends from 20%-or-more-owned domestic corporations that are subject to the 80% deduction (other than debt-financed stock)		80	
3	Dividends on debt-financed stock of domestic and foreign corporations (Section 246A)			
4	Dividends on certain preferred stock of less-than-20%-owned public utilities		42	
5	Dividends on certain preferred stock of 20%-or-more-owned public utilities		48	
6	Dividends from less-than-20%-owned foreign corporations and certain FSCs that are subject to the 70% deduction		70	
7	Dividends from 20%-or-more-owned foreign corporations and certain FSCs that are subject to the 80% deduction		80	
8	Dividends from wholly owned foreign subsidiaries subject to the 100% deduction (Section 245(b))		100	
9	**Total.** Add lines 1 through 8. See instructions for limitation			
10	Dividends from domestic corporations received by a small business investment company operating under the Small Business Investment Act of 1958		100	
11	Dividends from certain FSCs that are subject to the 100% deduction (Sec 245(c)(1))		100	
12	Dividends from affiliated group members subject to the 100% ded (Section 243(a)(3))		100	
13	Other dividends from foreign corporations not included on lines 3, 6, 7, 8, or 11			
14	Income from controlled foreign corporations under subpart F (attach Form(s) 5471)			
15	Foreign dividend gross-up (Section 78)			
16	IC-DISC and former DISC dividends not included on lines 1, 2, or 3 (Section 246(d))			
17	Other dividends			
18	Deduction for dividends paid on certain preferred stock of public utilities			
19	**Total dividends.** Add lines 1 through 17. Enter here and on line 4, page 1 ▶			
20	**Total special deductions.** Add lines 9, 10, 11, 12, and 18. Enter here and on line 29b, page 1 ▶			

Schedule E — Compensation of Officers (see instructions for line 12, page 1.)

Complete Schedule E only if total receipts (line 1a plus lines 4 through 10 on page 1, Form 1120) are $500,000 or more.

1	(a) Name of officer	(b) Social security number	(c) Percent of time devoted to business	(d) Common	(e) Preferred	(f) Amount of compensation
	Michael Williams	382-31-8401	100.0%	50.0%	%	35,000.
	Mary Roberts	336-58-5900	100.0%	50.0%	%	35,000.
			%	%	%	
			%	%	%	

2	Total compensation of officers	70,000.
3	Compensation of officers claimed on Schedule A and elsewhere on return	35,000.
4	Subtract line 3 from line 2. Enter the result here and on line 12, page 1	35,000.

Form **1120** (1998) ABC Corporation   36-6135404   Page **3**

Schedule J — Tax Computation (see instructions.)

1 Check if the corporation is a member of a controlled group (see Sections 1561 and 1563) .... ▶ ☐
  Important: Members of a controlled group, see instructions.
2a If the box on line 1 is checked, enter the corporation's share of the $50,000, $25,000, & $9,925,000 taxable income brackets (in that order):
  (1) $ _____   (2) $ _____   (3) $ _____
 b Enter the corporation's share of: (1) Additional 5% tax (not more than $11,750) ...... $ _____
                                       (2) Additional 3% tax (not more than $100,000) ..... $ _____
3 Income tax. Check if a qualified personal service corporation
  under Section 448(d)(2) (see instructions) .... ▶ ☐ | 3 | 14,951. |
4a Foreign tax credit (attach Form 1118) .... | 4a |
 b Possessions tax credit (attach Form 5735) .... | 4b |
 c Check: ☐ Nonconventional source fuel credit ☐ QEV credit (attach Form 8834) | 4c |
 d General business credit. Enter here and check which forms are attached: ☐ 3800
   ☐ 3468 ☐ 5884 ☐ 6478 ☐ 6765 ☐ 8586 ☐ 8830 ☐ 8826
   ☐ 8835 ☐ 8844 ☐ 8845 ☐ 8846 ☐ 8820 ☐ 8847 ☐ 8861 .. | 4d |
 e Credit for prior year minimum tax (attach Form 8827) .... | 4e |
5 **Total credits.** Add lines 4a through 4e .... | 5 |
6 Subtract line 5 from line 3 .... | 6 | 14,951. |
7 Personal holding company tax (attach Schedule PH (Form 1120)) .... | 7 |
8 Recapture taxes. Check if from: ☐ Form 4255   ☐ Form 8611 .... | 8 |
9 Alternative minimum tax (attach Form 4626) .... | 9 |
10 Add lines 6 through 9 .... | 10 | 14,951. |
11 Qualified zone academy bond credit (attach Form 8860) .... | 11 |
12 **Total tax.** Subtract line 11 from line 10. Enter here and on line 31, page 1 .... | 12 | 14,951. |

Schedule K — Other Information (see instructions.)

1 Check method of accounting: **a** ☐ Cash
  b ☒ Accrual **c** ☐ Other (spec) ▶ _____
2 See the instructions and state the:
 a Business activity code no. (New) ▶ 339900
 b Business activity ▶ Manufacturing
 c Product or service ▶ Toys

3 At the end of the tax year, did the corporation own, directly or indirectly, 50% or more of the voting stock of a domestic corporation? (For rules of attribution, see Section 267(c).) .... **No: X**

  If 'Yes,' attach a schedule showing: **(a)** name and identifying number, **(b)** percentage owned, and **(c)** taxable income or (loss) before NOL and special deductions of such corporation for the tax year ending with or within your tax year.

4 Is the corporation a subsidiary in an affiliated group or a parent-subsidiary controlled group? .... **No: X**
  If 'Yes,' enter employer identification number and name of the parent corporation ▶ _____

5 At the end of the tax year, did any individual, partnership, corporation, estate or trust own, directly or indirectly, 50% or more of the corporation's voting stock? (For rules of attribution, see Section 267(c).) ... **Yes: X**

  If 'Yes,' attach a schedule showing name and identifying number. (Do not include any information already entered in **4** above.)
  Enter % owned ▶ ____ 50.00

6 During this tax year, did the corporation pay dividends (other than stock dividends and distributions in exchange for stock) in excess of the corporation's current and accumulated earnings and profits? (See Sections 301 and 316.) .... **No: X**

  If 'Yes,' file Form 5452. If this is a consolidated return, answer here for the parent corporation and on **Form 851**, Affiliations Schedule, for each subsidiary.

7 Was the corporation a U.S. shareholder of any controlled foreign corporation? (See Sections 951 and 957.) .... **No: X**
  If 'Yes,' attach Form 5471 for each such corporation.
  Enter no. of Forms 5471 attached ▶ _____

8 At any time during the 1998 calendar year, did the corporation have an interest in or a signature or other authority over a financial account (such as a bank account, securities account, or other financial account) in a foreign country? .... **No: X**
  If 'Yes,' the corporation may have to file Form TD F 90-22.1.
  If 'Yes,' enter name of foreign country ▶ _____

9 During the tax year, did the corporation receive a distribution from, or was it the grantor of, or transferor to, a foreign trust? If 'Yes,' the corporation may have to file Form 3520 ... **No: X**

10 At any time during the tax year, did one foreign person own, directly or indirectly, at least 25% of: **(a)** the total voting power of all classes of stock of the corporation entitled to vote, or **(b)** the total value of all classes of stock of the corporation? .... **No: X**
   If 'Yes,'
   a Enter percentage owned ▶ _____
   b Enter owner's country ▶ _____
   c The corporation may have to file Form 5472. Enter number of Forms 5472 attached ▶ _____

11 Check this box if the corporation issued publicly offered debt instruments with original issue discount .... ▶ ☐
   If so, the corporation may have to file Form 8281.

12 Enter the amount of tax-exempt interest received or accrued during the tax year ▶ $ _____ 0.

13 If there were 35 or fewer shareholders at the end of the tax year, enter the number ▶ _____ 2

14 If the corporation has an NOL for the tax year and is electing to forego the carryback period, check here .... ▶ ☐

15 Enter the available NOL carryover from prior tax years (do not reduce it by any deduction on line 29a).
   ▶ $ _____ 0.

BAA   CPCA0234 12/13/98

3-22   2000/CORPORATIONS, PARTNERSHIPS, ESTATES, AND TRUSTS

Form 1120 (1998)   ABC Corporation   36-6135404   Page 4

Schedule L — Balance Sheets per Books

Assets	Beginning of tax year (a)	Beginning of tax year (b)	End of tax year (c)	End of tax year (d)
1 Cash		11,338.		32,408.
2a Trade notes and accounts receivable	23,100.		65,595.	
b Less allowance for bad debts		23,100.		65,595.
3 Inventories		61,621.		46,718.
4 U.S. government obligations				
5 Tax-exempt securities (see instructions)				
6 Other current assets (attach schedule)				49.
7 Loans to stockholders				
8 Mortgage and real estate loans				
9 Other investments (attach schedule)				
10a Buildings and other depreciable assets	90,500.		90,500.	
b Less accumulated depreciation	13,561.	76,939.	36,550.	53,950.
11a Depletable assets				
b Less accumulated depletion				
12 Land (net of any amortization)				
13a Intangible assets (amortizable only)				
b Less accumulated amortization				
14 Other assets (attach schedule)				
15 Total assets		172,998.		198,720.

Liabilities and Stockholders' Equity

	(a)	(b)	(c)	(d)
16 Accounts payable		48,810.		23,325.
17 Mortgages, notes, bonds payable in less than 1 year				
18 Other current liabilities (attach sch)				
19 Loans from stockholders				
20 Mortgages, notes, bonds payable in 1 year or more				
21 Other liabilities (attach schedule)				
22 Capital stock: a Preferred stock				
b Common stock	100,000.	100,000.	100,000.	100,000.
23 Additional paid-in capital				
24 Retained earnings — Approp				
25 Retained earnings — Unappropriated		24,188.		75,395.
26 Adjustments to shareholders' equity				
27 Less cost of treasury stock				
28 Total liabilities and stockholders' equity		172,998.		198,720.

Note: You are not required to complete Schedules M-1 and M-2 below if the total assets on line 15, column (d) of Schedule L are less than $25,000.

Schedule M-1 — Reconciliation of Income (Loss) per Books With Income per Return (see instructions.)

1 Net income (loss) per books	63,207.	7 Income recorded on books this year not included on this return (itemize):		
2 Federal income tax	14,951.	Tax-exempt interest $ _____ 0.		
3 Excess of capital losses over capital gains				
4 Income subject to tax not recorded on books this year:				0.
		8 Deductions on this return not charged against book income this year (itemize):		
5 Expenses recorded on books this year not deducted on this return (itemize):		a Depreciation .. $ _____		
a Depreciation .... $ _____		b Contrib carryover . $ _____		
b Contributions carryover .. $ _____				
c Travel & entertainment .. $ 375.				
	375.	9 Add lines 7 and 8		0.
6 Add lines 1 through 5	78,533.	10 Income (line 28, page 1) — line 6 less line 9		78,533.

Schedule M-2 — Analysis of Unappropriated Retained Earnings per Books (Line 25, Schedule L)

1 Balance at beginning of year	24,188.	5 Distributions .... a Cash		12,000.
2 Net income (loss) per books	63,207.	b Stock _____ c Property		
3 Other increases (itemize): _____		6 Other decreases (itemize):		
		7 Add lines 5 and 6		12,000.
4 Add lines 1, 2, and 3	87,395.	8 Balance at end of year (line 4 less line 7)		75,395.

CPCA0234 12/13/98

CORPORATIONS: ORGANIZATION AND CAPITAL STRUCTURE   3-23

Form **4562**	**Depreciation and Amortization** (Including Information on Listed Property) ► See instructions. ► Attach this form to your return.	OMB No. 1545-0172 **1998**
Department of the Treasury Internal Revenue Service (99)		67
Name(s) Shown on Return: ABC Corporation	Business or Activity to Which This Form Relates: Form 1120 Line 20	Identifying Number: 36-6135404

Part I — Election to Expense Certain Tangible Property (Section 179)
(Note: If you have any 'listed property,' complete Part V before you complete Part I.)

1	Maximum dollar limitation. If an enterprise zone business, see instructions	1	$18,500.
2	Total cost of Section 179 property placed in service. See instructions	2	
3	Threshold cost of Section 179 property before reduction in limitation	3	$200,000.
4	Reduction in limitation. Subtract line 3 from line 2. If zero or less, enter -0-	4	
5	Dollar limitation for tax year. Subtract line 4 from line 1. If zero or less, enter -0-. If married filing separately, see instructions	5	

6	(a) Description of property	(b) Cost (business use only)	(c) Elected cost

7	Listed property. Enter amount from line 27	7	
8	Total elected cost of Section 179 property. Add amounts in column (c), lines 6 and 7	8	
9	Tentative deduction. Enter the smaller of line 5 or line 8	9	
10	Carryover of disallowed deduction from 1997. See instructions	10	
11	Business income limitation. Enter the smaller of business income (not less than zero) or line 5 (see instrs)	11	
12	Section 179 expense deduction. Add lines 9 and 10, but do not enter more than line 11	12	
13	Carryover of disallowed deduction to 1999. Add lines 9 and 10, less line 12 ► 13		

Note: *Do not use Part II or Part III below for listed property (automobiles, certain other vehicles, cellular telephones, certain computers, or property used for entertainment, recreation, or amusement). Instead, use Part V for listed property.*

Part II — MACRS Depreciation for Assets Placed in Service Only During Your 1998 Tax Year
(Do Not Include Listed Property)

Section A — General Asset Account Election

14 If you are making the election under Section 168(i)(4) to group any assets placed in service during the tax year into one or more general asset accounts, check this box. See instructions ► ☐

Section B — General Depreciation System (GDS) (See instructions)

(a) Classification of property	(b) Month and year placed in service	(c) Basis for depreciation (business/investment use only — see instructions)	(d) Recovery period	(e) Convention	(f) Method	(g) Depreciation deduction
15a 3-year property						
b 5-year property						
c 7-year property						
d 10-year property						
e 15-year property						
f 20-year property						
g 25-year property			25 yrs		S/L	
h Residential rental property			27.5 yrs	MM	S/L	
			27.5 yrs	MM	S/L	
i Nonresidential real property			39 yrs	MM	S/L	
				MM	S/L	

Section C — Alternative Depreciation System (ADS) (See instructions)

16a Class life					S/L	
b 12-year			12 yrs		S/L	
c 40-year			40 yrs	MM	S/L	

Part III — Other Depreciation (Do Not Include Listed Property) (See instructions)

17	GDS and ADS deductions for assets placed in service in tax years beginning before 1998	17	19,469.
18	Property subject to Section 168(f)(1) election	18	
19	ACRS and other depreciation	19	

Part IV — Summary (See instructions)

20	Listed property. Enter amount from line 26	20	3,520.
21	Total. Add deductions on line 12, lines 15 and 16 in column (g), and lines 17 through 20. Enter here and on the appropriate lines of your return. Partnerships and S corporations — see instructions	21	22,989.
22	For assets shown above and placed in service during the current year, enter the portion of the basis attributable to Section 263A costs	22	

BAA For Paperwork Reduction Act Notice, see the separate instructions.   FDIZ0812   07/23/98   Form **4562** (1998)

Form 4562 (1998) ABC Corporation 36-6135404 Page 2

Part V — Listed Property — Automobiles, Certain Other Vehicles, Cellular Telephones, Certain Computers, and Property Used for Entertainment, Recreation, or Amusement

Note: *For any vehicle for which you are using the standard mileage rate or deducting lease expense, complete **only** 23a, 23b, columns (a) through (c) of Section A, all of Section B, and Section C if applicable.*

Section A – Depreciation and Other Information (Caution: See instructions for limits for passenger automobiles.)

23a Do you have evidence to support the business/investment use claimed? .... [X] Yes [ ] No   23b If 'Yes,' is the evidence written? ...... [X] Yes [ ] No

(a) Type of property (list vehicles first)	(b) Date placed in service	(c) Business/ investment use percentage	(d) Cost or other basis	(e) Basis for depreciation (business/investment use only)	(f) Recovery period	(g) Method/ Convention	(h) Depreciation deduction	(i) Elected Section 179 cost
24 Property used more than 50% in a qualified business use (see instructions):								
truck	01/02/97	100.00	11,000.	11,000.	5.00	200DB/HY	3,520.	
25 Property used 50% or less in a qualified business use (see instructions):								

26 Add amounts in column (h). Enter the total here and on line 20, page 1 .... | 26 | 3,520.
27 Add amounts in column (i). Enter the total here and on line 7, page 1 .... | 27 |

Section B — Information on Use of Vehicles

Complete this section for vehicles used by a sole proprietor, partner, or other 'more than 5% owner,' or related person.
If you provided vehicles to your employees, first answer the questions in Section C to see if you meet an exception to completing this section for those vehicles.

	(a) Vehicle 1	(b) Vehicle 2	(c) Vehicle 3	(d) Vehicle 4	(e) Vehicle 5	(f) Vehicle 6
28 Total business/investment miles driven during the year (**Do not** include commuting miles)						
29 Total commuting miles driven during the year						
30 Total other personal (noncommuting) miles driven						
31 Total miles driven during the year. Add lines 28 through 30						
	Yes No	Yes No	Yes No	Yes No	Yes No	Yes No
32 Was the vehicle available for personal use during off-duty hours?						
33 Was the vehicle used primarily by a more than 5% owner or related person?						
34 Is another vehicle available for personal use?						

Section C — Questions for Employers Who Provide Vehicles for Use by Their Employees

*Answer these questions to determine if you meet an exception to completing Section B for vehicles used by employees who **are not** more than 5% owners or related persons.*

	Yes	No
35 Do you maintain a written policy statement that prohibits all personal use of vehicles, including commuting, by your employees?		
36 Do you maintain a written policy statement that prohibits personal use of vehicles, except commuting, by your employees? See instructions for vehicles used by corporate officers, directors, or 1% or more owners		
37 Do you treat all use of vehicles by employees as personal use?		
38 Do you provide more than five vehicles to your employees, obtain information from your employees about the use of the vehicles, and retain the information received?		
39 Do you meet the requirements concerning qualified automobile demonstration use? See instructions		

Note: *If your answer to 35, 36, 37, 38, or 39 is 'Yes,' you need not complete Section B for the covered vehicles.*

Part VI — Amortization

(a) Description of costs	(b) Date amortization begins	(c) Amortizable amount	(d) Code Section	(e) Amortization period or percentage	(f) Amortization for this year
40 Amortization of costs that begins during your 1998 tax year:					

41 Amortization of costs that began before 1998 .... | 41 |
42 **Total.** Enter here and on 'Other Deductions' or 'Other Expenses' line of your return .... | 42 |

FDIZ0812 07/23/98

ABC Corporation 36-6135404
Form 1120 12/31/98

Page 2, Schedule A, Line 5, Other Costs:

Depreciation	18,367
Heat & electric 85% (16,000)	13,600
Insurance	10,000
Maintenance	2,200
Materials & supplies	5,000
Payroll taxes	15,650
Rent	51,000
Small tools	1,200
	117,017

Page 1, Line 26, Other Deductions:

Delivery	2,400
Dues & subscriptions	725
Entertainment 50% (750)	375
Heat & electric 15% (16,000)	2,400
Insurance	2,000
Legal & accounting	1,000
Office supplies	2,500
Packaging	7,000
Telephone	4,800
	23,200

CHAPTER 4

CORPORATIONS: EARNINGS & PROFITS AND DIVIDEND DISTRIBUTIONS

LEARNING OBJECTIVES

After completing Chapter 4, you should be able to:

1. Understand the role that earnings and profits plays in determining the tax treatment of distributions.

2. Compute a corporation's earnings and profits.

3. Apply the rules for allocating earnings and profits to distributions.

4. Understand the tax impact of property dividends on the recipient shareholder and the corporation making the distribution.

5. Understand the nature and treatment of constructive dividends.

6. Distinguish between taxable and nontaxable stock dividends and stock rights.

KEY TERMS

Accumulated earnings and profits	Earnings and profits	Stock rights
Constructive dividend	Property dividend	Unreasonable compensation
Current earnings and profits	Stock dividend	

OUTLINE

I. TAXABLE DIVIDENDS - IN GENERAL

   A. Distributions are presumed to be dividends unless the parties can show otherwise.

   B. Dividend income is limited to the amount of E & P of the distributing corporation.

   C. Distributions not taxed as dividends, because of insufficient E & P, are return of capital to the extent of stock basis and any remainder is gain.

   D. E & P represents the corporation's economic ability to pay a dividend without impairing its capital.

II. EARNINGS AND PROFITS

   A. Computation of E & P begins with taxable income
      1. E & P is increased by:
         a. all previously excluded items of income
         b. deferred gain on installment sales, in the year of sale
      2. E & P is decreased by:
         a. excess capital losses.
         b. expenses to produce tax-exempt income.
         c. Federal income taxes paid.
         d. non-deductible insurance premiums, fines, and penalties.
         e. related party losses
      3. Timing adjustments
         a. Charitable contribution carryovers
         b. net operating loss carryovers
         c. capital loss carryovers
      4. Accounting method adjustments
         a. deferred gain on installment sales
         b. depreciation, for E & P, must be computed using the straight-line method over the assets ADR midpoint life; §179 expense are deducted over 5 years.
         c. depletion, for E & P, must be computed using the cost depletion method.
         d. the percentage completion method of accounting for long-term contracts is required for E & P purposes.
         e. intangible drilling costs, for E & P, are amortized over 60 months.
         f. mine exploration and development costs, for E & P, are amortized over 120 months.

B. E & P measures the earnings of the corporation that are treated as available for distribution to shareholders as dividends.

C. Current versus Accumulate E & P
1. Current E & P is determined by making a series of adjustments to the corporation's taxable income.
2. Current E & P is allocated on a pro rata basis to distributions made during the year.
3. Accumulated E & P is the total of all previous years' current E & P, since February 28, 1913, as computed on the first day of each tax year, reduced by distributions made.
4. Accumulated E & P is applied, to the extent necessary, in chronological order beginning with the earliest distribution.

D. Allocating E & P To Distributions
1. Positive current E & P + positive accumulated E & P = dividend.
2. Positive current E & P + deficient accumulated E & P = dividend to extent of current E & P.
3. Deficient current E & P + positive accumulated E & P = Net E & P.
   a. if positive, distribution is a dividend, to the extent of the balance;
   b. if negative, distribution is return of capital.

III. PROPERTY DIVIDENDS

A. Property Dividends - Effect on the Shareholder
1. The amount of the distribution is the fair market value of the property on the date of distribution, reduced by liabilities of the corporation assumed by the shareholder.
2. The shareholder's basis in the property is the fair market value of the property on the date of distribution.

B. Property Dividends - Effect on the Corporation
1. All distributions of appreciated property cause gain recognition, the property is treated as sold for its fair market value.
2. On distributions of property having a tax basis in excess of its fair market value the corporation cannot recognize a loss.
3. If distributed property is subject to a liability in excess of basis, the fair market value of the property for determining gain on the distribution cannot be less than that liability.

C. Effect of Corporate Distributions on E & P
1. E & P is reduced by the amount of money, or, if property, the greater of the fair market value or the adjusted basis minus any liability.

2. E & P is increased by gain recognized on appreciated property distributions.
3. Under no circumstances can a distribution generate or add to a deficit in E&P.

IV. CONSTRUCTIVE DIVIDENDS

A. Types of Constructive Dividends
1. The key factor determining dividend status is that a measurable economic benefit is conveyed to the shareholder.
2. The most frequent constructive dividend situations are:
   a. shareholder use of corporate-owned property,
   b. bargain sale of corporate property to a shareholder,
   c. bargain rental of corporate property,
   d. payments for the benefit of a shareholder,
   e. unreasonable compensation,
   f. loans to shareholders,
   g. loans to a corporation by shareholders.

B. Tax Treatment of Constructive Dividends
1. Constructive distributions are, for tax purposes, treated the same as actual distributions.
2. The constructive distribution is taxable dividend income to the extent of the corporation's current and accumulated E & P.

V. STOCK DIVIDENDS AND STOCK RIGHTS

A. Stock Dividends
1. Stock dividends are not taxable if they are pro rata distributions on common stock.
2. Five exceptions to nontaxability of stock dividends apply for distributions which can change proportionate ownership:
   a. distributions payable either in stock or property.
   b. distributions resulting in the receipt of property by some shareholders and an increase in the proportionate interest of other shareholders in the assets or E & P of the distributing corporation.
   c. distributions of preferred stock to some common stock shareholders and common stock to other common shareholders.
   d. distributions on preferred stock other than an increase in the conversion ratio of convertible preferred stock made solely to account for a stock dividend or stock split with respect to stock into which the preferred stock is convertible.

    e. distributions of convertible preferred stock, unless it can be shown that the distribution will not result in a disproportionate distribution.
   3. E & P is not reduced for nontaxable stock dividends.
   4. Taxable stock dividends are treated, by the corporation, the same as any other property distribution.
   5. The shareholder's basis in a taxable stock dividend is fair market value.
   6. The shareholder's basis in the stock on which a nontaxable stock dividend is distributed is reallocated to all the shares.

  B. Stock Rights are subject to the same rules as stock dividends for determining taxability.

VI. TAX PLANNING CONSIDERATIONS

  A. Corporation Distributions
   1. An E & P account should be established and maintained because E & P is the measure of dividend income to shareholders.
   2. There is no statute of limitations on the computation of E & P.

  B. Constructive Dividends
   1. Shareholders should try to structure their dealings with the corporation on an arm's length basis.
   2. Dealings between shareholders and closely held corporations should be as formal as possible.

Section 301-Property Distributions Effect on the Shareholder

Amount Distributed equals FMV of property minus liabilities assumed and any liabilities to which the property is subject immediately before and after distribution

↓

Is the existing E & P greater than the distribution amount? —No→ **Is the distribution greater than the existing E&P, and is the distribution less than the existing E&P plus the shareholders basis in the stock investment?** —No→ **Is the FMV of the distribution greater than the corporation's existing E&P plus the shareholders basis in the stock investment?**

↓Yes ↓Yes ↓Yes

Treat the entire distribution as dividend income.

Treat all of the distribution covered by existing E&P as dividend income, and the rest as return of capital

Treatment:
(1) Distribution covered by E&P is dividend income.
(2) Return of capital until basis of stock investment is zero.
(3) Remainder is capital gain

↓

Basis of property assumed by the shareholder:

FMV of the property on the distribution date.

CORPORATIONS: EARNINGS & PROFITS AND DIVIDEND DISTRIBUTIONS

Section 311-Property Distributions Effect on the Corporation

```
                    ┌─────────────────────────────┐
                    │ Is gain or loss recognized? │
                    │ Does Distribution affect E&P?│
                    └─────────────────────────────┘
                                  │
        ┌─────────────────────────┼─────────────────────────────┬─────────────────────────────────┐
        │                         │                             │                                 │
┌───────────────────┐   No   ┌──────────────────────┐   No   ┌──────────────────────────┐   No
│ Is it appreciated │───────▶│ Does the tax basis   │───────▶│ Is property subject to   │────────▶
│ property?         │        │ exceed FMV?          │        │ liability in excess of   │
└───────────────────┘        └──────────────────────┘        │ basis?                   │
        │ Yes                         │ Yes                  └──────────────────────────┘
        ▼                             ▼                             │ Yes
┌────────────────────────┐    ┌──────────────────────┐              ▼
│ Recognize gain as if   │    │ No loss is recognized│     ┌──────────────────────────┐
│ property were sold for │    └──────────────────────┘     │ Recognize gain FMV ≠     │
│ FMV on distribution    │                                 │ liability                │
│ date                   │                                 └──────────────────────────┘
└────────────────────────┘
                                      ▼
                            ┌──────────────────────┐
                            │ E&P increased by     │◀────────────────
                            │ gain recognized      │
                            └──────────────────────┘
                                      │
                                      ▼
                            ┌────────────────────────────┐
                            │ E&P reduced by amount of   │◀────────────
                            │ money or, the greater: FMV │
                            │ or adjusted basis less any │
                            │ liability                  │
                            └────────────────────────────┘
                                      │
                                      ▼
                            ┌────────────────────────────┐
                            │ Limitations on E&P         │
                            │ no distribution may generate│
                            │ or add to a deficit in E&P │
                            └────────────────────────────┘
```

≠ means is not less than

Section 305-Stock Dividends

Shareholder receives a stock dividend or rights to acquire stock

↓

Was distribution payable in either stock or property at the option of shareholder?
- No ↓
- Yes → Include in gross Income of shareholder

Did it result in a receipt of property (cash) by some shareholders and an increase in assets or E&P to others (stock dividend)?
- No ↓
- Yes → Include in gross Income of shareholder

Did some common shareholders receive common stock and others receive preferred?
- No ↓
- Yes → Include in gross Income of shareholder

Was it a distribution on preferred stock other than an increase in the conversion ratio of convertible preferred stock made solely to take in account a stock dividend or split into which is convertible?
- No ↓
- Yes → Include in gross Income of shareholder

Did distribution of convertible preferred stock result in a disproportionate distribution?
- No ↓
- Yes → Include in gross Income of shareholder

Stock dividend is not includible in gross income of shareholder

CORPORATIONS: EARNINGS & PROFITS AND DIVIDEND DISTRIBUTIONS 4-9

TEST FOR SELF-EVALUATION

True or False

T F 1. Gem Corporation has two classes of stock, Class A common and Class B preferred. Class B preferred stock CANNOT be converted into Class A common stock. If Gem declares a common stock dividend on the Class A stock pro rata among the shareholders, Class A shareholders must include the dividend in gross income. (IRS 96 3A-9)

T F 2. The current earnings and profits of a corporation at the time of a distribution by the corporation, do NOT necessarily determine whether the distribution is a taxable dividend. (IRS 95 3A-9)

T F 3. Generally, a shareholder will NOT include in gross income a distribution of stock or stock rights in a corporation if it is a distribution on preferred stock. (IRS 95 3A-10)

T F 4. If a corporation distributes property subject to a liability which is greater than the property's adjusted basis, the fair market value of the property is treated as NOT less than the liability assumed or acquired by the shareholder. (IRS 95 3A-11)

T F 5. A shareholder holding solely common stock does NOT include a distribution of common stock in gross income if other common shareholders received preferred stock in the same distribution. (IRS 94 3A-4)

T F 6. Corporation Y has a dividend reinvestment plan that allows its shareholders to use its dividends to buy more shares of stock in Corporation Y rather than receiving the dividend in cash. If shareholder W uses his dividends to buy more stock at a price equal to its fair market value, he does NOT report the dividends as income. (IRS 94 1A-7)

T F 7. A shareholder does NOT include in gross income a distribution of stock or rights to acquire stock in the distributing corporation if any shareholder may elect to receive money in lieu of the stock or rights. (IRS 93 3A-9)

T F 8. Generally, additional shares of stock received from nontaxable stock dividends or stock splits results in a per share reduction in the basis of the original stock. (IRS 93 1A-10)

Fill in the Blanks

1. The key factor in determining whether a dividend has in fact been paid is the measure of _____ conveyed to the shareholder.

4-10   2000/CORPORATIONS, PARTNERSHIPS, ESTATES, AND TRUSTS

2. Distributions by a corporation are presumed to be _____ unless the parties can prove otherwise.

3. When stock dividends are taxable, the basis to the shareholder-distributee is the _____.

4. The rules for determining the taxability of _____ are identical to those for determining taxability of stock dividends.

Multiple Choice

_____ 1. Cavalier, a calendar year C corporation, had accumulated earnings and profits of $30,000 as of January 1, 1996. On April 1, 1996 Cavalier distributed $55,000 in cash to Cavalier's sole shareholder. For 1996, Cavalier had earnings and profits of $20,000. The shareholder's adjusted basis in Cavalier's stock was $12,000 before the distribution. As a result of this distribution, what is the amount of the shareholder's ordinary dividend income and return of capital? (IRS 97 3C-69)

	Dividend Income	*Return of Capital*
a.	$50,000	$5,000
b.	$55,000	$0
c.	$30,000	$25,000
d.	$50,000	$12,000

_____ 2. Badger Corporation had $64,000 of earnings and profits before accounting for the following distributions to its sole shareholder:

Cash		$ 25,000
Real estate:	Adjusted Basis	70,000
	Fair market value	98,000
	Subject to a mortgage of	40,000

The shareholder assumes the $40,000 mortgage on the property. Without considering federal income taxes, what is the net reduction to Badger's earnings and profits? (IRS 97 3C-70)

a. $28,000
b. $55,000
c. $64,000
d. $68,000

_____ 3. On July 1, 1996, Rose, a calendar year C corporation, distributed an auto used 100% in its business to its sole shareholder. At the time of the distribution, the auto, which originally cost $18,000, had an adjusted basis of $6,000 and a fair market value of $5,000. There were no liabilities attached to the auto. No other distributions were made during 1996. As of January 1, 1996, Rose's earnings and profits were $8,000. By what amount will Rose reduce its earnings and profits as a result of the distribution of the auto? (IRS 97 3C-71)

a. $3,000
b. $4,000
c. $5,000
d. $6,000

_____ 4. Terre Corporation distributed depreciable personal property having a fair market value of $9,500 to its shareholders. The property had an adjusted basis of $5,000 to the corporation. Terre had correctly deducted $3,000 in depreciation on the property. What is the amount of Terre's TOTAL recognized gain on the distribution and how much of this gain will be considered ordinary income?
(IRS 97 3C-72)

	Total recognized Gain	Ordinary Income
a.	$4,500	$0
b.	$4,500	$3,000
c.	$4,500	$4,500
d.	$9,500	$0

_____ 5. Noble, a calendar-year accrual basis corporation, distributed shares of Reitz Corporation stock to Noble's employees in lieu of salaries. The salary expense would have been deductible as compensation if paid in cash. On the date of the payment, Noble's adjusted basis in the Reitz Corporation stock distributed was $25,000 and the stock's fair market value was $85,000. What is the tax effect to Noble Corporation? (IRS 97 3C-73)

a. $25,000 deduction
b. $25,000 deduction; $60,000 recognized gain
c. $85,000 deduction
d. $85,000 deduction; $60,000 recognized gain

_____ 6. For 1995, Roberts Corporation had a beginning balance of unappropriated retained earnings of $100,000 and net income per books of $125,000. During 1995 it paid cash dividends of $60,000, had a loss on sale of securities of $3,600, and received a refund of 1994 income taxes of $6,000. What is its ending balance of unappropriated retained earnings for 1995? (IRS 96 3C-55)

a. $225,000
b. $174,600
c. $171,000
d. $161,400

____ 7. Camden, Inc., a calendar year C corporation that began conducting business in 1983, had accumulated earnings and profits of $20,000 as of January 1, 1995. On October 1, 1995, Camden distributed $25,000 in cash to Beaufort, Camden's sole shareholder. Camden had a $20,000 DEFICIT in earnings and profits for 1995. Beaufort had an adjusted basis of $8,000 in his stock before the distribution. What is the amount of Beaufort's ordinary dividend income and capital gain as of the date of the distribution? (IRS 96 3C-57)

	Dividend Income	*Capital Gain*
a.	$ 0	$25,000
b.	$25,000	$ 0
c.	$ 5,000	$12,000
d.	$ 5,000	$ 8,000

____ 8. Elk Corporation, a calendar year C corporation, had accumulated earnings and profits of $60,000 as of January 1, 1995, the beginning of its tax year. Elk had an operating loss of $70,000 for the first 6 months of 1995, but had earnings and profits of $6,000 for the entire tax year 1995. Elk distributed $15,000 to its shareholders on July 1, 1995. What portion of the $15,000 distribution would be an ordinary dividend? (IRS 96 3C-58)

a. $15,000
b. $10,600
c. $6,000
d. $0

____ 9. Ball, a calendar year C corporation, had accumulated earnings and profits of $50,000 as of January 1, 1995. Ball had a deficit in earnings and profits for 1995 of $65,000. Ball distributed $25,000 to its shareholders on July 1, 1995. What is Ball Corporation's accumulated earnings and profits as of December 31, 1995? (IRS 96 3C-59)

a. $0
b. ($15,000)
c. ($32,500)
d. ($40,000)

____ 10. Which of the following statements is CORRECT? (IRS 95 1B-30)
a. Stock dividends are distributions made by a corporation of another corporation's stock.
b. In computing basis for new stock received as a result of a nontaxable dividend, it is immaterial whether the stock received is identical or not to the old stock.
c. If a stock dividend is taxable, the basis of the old stock does NOT change.
d. If you receive nontaxable stock rights and allow them to expire, you have a loss equal to the fair market value of the rights.

CORPORATIONS: EARNINGS & PROFITS AND DIVIDEND DISTRIBUTIONS 4-13

___ 11. E-Z Corporation, which has a dividend reinvestment plan, paid dividends of $20 per share during 1994. Carlos, who owned 100 shares of E-Z Corporation prior to the distribution, participated in the plan by using ALL the dividends to purchase 20 additional shares of stock. He purchased the stock for $100 per share when the fair market value was $125 per share. How much dividend income must Carlos report on his 1994 income tax return? (IRS 95 1C-48)

    a. $2,500
    b. $2,000
    c. $500
    d. $0

___ 12. In 1992, Chim purchased 100 shares of preferred stock of Donald Corporation for $5,000. In 1994, she received a stock dividend of 20 additional shares of preferred stock in Donald. On the date of the distribution, the preferred stock had a fair market value of $40 per share. What is Chim's basis in the new stock she received as a result of the stock dividend? (IRS 95 1C-60)

    a. $1,000
    b. $833
    c. $800
    d. $0

___ 13. In 1993, Corey bought 200 shares of ABC stock at $10 a share. In 1994, Corey bought an additional 100 shares of ABC stock at $20 a share. In 1995, ABC declared a 2-for-1 stock split. How many shares of ABC stock does Corey own and what is the basis of the stock? (IRS 96 1C-58)

    a. 400 shares at $5 a share and 200 shares at $10 a share
    b. 400 shares at $10 a share and 200 shares at $20 a share
    c. 200 shares at $20 a share and 100 shares at $40 a share
    d. 600 shares at $6.67 per share

___ 14. On January 3, 1995, Susan purchased 300 shares of common stock in Corporation Y for $120 per share. Four months later she purchased 100 additional shares at $180 per share. On December 10, 1995, Susan received a 20% nontaxable stock dividend. The new and the old stock are identical. What is the amount of Susan's basis in each share of Corporation Y stock after the stock dividend?
(IRS 96 1C-59)

    a. 480 shares at $112.50 a share
    b. 360 shares at $120 a share and 120 shares at $180 a share
    c. 360 shares at $120 a share and 120 shares at $150 a share
    d. 360 shares at $100 a share and 120 shares at $150 a share

____ 15. In 1993, Nancy bought 100 shares of Trauna, Inc. for $5,000 or $50 a share. In 1994, Nancy bought 100 shares of Trauna stock for $8,000 or $80 a share. In 1995, Trauna declared a 2-for-1 stock split. Nancy sold 50 shares of the stock she received from the stock split for $2,000. She could NOT definitely identify the shares she sold. What is the amount of Nancy's net capital gain from this sale for 1995?   (IRS 96 1C-68)

   a. $0
   b. $750
   c. $1,625
   d. $2,000

CORPORATIONS: EARNINGS & PROFITS AND DIVIDEND DISTRIBUTIONS 4-15

Comprehensive Problem

In its financial statements for 1998, JD Corporation showed $300,000 of pre-tax accounting income. Indicate any adjustments for the following recorded transactions and determine JD Corporation's taxable income and net increase (decrease) in E & P for the year.

	Per Book	Taxable	E & P
Pre-tax accounting income:	$300,000		
1. Insurance Premium Expense:			
a. fire & casualty	15,000		
b. employee group life (employee named beneficiary)	20,000		
c. term life on John Doe, Pres. (JD Corp. is beneficiary)	7,000		
2. Interest Income:			
a. University City bonds	15,000		
b. CD, National Bank	10,000		
3. Dividend Income:			
a. Fuji Photo, Tokyo	3,000		
b. Sears Roebuck, Chicago	8,000		
4. Charitable Contributions:			
a. United Way	7,000		
b. bowling team shirts	350		
c. University City Park District (unimproved land, FMV $50,000; cost $35,000)	35,000		
5. Depreciation (straight-line for book accelerated for tax)	40,000	70,000	
6. Dividend Payments:			
a. cash 20,000			
b. common stock, 1 for 3 $12 par value			
TAXABLE INCOME		_____	
7. Federal Income Taxes:		_____	_____
NET CHANGE IN E & P			_____

SOLUTIONS

True or False

1. F (p. 4-16; distribution does not change proportionate common interest)
2. T (p. 4-7)
3. F (p. 4-16; distributions on preferred stock are generally taxable)
4. T (p. 4-11)
5. F (p. 4-16; distribution changes proportionate common interest)
6. F (p. 4-16; dividend income is used to purchase additional stock)
7. F (p. 4-16; taxable - can alter proportionate interests)
8. T (p. 4-16)

Fill in the Blanks

1. economic benefit (p. 4-3)
2. dividends (p. 4-2)
3. fair market value (p. 4-16)
4. stock rights (p. 4-17)

Multiple Choice

1. a (p. 4-8; presumed that current E&P cover all distributions until shown otherwise)
2. b (p. 4-12; + 28,000 gain, - 25,000 cash, - 98,000 FMV, + 40,000 mortgage)
3. d (p. 4-12; adjusted basis > FMV, no loss recognized)
4. b (total gain: 9,500 - 5,000 = 4,500; depreciation recap is ordinary income)
5. d (gain: 85,000 FMV - 25,000 basis; salary deduction is FMV)
6. c (begin balance + net income per books - dividends paid = 165,000; official answer, 171,000 assumes Roberts is a cash basis taxpayer and the refund arose only in 1995)
7. c (p. 4-9; accumulated, 20,000 - ¾(20,000) = 5,000 dividend; 25,000 distribution - 5,000 dividend - 8,000 basis = 12,000 capital gain)
8. a (see #1)
9. c (p. 4-9; accumulated 50,000 - ½(65,000) = 18,500 dividend; 25,000 distribution - 18,500 dividend = 6,500 return of capital. 7/1/95 balance in E&P is zero; 12/31 balance is 32,500 or remaining ½(65,000))
10. c (4-16; for taxable stock dividends, basis is FMV)
11. a (p. 4-14; FMV of stock over actual investment is constructive dividend)
12. c (p. 4-16; distributions of stock to preferred shareholders are taxable, 20 shares X $40 per share)
13. a (p. 4-16; basis is reallocated: $2,000 over 400 shares plus $2,000 over 200 shares)
14. d (p. 4-16; basis is reallocated: $36,000 over 360 shares plus $18,000 over 120shares)
15. b (without specific identification, FIFO applies: 50 shares at $25 per share = 1,250 basis; 2,000 proceeds - 1,250 basis = 750 gain)

Comprehensive Problem

For tax:

1. + 7,000 expense to produce tax-exempt income
2. - 15,000 tax-exempt municipal
3. - 5,600 dividend received 70% (8,000) unrelated, domestic corporation
4. + 11,600 contribution before limitation is 7,000 + 50,000 the 10% limitation is applied to taxable income before dividends received deduction or any charitable deduction, in this problem, $30,400; $57,000 - $30,400 results in a $26,600 carry forward; the $350 could be deducted as a promotional expense.
5. - 30,000 net change

TAXABLE INCOME: $268,000

7. $87,770; .15(50,000) + .25(25,000) + .34(193,000) + .05(168,000)

For E & P

4. -15,000 57,000 allowable - 42,000 taken
5. -20,000 dividend payment
7. -87,770 federal income tax

NET CHANGE IN E & P: 177,230 increase

CHAPTER 5

CORPORATIONS: REDEMPTIONS AND LIQUIDATIONS

LEARNING OBJECTIVES

After completing Chapter 5, you should be able to:

1. Identify the stock redemptions that are treated as sales or exchanges of stock rather than as dividend income.

2. Recognize that some redemption transactions do not qualify for sale or exchange treatment.

3. Understand the tax consequences when a parent corporation distributes stock and securities of its subsidiary.

4. Understand the tax consequences of complete liquidations for both the corporation and its shareholders.

5. Identify tax planning opportunities available to minimize the tax impact in stock redemptions and complete liquidations.

KEY TERMS

Attribution	Not essentially equivalent	Redemption to pay death taxes
Complete termination redemptions	redemption	Residual method
Corporate liquidation	Partial liquidation	Section 338 election
Disproportionate redemption	Preferred stock bailout	Stock redemption
Meaningful reduction test		

OUTLINE

I. STOCK REDEMPTIONS - IN GENERAL

   A. In a stock redemption, a corporation buys or exchanges property for its own stock, from a shareholder.

   B. Only qualifying stock redemptions are treated as a sale or exchange for tax purposes; other redemptions are treated as dividend distributions.
      1. Qualifying stock redemptions are defined in the Code.
      2. Generally, in a qualified stock redemption, a substantial reduction in the shareholder's ownership of the corporation must occur.

II. STOCK REDEMPTIONS - SALE OR EXCHANGE TREATMENT

   A. Five major types of stock redemptions qualify for sale or exchange treatment:
      1. Not essentially equivalent to a dividend
      2. Substantially disproportionate in terms of shareholder effect
      3. Complete termination of a shareholder's interest
      4. Partial liquidation of a corporation
      5. To pay a shareholder's death taxes.

   B. Stock Attribution Rules
      1. Stock attribution rules treat a shareholder as the owner of stocks held by certain related parties, in addition to the stocks owned personally.
      2. For an individual, redeeming stock, the following are related parties:
         a. <u>family</u>: spouse, children, grandchildren, parents = deemed 100% owned by the individual.
         b. <u>Partnership</u>: partnership's stock times the partner's proportionate share in the partnership = % deemed owned by the individual.
         c. <u>estate or trust</u>: estate or trust's stock times the beneficiary's proportionate interest in the estate or trust = % deemed owned by the individual.
         d. <u>corporation</u>: if a more than 50% shareholder, corporate stock times the shareholder's proportionate interest in the corporation = % deemed owned by the individual.
      3. Stock attribution rules also apply to partnerships, estates, trusts and corporations redeeming stock:
         a. <u>partnership</u> stock of partner is deemed 100% owned.
         b. <u>estate or trust</u> stock of beneficiary is deemed 100% owned.
         c. <u>corporation</u> stock of 50% or more shareholder, is deemed 100% owned.

C. Not Essentially Equivalent Redemptions
1. A meaningful reduction in the shareholder's proportionate ownership must take place.
2. A decrease in the redeeming shareholder's voting control is considered the most important factor in determining whether or not a meaningful reduction has occurred.

D. Disproportionate Redemptions
1. After the distribution, the shareholder must own less than 80% of his interest in the corporation before the redemption.
2. After the distribution, the shareholder must own less than 50% of the total combined voting power of all classes of stock entitled to vote.

E. Complete Termination Redemptions
1. Family attribution rules do not apply if both the following conditions are met:
   a. the former shareholder has no interest, other than as a creditor, in the corporation for at least 10 years after the redemption, and
   b. the former shareholder files an agreement to notify the IRS of any acquisition of a prohibited interest within the 10 year period.
2. The former shareholder may reacquire an interest in the corporation through a bequest or inheritance but in no other manner.

F. Redemptions in Partial Liquidation
1. A noncorporate shareholder is allowed exchange treatment when:
   a. the distribution is not essentially equivalent to a dividend, or
   b. an active business is terminated.
2. The not essentially equivalent to a dividend requirement tests the effect of the distribution on the corporation, not the shareholder; there must be a genuine contraction of the business of the corporation.
3. The complete termination of a business test requires:
   a. the corporation has more than one trade or business and two or more of the businesses have been in existence for at least 5 years.
   b. the corporation terminates one trade or business that has been in existence for at least 5 years while continuing a remaining business that has been in existence for at least 5 years.
   c. the terminated trade or business was not acquired in a taxable transaction within the 5 year period.
4. Any distribution must be made within the taxable year in which the plan is adopted or within the succeeding taxable year.

G. Redemptions to Pay Death Taxes
1. A redemption which qualifies as a redemption to pay death taxes is not subject to the not essentially equivalent to a dividend or substantially disproportionate tests.
2. The value of the stock in the gross estate of a decedent must exceed 35% of the value of the adjusted gross estate.
3. The distribution is limited to the sum of death taxes, funeral, and certain estate administration expenses.

H. Effect on the Corporation Redeeming Its Stock
1. Loss is not recognized on purchases or repurchases of stock, these are capital transactions.
2. The E & P account of a corporation is reduced by a stock redemption in proportion to the amount of the corporation's outstanding stock that is redeemed. The amount of the reduction cannot exceed the ratable share of the E & P attributable to the stock redeemed.

III. STOCK REDEMPTIONS - NO SALE OR EXCHANGE TREATMENT

A. Redemptions that do not qualify for exchange treatment as provided for in the Code are considered dividends to the extent of the corporation's E & P.

B. The Problem
1. Clever taxpayers devised a scheme to bail out corporate profits.
   a. A corporation would issue a nontaxable, nonvoting preferred stock dividend on common stock.
   b. The shareholder would assign a portion of his common stock basis to the preferred stock.
   c. The shareholder would then sell the preferred stock to a third party.
2. The sale of the preferred stock bailed out corporate profits as capital gains without reducing the shareholder's percentage ownership of the corporation.

C. §306 Stock Bailout Solution
1. The shareholder has ordinary income on the sale of the preferred stock to a third party, to the extent that, the fair market value of the preferred stock, on the date of distribution, would have been a dividend.
2. No loss is recognized on the sale of the preferred stock by the shareholder.
3. If the corporation redeems the preferred stock, the proceeds constitute dividend income to the extent of the corporation's E & P on the date of the redemption.

D. §306 Stock is stock other than common that:
1. is received as a nontaxable stock dividend.
2. is received tax-free in a corporate reorganization which is substantially the same as a stock dividend.
3. is received in exchange for §306 stock.
4. has a basis determined by reference to §306 stock.
5. If a corporation has no E & P on the date of a nontaxable preferred stock dividend, the stock will not be §306 stock.

E. Redemption Through Use of Related Corporations
1. When a shareholder controls two corporations and sells stock of one corporation to the other corporation, the sale may be treated as a redemption subject to the not essentially equivalent and disproportionate redemption rules.
   a. control is 50% of the combined voting power, or 50% of the total value of all classes of stock.
   b. stock attribution rules apply in determining the degree of control.
2. If the rules are not satisfied, the exchange is treated as a taxable dividend to the extent of the corporations' E & P.
   a. first reducing the E & P of the acquiring corporation, then, if necessary, the E & P of the issuing corporation.
   b. the acquiring corporation treats the stock received as a contribution to capital, having the same basis as the transferring shareholder had.
   c. the individual's basis in the stock of the acquiring corporation is increased by his basis in the stock surrendered.
3. If the rules are satisfied, the sale is recast as a redemption of the stock of the acquiring corporation.

IV. DISTRIBUTION OF STOCK AND SECURITIES OF A CONTROLLED CORPORATION

A. Stock in an existing subsidiary corporation can be distributed to the shareholders of the parent tax-free, if the requirements of Section 355 are met.

B. §355 applies only:
1. To distributions which involve at least 80% of the stock of the subsidiary.
2. When, following the distribution, both the parent and the subsidiary are engaged in an active trade or business in which they had been so engaged for at least 5 years prior to the distribution, and
3. When the parent has held stock in the subsidiary for at least 5 years prior to the distribution.

C. The distribution must be motivated by a sound business purpose.

D. The distribution can be in the form of:
1. Spin-off: distribution of subsidiary stock to parent shareholders, giving control of the subsidiary to those shareholders.
2. Split-off: distribution of subsidiary stock in exchange for some parent corporation stock.
3. Split-up: stock of two subsidiary corporations is distributed to parent shareholders and the parent corporation is liquidated.

E. Tax Consequences of a §355 Distribution at the Shareholder Level
1. A shareholder can receive only stock or securities tax-free.
2. If the principal amount of securities received is greater than the principal amount of the securities surrendered, or if no securities were given up, the fair market value of the excess principal received is treated and taxed as boot.
3. The basis of stock held before the exchange is allocated among all stocks held immediately after the transaction in proportion to their relative fair market values.

V. LIQUIDATIONS

A. A corporate liquidation occurs, for tax purposes, when a corporation ceases to be a going concern.

B. Legal dissolution under state law is not required for Federal tax purposes.

VI. LIQUIDATIONS - EFFECT ON THE DISTRIBUTING CORPORATION

A. A liquidating corporation recognizes gain and/or loss on the distribution of property.
1. The property distributed is treated as if sold at its fair market value.
2. If subject to a liability, the fair market value cannot be less than that liability.

B. Two exceptions prohibit loss recognition when either of the following situations exist:
1. Related-party, 50% shareholder ownership, and
   a. the distribution is not pro rata, or
   b. the property distributed is disqualified property.
2. Built-in loss property distributions
   a. for property held for 2 years or less, it is assumed that the property was contributed to the corporation for the purpose of providing a loss.

b. the restriction applies only to the amount of the built-in loss.
 3. Disqualified property is property acquired by the corporation as a capital contribution or §351 exchange during the five year period before the liquidating distribution.

VII. LIQUIDATIONS - EFFECT ON THE SHAREHOLDER

 A. Generally, gain or loss is recognized as though the shareholder sold his stock.

 B. The shareholder's gain recognition on the receipt of notes from corporate installment sales of capital assets may be deferred and recognized as received.

VIII. LIQUIDATIONS - PARENT SUBSIDIARY SITUATIONS

 A. If a parent corporation liquidates a subsidiary, under §332, no gain or loss is recognized by the parent or by the subsidiary for property distributed to the parent. §332 requires:
  1. The parent must own at least 80% of the voting stock and 80% of the total value of all subsidiary stock on the date the plan of liquidation is adopted and thereafter until all property is distributed.
  2. The subsidiary must distribute all its property within the taxable year or within 3 years from the close of the tax year when the plan was adopted and the first distribution was made.
  3. The subsidiary must be solvent.

 B. Tax Treatment When a Minority Interest Exists
  1. Distributions to minority shareholders cause gain, but not loss, recognition to the distributing corporation.
  2. The minority shareholder recognizes gain or loss as on a stock sale.

 C. Indebtedness of Subsidiary to Parent
  1. The subsidiary does not recognize gain or loss on property transferred to the parent in a §332 liquidation.
  2. Realized gain or loss is recognized by the parent on property received to satisfy a debt of the subsidiary.

 D. Basis of Property Received by the Parent Corporation
  1. Property received by the parent retains the same basis as it had in hands of the subsidiary. The parent's basis in the subsidiary's stock disappears.
  2. When a parent liquidates a subsidiary shortly after a qualified stock purchase and elects under §338, it will have a basis in subsidiary assets equal to its basis in subsidiary stock.

E. A §338 election is irrevocable but liquidation of the subsidiary is not required. To qualify:
1. At least 80% of the voting power and value must be acquired by the purchasing corporation.
2. Acquisition takes place within a 12 month period beginning with the first purchase of stock.
3. The stock must be acquired in a taxable transaction.
4. The election must be made by the 15th day of the 9th month after the month in which the purchase occurred.

F. Under §338, the acquired corporation is deemed to have sold its assets for the amount of the purchasing corporation's "grossed up" basis in the stock, adjusted for liabilities of the subsidiary.
1. The grossed up basis is the parent's basis in the subsidiary stock times 1 over the percentage of value held by the purchasing corporation, on the acquisition date.
2. This basis is allocated among the assets of the subsidiary using the residual method. Purchase price in excess of the total fair market value of identifiable assets is allocated to goodwill or going concern value.
3. The subsidiary is treated as having sold all assets for their fair market value on the acquisition date and recognizes gain or loss.
4. The day after acquisition, the subsidiary is treated as a new corporation that purchased all of the assets and, if not liquidated, the holding period begins anew. If the subsidiary is liquidated, the parent's holding period begins on the date the parent acquired the subsidiary's stock.

TEST FOR SELF-EVALUATION

True or False

T F 1. Liquidating distributions, sometimes called liquidating dividends, are, at least in part, one form of a return of capital, assuming the distributee has at least some adjusted basis in the stock. (IRS 91 1A-5)

T F 2. A corporation will recognize a gain or loss on the distribution of its property to its noncorporate shareholders in complete liquidation of the corporation, the same as if the corporation had sold the property to its shareholders at fair market value. (IRS 90 3A-17)

T F 3. A proportionate distribution to a corporate shareholder by a corporation in partial redemption of stock, pursuant to a plan of partial liquidation, is treated as a dividend to the extent of earnings and profits of the distributing corporation. (IRS 90 3A-18)

T F 4. When a corporation does not cancel redeemed stock but holds the stock in its treasury, the corporation will recognize a gain or loss on its retransfer or redistribution. (IRS 92 3A-9)

T F 5. Corporation W has 2,000 shares of its only class of stock outstanding. Mr. D owns 1,500 shares and his son, Randy, owns 500 shares. W redeemed all 1,500 shares from Mr. D for $45,000. Mr. D kept his position in W as an officer and director. This redemption qualifies for capital gain treatment by Mr. D since all of his ownership in W has been terminated. (IRS 90 3A-19)

T F 6. Corporation K distributed land use in its business to its shareholders in a qualified redemption of stock. At the time of the distribution, the land had an adjusted basis to K of $200,000, and a fair market value of $500,000. Corporation K does not recognize any gain on this distribution. (IRS 90 3A-20)

T F 7. In a complete liquidation of a corporation, the character of a shareholder's gain or loss is generally determined by the character of the asset(s) in the hands of the corporation before distribution to the shareholder. (IRS 91 3A-18)

T F 8. The gain or loss to a shareholder from a distribution in liquidation of a corporation is to be determined by comparing the amount of the distribution with the adjusted basis of the stock regardless of whether the distribution is in partial or complete liquidation of the corporation. (IRS 91 3A-19)

T F   9.   After a stock redemption, if a shareholder's ownership percentage of all voting stock is less than 80% of his percentage of all voting stock held before the redemption, and the shareholder owns less than 50% of all voting stock of the corporation after the redemption, the redemption is considered substantially disproportionate. (IRS 91 3A-20)

T F 10.   In May, 1992, Lion Corporation distributed property in proportionate redemption of its stock in partial liquidation. Lion distributed land to Peter, a 50% shareholder. Lion distributed a building to Black Corporation, a 50% shareholder. The distribution was NOT essentially equivalent to a dividend and was made pursuant to a plan adopted in March of 1992. This transaction meets the requirements of Internal Revenue Code Section 302 and would be treated as a distribution of corporate assets in exchange for stock. (IRS 93 3A-10)

T F 11.   Under the constructive ownership rules that apply to a partial stock redemption, a waiver of family attribution may qualify a redemption for exchange treatment. (IRS 92 3A-10)

Fill in the Blanks

1. Generally, in the application of Section 332 to the liquidation of a subsidiary by a parent corporation, the property received by the parent carries the _____ basis in the hands of the parent as it did in the hands of the subsidiary.

2. Section 332 _____ apply to an insolvent subsidiary.

3. The effect of Section 338 is to give the assets acquired by a parent corporation in the liquidation of its subsidiary the _____ basis as the stock which the parent held in the subsidiary.

4. Liquidations and _____ parallel each other concerning their effect on the E & P of the distributing corporation.

5. Section 306 was enacted to preclude individuals from pulling earnings out of a corporation via the _____.

6. Stock redemptions which qualify for exchange treatment include distributions that are: _____ to a dividend, _____, in _____ of a shareholder's interest and, to pay _____.

7. A stock redemption is treated as "substantially disproportionate" if, after the distribution, the shareholder owns less than _____ of his holdings prior to the distribution and less than _____ of the combined voting power of all stock.

8. A subsidiary does not recognize gain or loss on a liquidating distribution to a parent corporation that directly owns _____ of the subsidiary's stock.

Multiple Choice

_____ 1. Under a plan of complete liquidation, Jayhawk Corporation distributed land, having an adjusted basis of $26,000, to its sole shareholder. The land was subject to a liability of $38,000 which the shareholder assumed for legitimate business purposes. The fair market value of the land on the date of distribution was $35,000. What is the amount of Jayhawk's recognized gain or loss?
(IRS 97 3C-74)

    a. $9,000
    b. $12,000
    c. ($3,000)
    d. ($29,000)

_____ 2. Anne owned 1,000 shares of Oswego Corporation. Anne had purchased the stock in 1988 at $100 per share. Pursuant to Oswego's plan of complete liquidation, Anne received land with a fair market value of $75,000 and an adjusted basis of Oswego of $50,000 on December 1, 1995, and she received $50,000 cash on January 15, 1996. The distributions resulted in complete liquidation of Oswego Corporation. What is the amount of Anne's long-term capital gain for 1995 and 1996?
(IRS 97 3C-75)

	1995	1996
a.	$ 0	$ 0
b.	$12,500	$12,500
c.	$ 0	$25,000
d.	$15,000	$10,000

_____ 3. Burke Corporation had earnings and profits of $500,000 before distributions. Due to economic conditions, Burke, in partial liquidation, distributed land having an adjusted basis to Burke of $135,000 and a fair market value of $150,000 to Mr. Ashby for 95% of his interest in Burke. Mr. Ashby's adjusted basis in the stock at the time of the distribution was $180,000. What is the amount of Burke Corporation's recognized gain or (loss)?
(IRS 97 3C-76)

    a. $0
    b. $15,000
    c. ($30,000)
    d. ($45,000)

_____ 4. Two unrelated individuals, Tom and Dave, own all the stock of Huskie Corporation, which has earnings and profits of $400,000. Because of his inactivity in the business for the last several years, Tom has decided to retire from the business completely and move to Hawaii. Accordingly, Huskie Corporation will redeem all the stock owned by Tom and, in return, Tom will receive a distribution of $500,000. Tom's adjusted basis in the stock is $250,000. What will be the tax effect to Tom? (IRS 97 3C-77)

a. $400,000 dividend
b. $500,000 dividend
c. $100,000 capital gain
d. $250,000 capital gain

_____ 5. You may receive a return of capital distribution based on your stock. All of the following are true except: (IRS 96 1B-28)

a. A return of capital reduces the basis of your stock.
b. When the basis of your stock has been reduced to zero, report any additional return of capital as a capital loss.
c. Any liquidating distribution you receive is NOT taxable to you until you have recovered the basis of your stock.
d. If the total liquidating distributions you receive are less than the basis of your stock, you may have a capital loss.

_____ 6. Ranger Corporation's only class of stock is owned as follows:

Matthew	40%
Darlene, Matthew's sister	25%
Matthew's and Darlene's father	25%
Matthew's and Darlene's grandfather	10%

What is Matthew's percentage of stock ownership under the attribution rules for stock redemptions? (IRS 96 3B-26)

a. 65%
b. 75%
c. 90%
d. 100%

_____ 7. Heritage Corporation distributed an antique automobile to Rene, its sole shareholder. On the date of the distribution, the automobile had a fair market value of $30,000 and an adjusted basis to Heritage of $22,000. What is the amount of Heritage Corporation's recognized gain on the distribution?
(IRS 96 3C-60)

a. $30,000
b. $12,000
c. $8,000
d. $0

_____ 8. Ann owned two blocks of Biddle Corporation stock which had the following characteristics:

Block	Shares	Acquired	Basis
1	200	06/01/94	$20,000
2	50	07/01/95	$12,500

Ann's two blocks of stock combined represented 10% of Biddle's only class of stock outstanding. Pursuant to Biddle's complete liquidation, Ann received a $50,000 cash distribution on December 1, 1995 in exchange for her 250 shares. Biddle's earnings and profits balance immediately before any liquidating distribution was $50,000. What is the amount and character of Ann's gain or loss?
(IRS 96 3C-61)

a. $50,000 dividend income
b. $17,50 long-term capital gain
c. $20,000 long-term capital gain and $2,500 short-term capital loss
d. No gain or loss

_____ 9. Daring Corporation, pursuant to a plan of complete liquidation, distributed land acquired in 1990 to Maria, its sole shareholder. The land had a fair market value of $120,000, an adjusted basis to Daring of $90,000, and was subject to a liability of $125,000 which was assumed by Maria. Maria owned 500 shares of Daring which she had purchased in 1988 for $50,000. Daring does NOT qualify as a small business corporation. What is the character and the amount of the gain or (loss) recognized by Maria and Daring Corporation? (IRS 96 3C-62)

	Maria	Daring
a.	$50,000 ordinary loss	$30,000 ordinary gain
b.	$50,000 long-term capital loss	$35,000 long-term capital gain
c.	$55,000 long-term capital loss	$30,000 long-term capital gain
d.	$55,000 long-term capital loss	$35,000 long-term capital gain

_____ 10. Mouse Corporation owns as an investment, 10% of the stock of Salem Corporation with an adjusted basis of $4,000 and a fair market value of $44,000. Mouse uses the Salem stock to redeem approximately 1%, or $10,000 par value, of its own outstanding stock from unrelated, noncorporate shareholders. As a result of this transaction, Mouse must report gain of: (IRS 96 3C-64)

a. $0
b. $2,000
c. $40,000
d. $44,000

_____ 11. Diana, the sole shareholder of Ancient Corporation's only class of stock, owns 1000 shares which she purchased in 1984. Diana's basis in the stock is $2,000,000. During 1995, Ancient, which had earnings and profits of $5,000,000, redeeemed 900 shares for $4,500,000. What is the amount and character of Diana's gain? (IRS 96 3C-65)

a. $4,500,000 dividend
b. $4,500,000 capital gain
c. $2,700,000 dividend
d. $2,700,000 capital gain

SOLUTIONS

True or False

1. T (p. 5-23)
2. T (p. 5-24)
3. T (p. 5-11; sale or exchange treatment in partial liquidations apply only to noncorporate shareholders)
4. F (p. 5-15; capital transaction)
5. F (p. 5-10; no interest other than as a creditor)
6. F (p. 5-15; FMV - adjusted basis)
7. F (p. 5-29; in the hands of the shareholder)
8. T (p. 5-4, 29)
9. T (p. 5-8)
10. F (p. 5-11; only noncorporate shareholders)
11. T (p. 5-6; attribution waived only for complete termination redemptions)

Fill in the Blanks

1. same (p. 5-35)
2. doesn't (p. 5-30)
3. same (p. 5-35)
4. stock redemptions (p. 5-23)
5. preferred stock bail-out approach (p. 5-16)
6. not essentially equivalent; substantially disproportionate; termination; shareholder's death taxes (p. 5-6)
7. 80%; 50% (p. 5-8)
8. 80% or more (p. 5-30)

Multiple Choice

1. b (FMV not less than liability, $38,000 - 26,000)
2. c (original basis: $100,000 - $75,000 received in 1995; remaining basis $25,000 - $50,000 received in 1996)
3. b (FMV minus adjusted basis)
4. d (complete termination redemption)
5. b (additional return of capital would be capital gain)
6. a (spouse, children, grandchildren and parents, not sibling or grandparent)
7. c (30,000 - 22,000)
8. c (distribution @ $200 per share, 200 shares @ $100 per share, long-term, 50 shares @ $250, short-term)
9. d (Maria,: 120,000 FMV-50,000 basis = 70,000 gain - 125,000 liability = 55,000 loss Daring: 125,000 liability - 90,000 basis)
10. c (FMV - basis)
11. a (no reduction in proportionate ownership and adequate E & P)

CHAPTER 6

ALTERNATIVE MINIMUM TAX AND CERTAIN PENALTY TAXES IMPOSED ON CORPORATIONS

LEARNING OBJECTIVES

After completing Chapter 6, you should be able to:

1. Explain the reason for the alternative minimum tax.

2. Calculate the alternative minimum tax applicable to corporation.

3. Understand the function of adjusted current earnings (ACE).

4. Appreciate the purpose of the accumulated earnings tax.

5. Determine the reasonable needs of the business.

6. Compute the accumulated earnings tax.

7. Discuss the reason for the personal holding company tax.

8. Recognize the requirements for personal holding company status.

9. Compute the personal holding company tax.

10. Compare the accumulated earnings and personal holding company taxes.

KEY TERMS

Accumulated earnings credit	Bardahl formula	Ordinary gross income
Accumulated earnings tax	Consent dividend	Personal holding company
Adjusted current earnings	Deficiency dividend	(PHC)
Adjusted ordinary gross income	Dividends paid deduction	Reasonable needs of a
Alternative minimum tax	Minimum credit (AET)	business
Alternative minimum taxable income	Minimum tax credit (AMT)	Tax preference items

OUTLINE

I. ALTERNATIVE MINIMUM TAX

A. C corporations are subject to an alternative minimum tax (AMT).
   1. Qualified 'small corporations' having average gross receipts of $5 million or less, in the preceding 3 years, are not subject to the AMT for tax years beginning after December 31, 1997.
   2. If the corporation did not exist for three years, the gross receipts test is applied on the basis of the period during which it did exist.
   3. A corporation that passes the $5 million average gross receipts test will continue to qualify as a small corporation as long as average gross receipts for three years preceding the tax year do not exceed 7.5 million.

B. AMT calculation:
   Regular Taxable Income Before NOL Deduction

   +/- Adjustments
   1. Depreciation of property placed in service after 1986 and before 1999:
      a. real property - the excess of regular tax depreciation over straight-line, 40 year life, mid-month convention.
      b. personal property - the excess of accelerated depreciation over the amount determined using 150% DB, ADS class life, same convention as for regular tax.
   2. After 1998, the depreciation adjustment for real estate is eliminated and the adjustment for personal property is applied to the difference between DDB and 150% DB over the property's MACRS recovery period.
   3. Amortization of mining and exploration costs - the difference between the costs incurred and what would have resulted if the costs were capitalized and amortized over 10 years.
   4. Adjusted gain or loss - the difference between AMT and regular tax gain or loss on asset dispositions.
   5. Long-term contracts for AMT purposes are determined under the percentage of completion method for contracts entered into after March 1, 1986.
   6. Passive activities losses of certain closely held and personal service corporations.

   + Preferences
   1. Amortization claimed on certified pollution control facilities.
   2. Accelerated depreciation on real property in excess of straight line for property placed in service before 1987.
   3. Tax-exempt interest from specified private activity bonds.
   4. Percentage depletion claimed in excess of the adjusted basis of property.
   = Unadjusted AMTI

+/- ACE adjustments
1. ACE depreciation for property placed in service prior to 1994.
2. Inclusion in ACE of items included in E & P, net of related expenses
   a. tax-exempt interest income
   b. death benefits from life insurance contracts
   c. tax benefit exclusions.
3. Disallowance of items not deductible from E & P: 70% dividends received deduction from a less than 20% owned corporation.
4. Other adjustments based on rules for determining E & P
   a. intangible drilling costs
   b. circulation expenditures
   c. amortization of organizational expenditures
   d. LIFO inventory adjustments
   e. installment sales

- AMT NOL (not more than 90% of AMTI)

= AMTI

    C.   Generally the AMT is 20% of alternative minimum taxable income (AMTI) which exceeds the exemption amount of $40,000. The exemption is reduced by 25% of AMTI in excess of $150,000.

    D.   Minimum Tax Credit
1. AMT paid in one tax year may be carried forward indefinitely and used as a credit against regular tax liability that exceeds its tentative minimum tax.
2. Minimum tax credit may not be carried back and may not be offset against any future minimum tax liability.

II. PENALTY TAX ON UNREASONABLE ACCUMULATIONS

    A.   The tax law is designed to discourage the retention of earnings in a corporation beyond the normal business needs. A penalty tax is imposed on corporations that retain a surplus amount of earnings which, had they been distributed to the shareholder, would have been taxed, §531.

    B.   The Element of Intent
1. Application of the penalty tax is triggered when a group of shareholders control corporate policy and withhold dividends with the INTENT to avoid personal, ordinary income taxes.
2. Tax avoidance need not be the controlling reason for retaining earnings in the corporation; it just has to be a contributing reason to result in the application of the accumulated earnings tax.

C. Imposition of the Tax and the Accumulated Earnings Credit
1. The AET is in addition to the regular corporate tax and the alternative minimum tax.
2. It is 39.6% of the current year's addition to the corporate accumulated earnings balance not needed for a reasonable business purpose.
3. The accumulated earnings credit is the greater of:
   a. current E & P for the tax year needed to meet the reasonable needs of the business less net long-term capital gains for the year.
   b. The minimum credit: the difference between $250,000 ($150,000 for certain personal service corporations) and accumulated E & P at the close of the previous year.

D. Reasonable Needs of the Business
1. Must be specific, definite and feasible, anticipated needs for
   a. working capital and
   b. noncurrent expenditures, i.e. capital expenditures and extraordinary expenses.
2. The "Bardahl" formula is the standard method used to determine the working capital needs of an inventory corporation.

      Inventory Cycle
+   Accounts Receivable Cycle
−   Accounts Payable Cycle
×   Operating expenses other than accrued Federal income tax, depreciation, profit sharing and charitable contributions.
=   Working Capital Needs

3. A formula to develop the working capital needs required in a noninventory corporation has not been resolved as of yet. It is assumed it will follow the Bardahl formula using a human resource accounting approach.

E. Mechanics of the Penalty Tax
1. The accumulated earnings tax is applied against accumulated taxable income
2. Accumulated taxable income equals:
   a. Taxable Income
   b. +/− Certain Adjustments
   c. − Dividends Paid Deduction
   d. − Accumulated Earnings Credit
3. The certain adjustments which are deducted are:
   a. Corporate income tax for the year.

        b.   Excess charitable contributions
        c.   Capital loss adjustment.
        d.   Excess of net long-term capital gain over net short-term capital loss, minus the capital gain tax and net capital losses from prior years.
    4.   The certain adjustments, which are added are:
        a.   Capital loss carryovers and carrybacks.
        b.   Net operating loss deductions.
        c.   The dividends received deduction.

III. PERSONAL HOLDING COMPANY PENALTY TAX

  A.   The Personal Holding Company Penalty Tax, §541, was imposed to discourage the sheltering of passive income in a personal holding company, PHC.

  B.   The PHC penalty tax is in addition to the regular corporate tax and is 39.6% of undistributed personal holding company income.

  C.   Definition
    1.   For a company to be classified as a PHC, that company must meet both of the following tests:
        a.   More than 50% of the value of the outstanding stock of the corporation must have been owned by five or fewer individuals at any time during the last half of the taxable year.
        b.   Sixty percent or more of the corporation's adjusted ordinary gross income must be composed of passive types of incomes: dividends, interest, rents, royalties or certain personal service income.
    2.   For the 50% test for stock ownership, very broad rules of constructive ownership apply, §544:
        a.   stock owned by a corporation, partnership, trust, or estate is considered to be owned proportionately by its stockholders, partners, or beneficiaries.
        b.   stock owned by members of an individual's family or by his or her partner is considered to be owned by the individual.
        c.   A stock option is regarded as stock.
        d.   A convertible security is considered stock.
    3.   For the gross income test adjusted ordinary gross income (AOGI) is gross income, less gains from the sale or disposition of capital assets, and expenditures attributable to income from rents and mineral royalties.

  D.   Rental income is normally classified as PHC income. However, it may be excluded if:
    1.   50% or more of the corporation's AOGI is "adjusted income from rents," and
    2.   the dividends paid during the year are equal to or greater than the amount by which the nonrent PHC income exceeds 10% of ordinary gross income.

E. Adjusted income from mineral, oil, and gas royalties may be excluded from PHC income classification if the following three tests are met:
1. 50% or more of AOGI must constitute income from royalties;
2. nonroyalty PHC income may not exceed 10% of OGI; and
3. Section 162 business expenses, other than compensation paid to stockholders, must be at least 15% of AOGI.

F. Income from personal service contracts is PHC income only if:
1. the individual who is to perform the service is designated by someone other than the corporation and
2. the person designated to perform owns 25% or more of the corporation directly or indirectly at some time during the year.

G. Calculation of the PHC Tax
1. The PHC tax is applied against undistributed PHC income.
2. Undistributed PHC income is:
   a. Taxable income
   b. Plus:
      1. Dividends received deductions.
      2. A net operating loss, other than from the preceding year
      3. The excess of business expenses and depreciation over the income from nonbusiness property owned by the corporation.
   c. Minus:
      1. Federal income tax accrued.
      2. Excess charitable contributions
      3. The excess of long-term capital gain over short-term capital loss (net of tax).
   d. Equals: Adjusted taxable income
   e. Minus: Dividends paid deduction
   f. Equals: Undistributed personal holding company income (UPHCI)

H. Dividends include the total of dividends paid during the year, dividends considered as paid on the last day of the tax year, and consent dividends.

IV. A COMPARISON OF ACCUMULATED EARNINGS AND PHC TAXES

   A. The imposition of §541 does not require intent.

   B. §541 is applied to newly formed as well as older corporations.

   C. The stock ownership test of §542(a)(2) is very explicit with regard to the PHC penalty tax. § 531, AET, is subjective.

   D. Sufficient dividend distributions can eliminate either tax.
       1. The dividends include actual dividends, consent dividends, and distributions made during the grace period.
       2. In the case of a PHC, a deficiency dividend procedure can be used.

   E. §541 is a self-assessed tax; §531 is assessed by the IRS.

V. TAX PLANNING

   A. A corporation cannot be subjected to Sections 531 and 541 taxes simultaneously.

   B. To avoid the accumulated earnings tax:
       1. justification of earnings accumulated should be:
           a. documented during the period of accumulation,
           b. sincere, and
           c. pursued to the extent feasible
       2. avoid the argument that loans to shareholders have no bona fide business purpose.
       3. payments of dividends demonstrate good faith and the lack of tax avoidance motivation.

   C. An S corporation election will circumvent the application of §531 tax. The election is prospective in nature and may not be applied retroactively.

   D. Avoiding the PHC tax may be accomplished by:
       1. failing either test to avoid PHC classification
           a. dispersion of stock ownership, or
           b. decreasing the percentage relationship of PHCI to AOGI (reduce PHCI or increase AOGI)
       2. where rents or royalties are involved, consider maximizing the adjusted income to exempt it from PHC treatment.
       3. properly timing dividend distributions.

TEST FOR SELF-EVALUATION

True or False

T F 1. A business that is a mere holding or investment company is of no consideration for the intent of tax avoidance.

T F 2. A corporation may have to pay the alternative minimum tax if taxable income for regular income tax purposes, when combined with certain adjustments and preference items that apply in computing the alternative minimum tax, total more than $40,000. (IRS 90 3A-10)

T F 3. The reasonable business needs of a corporation are precisely outlined by the IRS.

T F 4. If a corporation paid an alternative minimum tax in 1988 because of adjustments or preference items that defer its tax liability rather than cause a permanent avoidance of the tax, the corporation's 1988 alternative minimum tax is available to be claimed as credit against its regular income for 1989 and later years. (IRS 90 3A-11)

T F 5. The Bardahl Manufacturing Corporation formula is used to determine the reasonable needs of the business to the exclusion of other significant data.

T F 6. Long-term capital gains can be accumulated by a corporation without any penalty tax.

T F 7. Accumulation of income for exotic ventures into areas not related to the business are acceptable as long as the company stays under the $250,000 accumulated earnings credit.

T F 8. Assuming a company is close to being classified as a personal holding company, due to its proximity to the 60% PHC income rule, it would be wise for the company to hold growth stocks, as opposed to high yield stocks; this is because the high growth stocks will not enter into the PHC income calculation until they are sold and consequently taxed at a capital gains rate.

T F 9. For tax years beginning after 1989, the alternative minimum tax rules require that the 150% declining balance method of depreciation be used for property placed in service after 1989. (IRS 91 3A-12)

T F 10. In determining working capital needs, it has been firmly established that all assets should be evaluated at their fair market values.

T F 11. Corporation X carries its net operating loss for 1986 back to 1983 for which X incurred a minimum tax liability. Corporation X must recompute its minimum tax liability for 1983. (IRS 87 3A-17)

Fill in the Blanks

1. The penalty tax on unreasonable accumulation of income is known as the _____ tax.

2. The tax rate on the excess accumulated income in excess of the $250,000 credit is _____%.

3. The justifiable needs of a business may be classified into two categories: _____ and _____ expenditures.

4. Average inventory, divided by the cost of goods sold, equals the _____.

5. The _____ of the marketable securities should be used in determining whether a corporation has excess accumulated earnings.

6. Accumulated taxable income (ATI) is the result of taxable income, plus or minus certain adjustments, minus the dividend paid deduction and the _____.

7. The payment of dividends _____ the amount of accumulated earnings subject to the accumulated earnings tax.

8. A personal holding company (PHC) is defined as a corporation which meets _____ of the following tests:

9. More than _____% of the value of the outstanding stock must be owned by _____ or fewer individuals at any time during the _____ of the taxable year.

10. A substantial proportion, _____%, of the corporate income (AOGI) must be composed of passive type income.

Multiple Choice

_____ 1.   XYZ Corporation has the following items of income and expense during the year:

Dividend income	$ 30,000
Rent income	120,000
Depreciation expense	30,000
Mortgage interest	25,000
Real estate taxes	25,000
Salaries	15,000
Dividends paid (4 shareholders)	18,000
Corporate income tax liability?	

From the above data, AOGI would be:

a. $150,000
b. $132,000
c. $ 70,000
d. $ 55,000
e. None of the above

_____ 2. From the above data, the corporate income tax liability is:

a. 4,855
b. 4,560
c. 5,100
d. 3,750
e. None of the above

_____ 3. To meet the ten percent rental income test, XYZ Corporation must pay out how much in dividends?

a. $30,000
b. $15,000
c. $18,000
d. -0-
e. None of the above

_____ 4. Assume 1998 taxable income is $41,500, of which $1,500 is dividend income, after the dividend exclusion. The Section 11 tax is $6,225 and dividends paid are $2,000. The PHC tax liability would be:

a. $8,338
b. $14,563
c. $14,421
d. $15,821
e. None of the above

_____ 5. Given the following data, determine the accumulated taxable income of Z Corporation for 1998:

Tax liability	116,630
Excess charitable contributions	15,000
Long-term capital gain, adjusted	20,000
Dividends received	80,000
Dividends paid this year	30,000
Accumulated earnings (1/1/98)	110,000
Taxable income	342,000

        a. $ 76,370
        b. $104,370
        c. $ 84,730
        d. $ 67,930
        e. None of the above

___ 6.   Assume the accumulated taxable income of the Z Corporation in Question 5 was $110,500. The accumulated earnings tax would be:

        a. $43,758
        b. $41,580
        c. $31,542
        d. $40,387
        e. None of the above

___ 7.   To avoid the classification of rental income as PHC income, adjusted income from rents must be 50% or more of AOGI. In the following problem, what is that percentage?

Interest on mortgage	$ 3,000
Real estate property taxes	2,000
Depreciation	1,500
Salaries	5,000
Rental income	14,000
AOGI	18,000

        a. 61%
        b. 19%
        c. 42%
        d. 25%
        e. None of the above

___ 8.   Given the following data:

Annual revenues	$800,000
Average annual accounts receivable	80,000
Yearly expenses	700,000
Average accounts payable	60,000

        the operating capital needed for one business cycle would be:

        a. $10,010
        b. $80,000
        c. $60,000
        d. $70,000
        e. None of the above

____ 9. The accumulated earnings tax does not apply to corporations that:

    a. Are personal service corporations
    b. Are personal holding companies
    c. Are members of an affiliated group

____ 10. The personal holding company tax

    a. Is imposed on corporations having 15 or more equal stockholders
    b. Applies regardless of the extent of dividend distributions
    c. Is self-assessed
    d. May apply if the minimum credit of $150,000 is exceeded

____ 11. The accumulated earnings tax can be imposed

    a. Regardless of the number of stockholders of a corporation
    b. On personal holding companies
    c. On companies that make distributions in excess of accumulated earnings
    d. Only on conglomerates

____ 12. Ray Holding Corp. has 18 unrelated equal stockholders. For the year ended December 31, 1997, Ray's income was from the following:

Interest Income	$ 25,000
Merchandising Operations	$ 40,000
Dividends from taxable domestic corporations	$125,000

Deductible expenses for 1997 totaled $20,000. Ray paid no dividends for the past three years. Ray's liability for personal holding company tax for 1997 will be based on

    a. $102,500
    b. $ 12,500
    c. $ 90,000
    d. $ -0-

____ 13. If a corporation's tentative minimum tax exceeds the regular tax, the excess amount is: (IRS 95 3B-28)

    a. payable in addition to the regular tax.
    b. carried back to the third preceding tax year.
    c. carried back to the first preceding tax year.
    d. subtracted from the regular tax.

____ 14. Given the following facts, what is the amount of Wood Corporation's alternative minimum tax? (IRS 95 3C-59)

Taxable income before net operating loss deductions	$85,000
Total adjustments to taxable income	(2,000)
Total tax preference items	45,000
Regular income tax	17,150

a. $1,250
b. $850
c. $450
d. $-0-

____ 15. Barrett Corporation's 1994 alternative minimum taxable income was $200,000. The exempt portion of Barrett's 1994 alternative minimum taxable income was:
(IRS 95 3C-60)

a. $0
b. $12,500
c. $27,500
d. $40,000

SOLUTIONS

True or False

1. F (p. 6-13; prima facie evidence of tax avoidance)
2. T (p. 6-10)
3. F (p. 6-14)
4. T (p. 6-10, 11)
5. F (p. 6-14; working capital needs)
6. T (p. 6-20)
7. T (p. 6-13)
8. T (p. 6-27)
9. F (p. 6-4; after 1986)
10. F (p. 6-19; FMV of marketable securities)
11. T (p. 6-4; AMT NOL cannot exceed 90% of AMTI)

Fill in the Blanks

1. accumulated earnings (p. 6-12)
2. 39.6% (p. 6-12)
3. working capital; extraordinary (p. 6-14)
4. inventory cycle (p. 6-15)
5. fair market value (p. 6-18)
6. accumulated earnings credit (p. 6-18)
7. reduces (p. 6-19)
8. both (p. 6-20)
9. 50%; five; last half (p. 6-21)
10. 60% (p. 6-21)

Multiple Choice

1. c Example 28 ($30,000 + 120,000) - ($30,000 + $25,000 + $25,000) = $70,000
2. c

Dividend income	$ 30,000	
Rental income	120,000	$150,000
Less: Depreciation	$ 30,000	
Mortgage interest	25,000	
Real estate taxes	25,000	
Salaries	15,000	$ 95,000
		55,000
Less dividend received deduction		21,000
Taxable income		34,000
Tax: 15%(34,000)		5,100

3. b

Nonrental PHC income	$ 30,000
Less 10% of OGI	15,000
	$ 15,000

4. b Taxable income $41,500
       Plus dividend received deduction
       ($1,500/.30) - ($1,500)   3,500
                                                   45,000
       Less Section 11 tax   6,225
       Less dividends paid   2,000
                                                   36,775
                                                 x 39.6%
       PHC tax liability   14,563

5. a Taxable income   342,000
      Plus 70% dividend deduction   56,000
                                                  398,000
      Less: Tax liability   116,630
            Excess charitable contributions   15,000
            Net long-term capital gain   20,000
            Dividends paid   30,000
            Accumulated earnings credit carryover 140,000
            Accumulated taxable income   76,370

6. a 39.6% (110,500)
7. c $14,000 - ($3,000 + $2,000 + 1,500) = $7,500 adjusted income from rents.
      $7,500/$18,000 = 42%
8. a (($80,000/$800,000)-($60,000/$700,000))x$700,000 = (.1-.0857) x $700,000 = $10,010
9. b (p. 6-21)
10. c (p. 6-32)
11. a (p. 6-12)
12. d (p. 6-22; definition, 5 or fewer owning 50% or more)
13. a (p. 6-3)
14. c Taxable income before NOL   85,000
       Minus adjustments   2,000
       Plus preferences   45,000
       Minus exemption   40,000
       AMTI   88,000
       Times 20%   17,600
       Less Regular tax   17,150

15. c (p. 6-9; $40,000 reduced by 25% of AMTI in excess of $150,000; 40,000 - 25%(50,000))

CHAPTER 7

CORPORATIONS: REORGANIZATIONS

LEARNING OBJECTIVES

After completing Chapter 7, you should be able to:

1. Gain a general understanding of corporate reorganizations.

2. Identify and apply the tax consequences of a corporate reorganization.

3. Identify the statutory requirements for the different types of reorganizations.

4. Recognize the judicial and administrative conditions that complement the statutory requirements for a nontaxable corporate reorganization.

5. Use the rules applicable to the carryover of tax attributes in a corporate reorganization.

6. Structure corporate reorganizations to obtain the desired tax consequences.

KEY TERMS

Business purpose	Equity structure shift	Recapitalization
Consolidation	Long-term tax-exempt rate	Reorganization
Continuity of business enterprise	Merger	Step transaction
Continuity of interest test	Owner shift	

OUTLINE

I. REORGANIZATIONS - IN GENERAL

  A. Summary of the Different Types of Reorganizations
   1. Type A: a statutory merger or consolidation;
   2. Type B: an exchange of stock for voting stock;
   3. Type C: an exchange of assets for voting stock;
   4. Type D: a divisive reorganization
   5. Type E: a recapitalization;
   6. Type F: a change in identity, form, or place of organization;
   7. Type G: an insolvent corporation

  B. Summary of Tax Consequences in a Tax-Free Reorganization
   1. Gain or Loss
     a. generally, no gain or loss is recognized unless consideration other than stock or securities is received.
     b. gain is recognized on securities received if the principal amount received is more than the principal amount of the securities surrendered.
     c. if consideration other than stock or securities is received, it is considered boot; the recognized gain is the lesser of boot received or the realized gain.
     d. any gain is treated as a dividend to the extent of the shareholder's pro rata share of the corporations E & P.
     e. losses are not recognized.
   2. Basis
     a. the basis of property received by the acquiring corporation is the same basis as in the hands of the target increased by the amount of gain recognized by the target on the transfer.
     b. the basis of stock and securities surrendered carries over to the stock and securities received, decreased by the amount of boot received, and increased by the amount of gain and dividend income recognized, if any.

II. TYPES OF TAX-FREE REORGANIZATIONS

  A. Type A
   1. Type A reorganizations include statutory mergers and consolidations.
   2. Advantages
     a. Type A reorganizations permit the greatest flexibility of any of the tax-free organizations, because the use of voting stock is not required.

- b. The use of money or property will constitute "boot," which may require the recognition of a gain. However, this will not destroy the tax-free treatment if the continuity of interest test is satisfied: at least 50% of the consideration must be stock.
 3. Disadvantages
    - a. Statutory compliance usually requires a majority approval of all shareholders; dissenting shareholders have the right to have their shares appraised and bought.
    - b. The acquiring corporation must assume all liabilities of the acquired corporation.
    - c. The use of a subsidiary to acquire the stock of the target company may reduce these problems,
        1. because the parent corporation is the majority stockholder, only the board of directors' approval is required.
        2. the parent's asset will be protected from target's creditors.

B. Type B
 1. Type B reorganizations require the exchange of stock for voting stock.
    - a. the acquiring corporation must give up only voting stock, and
    - b. after the exchange must own at least 80% of all classes of the target corporation's stock.
 2. Voting stock must be the sole consideration; this requirement is strictly construed.

C. Type C
 1. Type C reorganizations require the exchange of substantially all the assets of the target corporation for the voting stock of the acquiring corporation.
 2. The target corporation must distribute the stock, securities, and other properties it receives in the reorganization, as well as its own properties to its shareholders. It then, generally, is liquidated.
 3. The "voting stock" requirement for a C reorganization is less strict than it is for a B reorganization.

D. Type D
 1. Acquisitive D reorganization
    - a. the acquiring corporation transfers assets to the target corporation in exchange for control, 50%, of the target.
    - b. all stock and property received by the acquiring corporation must be distributed to the acquiring corporation's shareholders.
    - c. the acquiring corporation is liquidated.

2. Divisive D reorganization
   a. the acquiring corporation transfers assets to the target corporation in exchange for control, 80%, of the target.
   b. all stock received by the acquiring corporation must be distributed to the acquiring corporation's shareholders as:
      1. a spin-off - the shareholders do not give up any stock in the distributing corporation.
      2. a split-off - the shareholders exchange stock in the distributing corporation for stock in the new corporation.
   c. in a split-up, the assets of one corporation are transferred to two or more new corporations
      1. the stock of the new corporations is distributed to the transferor corporation's shareholders.
      2. the transferor corporation is liquidated.

E. Type E
   1. E reorganizations are recapitalizations, an exchange of:
      a. bonds for stock
      b. stock for stock
      c. bonds for bonds
   2. Potential tax consequences affect the shareholders who exchange stock or securities, not the corporation.

F. Type F
   1. F reorganizations merely change the identity, form or place of organization.
   2. Because the surviving corporation is the same corporation as its predecessor, tax attributes carry over.
   3. F reorganizations are restricted to single operating corporations.
   4. An F reorganization does not jeopardize a valid S election or §1244 stock status.

G Type G
   1. All or part of the assets of a debtor corporation are transferred to an acquiring corporation in a bankruptcy proceeding.
   2. Debtor corporation creditors must receive voting stock of the acquiring corporation for debt representing 80% or more of the fair market value of the debt of the debtor corporation.

III. JUDICIAL DOCTRINES

A. Five judicially-created doctrines have become the basic requirements for a tax-free corporate reorganization. They are:
   1. Sound business purpose,

2. Continuity of interest,
3. Continuity of business enterprise,
4. Step transaction, and
5. Plan of reorganization.

B. Continuity of Interest
1. The seller must acquire an equity interest in the purchasing corporation.
2. Generally, this test is met if the shareholders of the target corporation receive stock in the purchasing corporation equal in value to at least 50% of all formerly outstanding stock of the target corporation.

C. Continuity of Business Enterprise
1. The acquiring corporation continues the historic business of the transferor corporation, or
2. The acquiring corporation uses a significant portion of the assets of the transferor in its business.

IV. CARRYOVER OF CORPORATE TAX ATTRIBUTES

A. Allowance of Carryovers
1. Section 381(c) lists specific tax attributes of an acquired corporation which can be carried over to a successor corporation.
2. Only the A, C, acquisitive D, F, and G reorganizations are subject to the rules.

B. Loss Carryovers
1. An NOL or capital loss carryover is permitted as a deduction of the successor corporation but, may be limited.
2. The amount of loss, in the year of transfer, is limited to the taxable income or capital gain of the acquiring corporation multiplied by a percentage representing the days remaining in that tax year.
3. An owner shift or equity structure shift causes imposition of a §382 limitation. This section limits the amount of a loss carryover which can be used on an annual basis.

C. Earnings and Profits
1. E & P of a predecessor corporation carries over to the successor corporation as of the date of the transfer.
2. A deficit can only offset E & P accumulated after the date of the transfer.

TEST FOR SELF-EVALUATION

True or False

T F 1. Generally, if a reorganization consists of only stocks and/or securities, there will no tax consequences to the security holders.

T F 2. The recognition of gain on a Section 368 reorganization is limited to the amount of cash received and the fair market value of other property.

T F 3. Even though a corporation distributes all the cash and securities it receives to its shareholders in a tax-free reorganization, it still must pay a tax to the Federal government.

T F 4. The Type B reorganization is restricted to the exchange of stock for assets.

T F 5. The effective control level which must be reached by the acquiring corporation in a Type B reorganization is at least 80% of the total combined voting power of all classes of stock entitled to vote, and at least 80% of the total number of shares of all other classes of stock of the corporation.

T F 6. A Type D reorganization is a mechanism through which a corporation can divide itself--that is, effect a spin-off, split-off, or split-up.

T F 7. The Type E reorganization is of significance to the shareholders only, and is of no consequence to the corporation.

T F 8. The IRS has ruled that if a reorganization qualifies as an A, C, or D reorganization, and at the same time as an F reorganization, Type F will prevail.

T F 9. A split-up involves three corporations, none of which are liquidated.

T F 10. In a Type B reorganization, the assumption of a liability will not violate the "solely for voting stock" requirement.

Fill in the Blanks

1. Section 382 limitations on NOL carryovers are triggered only if there is an _____ or _____.

2. The 382 limitations apply if there has been a change of more than _____% in the ownership of the loss corporation.

3. Earnings and profits and deficits carry over, but deficits reduce E & P only after _____.

4. In order to substantiate a reorganization as having a bona fide business purpose, it is practically mandatory to have a _____ of _____.

5. In an A-type reorganization, the use of a subsidiary to acquire another corporation requires compliance with _____.

Multiple Choice

____ 1. Green Corporation exchanges voting stock in Blue Corporation, its parent, for 91% of the stock in Yellow Corporation. This is an example of which type of reorganization?

   a. Type A
   b. Type B
   c. Type C
   d. Type D
   e. None of the above

____ 2. Jots Corporation is acquired in a merger with Tons Corporation. Tons, the surviving corporation, has a $40,000 deficit in E & P, while Jots has a $150,000 positive E & P. After the merger, Tons distributes $75,000 to its shareholders. The distribution will be treated as:

   a. $35,000 ordinary dividend
   b. $75,000 ordinary dividend
   c. $35,000 ordinary income and $40,000 long-term capital gain
   d. $75,000 long-term capital gain
   e. None of the above

____ 3. Taos Corporation, a Texas corporation, organizes Chilton Corporation in Oklahoma. It transfers all of its assets to Chilton and distributes the Chilton stock to its shareholders, who turn in their Taos stock. Consequently, Taos is liquidated. This is an example of which type of reorganization?

   a. Type A
   b. Type C
   c. Type D
   d. Type F
   e. None of the above

____ 4. Which one of the following is not a corporate reorganization as defined in Section 368?

a. Stock redemption
b. Recapitalization
c. Change in identity
d. Split off

____ 5. Thomas and Bond each own a 50% interest in TomBoy Corporation. TomBoy is merged into Gunnison Corporation. Thomas receives cash for his stock, while Bond receives stock in Gunnison. As a result:

a. Both Thomas and Bond are not taxed
b. Thomas is taxed but Bond is not
c. Bond is taxed but Thomas is not
d. Both Thomas and Bond are taxed
e. None of the above

____ 6. The above is an example of:
a. "Continuity of business purpose"
b. A step transaction
c. "Continuity of interest"
d. All of the above
e. None of the above

____ 7. In order to have the full tax advantage of a net operating loss carry-over between two corporations, one of which is the acquired corporation, the change in ownership of the acquired corporation cannot exceed:

a. 40%
b. 33 - 1/3%
c. 60%
d. 50%
e. None of the above

____ 8. Carter Corporation merges with Dutch Corporation, which has a $140,000 net operating loss. Carter acquires Dutch in order to obtain the $140,000 loss. Carter reports on a calendar year basis and had a profit of $200,000 for the year. Carter acquired Dutch Corporation on September 1. Carter will get a tax write-off for Dutch's loss of:

a. -0-
b. $66,667
c. $46,667
d. $140,000
e. $200,000

____ 9. Would you answer to Question 8 be any different if both firms had other business reasons for the merger?
a. Yes
b. No

____ 10. Tums Corporation has been engaged in two businesses over the last 12 years. It decides to transfer the assets from one of its businesses to a new corporation, and distributes the stock to the shareholders of Tums. This is an example of a:
a. Spin-off
b. Split-off
c. Split-up
d. Type A reorganization
e. None of the above

____ 11. Following a plan of corporate reorganization Mike exchanged 5,000 shares of Cable Corporation common stock for 900 shares of Wire Corporation common stock. Mike had paid $18,750 for the Cable stock. The fair market value of the Wire stock was $21,500 on the date of the exchange. How much was Mike's recognized gain?
a. $2,050
b. $4,100
c. $2,750
d. $-0-

____ 12. With regard to corporate reorganizations, which one of the following statements is not correct?

a. A mere change in identity, form, or place of organization of one corporation qualifies as reorganization.
b. The reorganization provisions can be used to provide tax-free treatment for corporate transactions.
c. A plan of reorganization is not required.
d. A Letter Ruling should be requested when planning a corporate reorganization.

____ 13. Following a plan of corporate reorganization adopted in February 1998, Lori exchanged 10 shares of Green Corp. common stock that she had purchased in March 1988 at a cost of $1,000 for 15 shares of Brown Corp. common stock having a fair market value of $1,200. Lori's recognized gain on this exchange was:

a. $-0-
b. $200 ordinary income
c. $200 short-term capital gain
d. $200 long-term capital gain

SOLUTIONS

True or False

1. T (p. 7-6)
2. T (p. 7-6)
3. F (p. 7-17, 18, 19; tax free)
4. F (p. 7-12; stock for voting stock)
5. T (p. 7-12; 80% of all classes of stock)
6. T (p. 7-17)
7. T (p. 7-20)
8. T (p. 7-20)
9. F (p. 7-17; original corporation is liquidated)
10. F (p. 7-14; would be considered 'boot')

Fill in the Blanks

1. (p. 7-24; owner shift or an equity structure shift)
2. (p. 7-25; 50%)
3. (p. 7-26; the date of transfer)
4. (p. 7-3; written plan of reorganization)
5. (p. 7-9; state law)

Multiple Choice

1. b (Figure 7-4)
2. b (Positive E & P of acquired, $150,000 cannot offset deficit of successor)
3. d (p. 7-20)
4. a (p. 7-4)
5. b (p. 7-22)
6. c (p. 7-22)
7. d (p. 7-25)
8. a (p. 7-27; tax avoidance scheme)
9. a
10. a (Figure 7-8)
11. d (no consideration other than stock was received)
12. c (p. 7-3; general requirement)
13. a (no consideration other than stock was received)

CHAPTER 8

CONSOLIDATED TAX RETURNS

LEARNING OBJECTIVES

After completing Chapter 8, you should be able to:

1. Apply the fundamental concepts of consolidated tax returns.

2. Identify the sources of the rules for consolidated taxable income.

3. Recognize the major advantages and disadvantages of filing consolidated tax returns.

4. Describe the corporations that are eligible to file on a consolidated basis.

5. Explain the compliance aspects of consolidated returns.

6. Compute a parent's investment basis in a subsidiary.

7. Account for intercompany transactions of a consolidated group.

8. Identify limitations that restrict the use of losses and credits of group members derived in separate return years.

9. Derive deductions and credits on a consolidated basis.

10. Demonstrate tax planning opportunities available to consolidated groups.

KEY TERMS

Affiliated group
Consolidated return
Excess loss account
Restoration event
Separate return limitation year
(SRLY)

OUTLINE

I. CONTEXT OF THE CONSOLIDATED RETURN RULES

    A. Motivations to Consolidate
        1. A desire to isolate assets of other group members from the liabilities of specific operating divisions.
        2. A need to carry out specific planning objectives.
        3. An opportunity to manage the combined tax liability of the group's members.

    B. Philosophy of Consolidated Return Rules
        1. The underlying purpose of the consolidated return rules is one of organizational neutrality.
        2. A group of closely related corporations should have neither a tax advantage nor a disadvantage compared to taxpayers who file separate corporate returns.

II. ASSESSING CONSOLIDATED RETURN STATUS

    A. Potential Advantages
        1. Operating and capital loss carryovers of one group member may be used to shelter income of other group members.
        2. Deferral of gain recognition on some intercompany transactions.
        3. Optimization of certain deductions and credits by using consolidated amounts to compute pertinent limitations.

    B. Potential Disadvantages
        1. The consolidated return election is binding on all subsequent years until an eligible group no longer exists or the IRS consents to revocation of the election.
        2. Capital and operating loss carryover to separate return year(s) may provide a greater tax benefit than applying the loss to consolidated income.
        3. Deferral of loss recognition on some intercompany transactions.
        4. Income bunching and creating short tax years for subsidiaries required to adopt the parent's tax year.
        5. Incurring additional administrative costs to comply with consolidated return regulations.

III. ELECTING CONSOLIDATED RETURN STATUS

    A. All members of a corporate group must meet three requirements:

1. The stock ownership criteria of an affiliated group,
   a. the identifiable parent must own 80% of the voting power and 80% of the value of the subsidiary.
   b. this ownership test must be satisfied on every day of the tax year.
2. Be statutorily eligible to make the consolidated election,
   a. noncorporate entities such as partnerships, trusts and estates are ineligible.
   b. foreign corporations, tax-exempt charitable corporations and insurance companies may be statutorily ineligible.
3. Satisfy the compliance requirements in making and maintaining the election.
   a. initially the election is made on Form 1122 attached to the first, consolidated Form 1120 tax return.
   b. subsequent consolidated returns must include Form 851, Affiliations Schedule.
   c. the group continues filing consolidated returns until an eligible group no longer exists, or, the parent applies for and is granted permission to terminate the consolidated election.

B. Liability for consolidated taxes is born by the members, individually and jointly.

C. Tax Accounting Periods and Methods
1. All consolidated group members must use the same tax year as the parent.
2. Consolidated group members need not adopt the tax accounting method, cash or accrual, of the parent. However, a cash-basis corporation may need to change to accrual basis reporting because the $5 million gross receipts test is applied to consolidated gross receipts.

IV. STOCK BASIS OF SUBSIDIARY

A. Upon acquisition of a subsidiary, the parent's basis is the acquisition price. At each consolidated year-end, stock basis adjustments are required to prevent double recording of gains and losses.
   1. Positive adjustments include:
      a. an allocable share of consolidated taxable income for the year.
      b. an allocable share of consolidated operating or capital loss of a subsidiary that could not use the loss through a carryback.
   2. Negative adjustments include:
      a. an allocable share of consolidated taxable loss for the year.
      b. an allocable share of any carryover operating or capital loss deducted on the consolidated return and not previously a reduction in stock basis.
      c. dividends paid by the subsidiary to the parent out of E & P.

B. An "excess loss account" is created when accumulated post-acquisition taxable losses of the subsidiary exceed the acquisition price.
   1. The losses of the subsidiary are recognized in the current year's consolidated return.
   2. The stock basis account is not negative.
   3. If the parent disposes of the subsidiary's stock, this account represents capital gain on disposition.

C. In a chain of subsidiaries, computation of stock basis begins with the lowest level subsidiary and proceeds up to the parent.

D. Consolidated tax liability is allocated in proportion to each group members' contribution to consolidated taxable income unless an election to use some other allocation method is made.

V. COMPUTING CONSOLIDATED TAXABLE INCOME

A. Computational Procedure
   1. Each group member first computes its taxable income as though a separate entity.
   2. This income is then split to eliminate some intercompany items, to remove transactions which must be accounted for as a group and to recognize certain transactions which receive deferral treatment.
   3. Consolidated taxable income is a combination of the revised separate taxable incomes and the resulting income/loss from group items and deferral/restoration events.

B. Typical Intercompany Transactions
   1. Transactions which generate income to one member and a deductible expense to another member are left in consolidated income as direct offsets.
   2. Adjustments may be required if all members do not use the same accounting method.
   3. Dividends received from other group members are removed from separate taxable incomes, these dividends cannot be considered for any dividends received deduction.

C. Computation of Group Items
   1. Transactions which are statutorily limited must be computed as though the consolidated entity is one corporation. Such items are:
      a. net capital gain/loss
      b. §1231 gain/loss
      c. casualty/theft gain/loss

d. charitable contributions
e. dividends received deduction
f. net operating loss
g. the general business and research credits
h. any recapture of those credits
i. the foreign tax credit
j. the percentage depletion deduction
k. alternative minimum tax elements
2. The limitations are applied to consolidated taxable income after adjusting for intercompany transactions.

D. Deferral and Restoration Events
1. Gain or loss on intercompany sales of assets is deferred until control of the asset leaves the group.
2. The entire deferred gain or loss is restored to consolidated income when the asset is transferred outside the group, the transferor leaves the group or the consolidation election is terminated.
3. An election may be made to include or deduct all intercompany gain or loss immediately; this election remains in effect until IRS permission for revocation is received.

VI. TAX PLANNING CONSIDERATIONS

A. Optimize overall tax benefits when choosing consolidated partners:
1. Loss and credit carryovers
2. Passive activity income, loss, or credits
3. Gains that can be deferred through intercompany sales
4. Contributions to consolidated ACE adjustments
5. Excess limitation amounts
6. Section 1231 gains, losses, and look-back profiles.

B. 100% Dividends Received Deduction is an alternative to filing consolidated returns.

TEST FOR SELF-EVALUATION

True or False

T F 1. The Code describes the various elements of consolidated tax return rules.

T F 2. All members of the consolidated group must have the same tax year.

T F 3. All members of the consolidated group must use the same accounting method.

T F 4. Financial accounting consolidated income is the same as tax-basis consolidated income.

T F 5. The most commonly encountered intercompany transactions are removed from member's separate taxable incomes for consolidated tax purposes.

T F 6. Members of an affiliated group must file consolidated income tax returns.

T F 7. Only the parent corporation is responsible for consolidated tax liabilities.

Fill in the Blanks

1. The general function of the consolidated return rules is _____.

2. Controlled groups of corporations include _____ and _____ groups.

3. An _____ group requires an identifiable parent having control of _____% of the voting stock _____ % of the value of the subsidiary.

4. The three basic requirements for consolidated return rules are: _____, _____, _____.

5. To qualify as a parent-subsidiary controlled group, the parent must own _____% of the voting stock _____% of the value of the subsidiary.

6. Upon acquiring a subsidiary, the parent corporation records a stock basis on its tax balance sheet equal to _____.

7. Adjustments to the parent's stock basis in the subsidiary are made on _____ of the consolidated return year, or _____.

8. An _____ is created when accumulated deficits in the subsidiary's post-acquisition E & P exceed the acquisition price.

Multiple Choice

_____ 1. Sub sold a building to Parent for $400,000. Sub had originally paid $300,000 for the building and had accumulated depreciation of $100,000. Parent, after six years, sold the building to an unrelated third party for $500,000. Sub's realized gain on the sale to parent was:

   a. $100,000
   b. $200,000
   c. $300,000
   d. $400,000

_____ 2. Sub's recognized gain on the sale to parent was:

   a. $-0-
   b. $100,000
   c. $200,000
   d. $300,000

_____ 3. Parent's realized gain on the sale to the third party was:

   a. $-0-
   b. $100,000
   c. $100,000 plus accumulated depreciation
   d. $100,000 minus accumulated depreciation

_____ 4. Parent Corporation acquired 100% of the stock of Sub Corporation on July 5, 1996. Both corporations intend to file a consolidated return immediately upon acquisition. Parent's tax year ends March 31; Sub's tax year ends July 30. The first consolidated return is due:

   a. October 15
   b. September 15
   c. June 15
   d. March 15

_____ 5. A parent corporation's adjustments to its stock basis in a consolidated subsidiary includes:

   a. an allocable share of the subsidiary's E & P
   b. dividends paid by the subsidiary
   c. both a and b
   d. neither a nor b

____ 6. In the current year Parent Corporation provided services to its 100% owned subsidiary valued at $75,000. Sub will pay Parent next year. Sub uses the cash method of accounting, Parent uses the accrual method. Is any adjustment required in computing consolidated taxable income?

a. No
b. Yes

____ 7. The filing of consolidated tax returns is available only to:

a. parent-subsidiary controlled groups
b. brother-sister controlled groups
c. affiliated groups
d. all of the above

____ 8. With regard to a controlled corporate group, all of the following statements are correct except: (IRS 94 3B-26)

a. The controlled group is allowed only ONE set of graduated income tax brackets.
b. Controlled groups are allowed ONE $80,000 exemption amount for alternative minimum tax purposes.
c. The controlled group is allowed ONE $250,000 accumulated earnings credit.
d. The tax benefits of the graduated rate schedule are to be allocated equally among the members of the group unless they all consent to a different apportionment.

SOLUTIONS

True or False

1. F (p. 8-5; most are found in the Regulations)
2. T (p. 8-15)
3. F (p. 8-16; can use tax accounting method in place prior to consolidation)
4. F (p. 8-6; correspond only slightly)
5. F (p. 8-19; remain and cancel each other on consolidated basis)
6. F (p. 8-10; may file separately and claim 100% dividend received deduction)
7. F (p. 8-14; members are jointly and severally liable)

Fill in the Blanks

1. (p. 8-5; organizational neutrality)
2. (p. 8-9; parent-subsidiary, brother-sister)
3. (p. 8-10; affiliated, 80%, and 80%)
4. (p. 8-6; stock ownership, statutory eligibility and compliance)
5. (p. 8-10; 80%, or 80%)
6. (p. 8-16; the acquisition price)
7. (p. 8-16; last day, date of disposition)
8. (p. 8-16; excess loss account)

Multiple Choice

1. b (p. 8-29; $400,000 sale price - (300,000 - 100,000) basis)
2. a (p. 8-29; deferral event)
3. c (p. 8-29; $500,000 sale price - basis)
4. c (p. 8-13)
5. c (p. 8-16)
6. b (p. 8-19; different methods of accounting requires adjustment)
7. c (p. 8-9)
8. b (p. 8-15; the exemption for computing AMTI is $40,000)

CHAPTER 9

TAXATION OF INTERNATIONAL TRANSACTIONS

LEARNING OBJECTIVES

After completing Chapter 9, you should be able to:

1. Use the foreign tax credit provisions.

2. Apply the rules for sourcing income and allocating deductions into U.S. and foreign categories.

3. Utilize the U.S. tax provisions concerning nonresident alien individuals and foreign corporations.

4. Appreciate the tax benefits available to certain U.S. individuals working abroad.

5. Apply the U.S. tax rules for foreign corporations controlled by U.S. persons.

6. Explain how foreign currency exchange affects the tax consequences of international transactions.

KEY TERMS

Branch profits tax	Foreign earned income exclusion	Nonresident alien
Controlled foreign corporation	Foreign sales corporation	Subpart F
Dividend equivalent amount	Foreign tax credit	Tax haven
Effectively connected income	Functional currency	Tax treaty
FIRPTA	Green card test	Treaty shopping
		U.S. shareholder

OUTLINE

I. **OVERVIEW OF INTERNATIONAL TAXATION**

   A. The United States retains the right to tax its citizens and residents on their worldwide taxable income.

   B. U.S. persons with international transactions encounter many of the same Federal tax laws as any U.S. taxpayer:
   1. Income is subject to U.S. taxation.
   2. Certain expenses and losses are deductible.
   3. Credits are available.
   4. Earnings of domestic corporations face double taxation.

   C. U.S. taxpayers with international transactions face another set of provisions that apply to international business; these laws:
   1. are meant to prevent two-country taxation.
   2. allow the U.S. to remain competitive internationally.
   3. prevent taxpayers from evading U.S. taxation by moving income-producing activities abroad.

II. **THE FOREIGN TAX CREDIT**

   A. Foreign tax credits are:
   1. Elective for any particular year.
   2. Applicable only to foreign tax levies which have the predominant character of an income tax in the U.S. sense.
   3. Based on the exchange rate in effect when the foreign tax is paid, if accrued, based on average exchange rate for the relevant tax year.

   B. A qualified taxpayer is allowed a credit for foreign income taxes paid.
   1. The direct credit is available only to the taxpayer who bears the legal incidence of the foreign tax.
   2. The indirect credit is available to corporate taxpayers who receive dividends from foreign corporations that have paid a foreign tax on earnings.

   C. FTC Limitations
   1. The general limitation limits the FTC to:
      a. the lesser of the actual foreign taxes paid or accrued, or
      b. U.S. taxes, before the FTC, on foreign-sourced taxable income.
   2. To prevent cross-crediting, separate limitations apply to certain categories of foreign-source taxable income and the related foreign income taxes.

a. a two-year carryback and a five-year carryover of excess foreign taxes are allowed.
b. the carryback and carryover provision is available only within the separate baskets.
c. refer to the list of categories in Concept Summary 9-1 of text.

D. Possessions Corporations
1. §936 allows a credit against the U.S. tax attributable to foreign-source taxable income from the active conduct of a trade or business in a U.S. possession.
2. Legislation passed in 1996 repeals the credit except for corporations conducting an active trade or business in a possession on October 13, 1995.
3. A §936 corporation that adds a new line of business after October 13, 1995 will cease to be eligible.
4. The credit will phase out by January 1, 2006.

III. SOURCING OF INCOME AND ALLOCATION OF DEDUCTIONS

A. Income sourced within the United States generally includes:
1. Interest received from the U.S. government, District of Columbia, noncorporate U.S. residents and domestic corporations.
2. Dividends received from domestic corporations.
3. Income from personal services performed within the U.S.
4. Income from rental of tangible property located within the U.S.
5. Income from royalties on intangible property used in the U.S.
6. Income from the sale or exchange of real property located in the U.S.
7. Income from the sale or exchange of personal property by U.S. residents.
8. Income from transportation beginning and ending in the U.S.
9. 50% of income from transportation beginning or ending in the U.S.
10. Space and ocean activities conducted by U.S. residents.
11. 50% of income from international communications between the U.S. and a foreign country.

B. Income sourced outside the United States is residual income.

C. Allocation and Apportionment of Deductions
1. Deductions directly related to an activity or property are allocated to those classes of income.
2. Specific rules apply to the allocation and apportionment of:
a. interest expense
b. research and development expenditures

        c. certain stewardship fees
        d. legal and accounting fees
        e. income taxes
        f. losses
   3. Deductions not definitely related to any class of gross income are ratably allocated to all classes of gross income and apportioned between sources.

IV. U.S. TAXATION OF NONRESIDENT ALIENS AND FOREIGN CORPORATIONS

   A. NRAs having U.S. source income are taxed at the same rate as U.S. residents on effectively connected income and at a flat, 30%, rate on noneffectively connected income.
      1. A U.S. trade or business is a prerequisite to having effectively connected income.
      2. Effectively connected income is determined under the
         a. asset-use test: derived from assets used in, or held for use in, the trade or business, or
         b. business-activities test: if the activities of the trade or business were a material factor in the production of the income.

   B. Foreign Corporations
      1. A foreign corporation is not a domestic corporation; a domestic corporation is created or organized in the U.S.
      2. U.S. source fixed, determinable, annual or periodic income of foreign corporations is taxed at a flat 30% rate.
      3. Effectively connected income of foreign corporations conducting a trade or business in the U.S. are subject to the same tax rates as domestic corporations.
      4. Any U.S. source income attributable to a U.S. office of a foreign corporation is deemed to be effectively connected.
      5. The branch profits tax may impose a 30% tax on the dividend equivalent amount for the taxable year on any foreign corporation operating through a U.S. subsidiary.

   C. The Foreign Investment in Real Property Tax Act
      1. Treats gains and losses realized by NRAs and foreign corporations from the sale or disposition of U.S. real property as effectively connected income.
      2. NRA individuals must pay a tax equal to the lesser of 26, or 28, percent of their AMTI, or regular U.S. rates on the net U.S. real property gain for the taxable year.
      3. Any direct interest in real property located in the U.S. and any equity interest in a domestic corporation are U.S. real property interests.

4. Stock regularly traded on an established securities market is not treated as USRPI where a person holds no more than 5% of the stock.
5. Anyone acquiring a USRPI from a foreign person must withhold 10% of the amount realized on the disposition.

D. Tax Treaties
1. Income tax treaties generally provide taxing rights with regard to the taxable income of residents of one treaty country who have income sourced in the other treaty country.
2. Treaties generally provide for primary taxing rights which require the other treaty partner to allow a credit for the taxes paid on the twice-taxed income.
3. Primary taxing rights are usually determined by the residence of the taxpayer or the presence of a permanent establishment in a treaty country to which the income is attributable.

V. U.S. TAXPAYERS ABROAD

A. Citizens and residents of the U.S. are subject to Federal taxation of their worldwide taxable income.

B. The Foreign Earned Income Exclusion
1. Is elective.
2. Is available to an individual whose tax home is in a foreign country and who is either
   a. a U.S. citizen and bona fide resident of a foreign country, or
   b. a citizen or resident of the U.S. who, during any 12 consecutive months, is physically present in a foreign country for at least 330 full days.
3. The general exclusion is available for foreign earned income and is limited to the lesser of:
   a. $74,000 for 1999
   b. foreign earned income less the housing cost amount exclusion
      1. the housing cost amount is equal to the qualified housing expenses of an individual less a base amount.
      2. the base amount is 16% of the salary of an employee of the U.S. government for Step 1 Grade GS-14.
      3. the housing cost amount exclusion is limited to foreign earned income but can be elected in addition to the foreign earned income exclusion.
   c. A self-employed individual is not eligible to exclude housing expenses, but may elect to deduct them.

VI. FOREIGN CORPORATIONS CONTROLLED BY U.S. PERSONS

　　A. Certain types of income generated by controlled foreign corporations must be included in current tax year gross income by U.S. shareholders.
　　　　1. A U.S. shareholder is a U.S. person who owns, or is considered to own, 10% or more of the total combined voting power of the foreign corporation.
　　　　2. Stock owned directly, indirectly or constructively is counted.

　　B. A CFC is any foreign corporation in which more than 50% of the combined voting power of all classes of voting stock or the total value of the stock of the corporation is owned by U.S. shareholders on any day during the taxable year.

　　C. For Subpart F to apply, the foreign corporation must have been a CFC for an uninterrupted period of 30 days or more during the taxable year.

　　D. U.S. shareholders must include their pro rata share of Subpart F income in their gross income to the extent of their ownership. Subpart F income consists of:
　　　　1. Insurance income
　　　　2. Foreign base company income
　　　　　　a. foreign personal holding company income
　　　　　　b. foreign base company sales income
　　　　　　c. foreign base company service income
　　　　　　d. foreign base company shipping income
　　　　　　e. foreign base company oil-related income
　　　　3. International boycott factor income
　　　　4. Illegal bribes
　　　　5. Income derived from §901(j) foreign country.

VII. TRANSFERRING OWNERSHIP TO A FOREIGN PERSON

　　A. U.S. persons transferring potential income property to foreign corporations outside the U.S. taxing jurisdiction in the following, domestically tax-free, situations recognize the gain realized at the time of transfer.
　　　　1. property transfers to a controlled foreign corporation, §351
　　　　2. liquidation of a domestic subsidiary into a foreign parent, §332,
　　　　3. acquisition of a domestic corporation by a foreign corporation, B reorganization,
　　　　4. acquisition of a domestic corporation's assets by a foreign corporation, C reorganization.

　　B. The character of any gain recognized depends on the character of the property transferred.

1. a deemed sale occurs when the following assets are transferred:
   a. inventory
   b. accounts receivable and installment obligations
2. any recapture potential, depreciation, etc., must be recognized to the extent of the gain realized.

VIII. FOREIGN CURRENCY TRANSACTIONS

A. Tax Concepts Dealing with Foreign Exchange
   1. Foreign currency is treated as property other than money.
   2. Gain or loss on the exchange of foreign currency is considered separate from the underlying transaction.
   3. No gain or loss is recognized until a transaction is closed.

B. Where a QBU, foreign branch, uses foreign currency as its functional currency, profit or loss is computed in the foreign currency and translated using a weighted average exchange rate for the year.

IX. REPORTING REQUIREMENTS

A. A domestic corporation that is 25% or more foreign owned must file an informational return and maintain certain records where they will be accessible to the IRS.

B. Any foreign corporation carrying on a trade or business in the U.S. must file an informational return and maintain certain records where they will be accessible to the IRS.

C. U.S. partners of a controlled foreign partnership must file an information return.

D. A foreign partnership with U.S. source or effectively connected with a U.S. trade or business income must file a partnership return.

E. Changes in 10% or more ownership of interests in a foreign partnership must be reported.

F. Creation of, or a transfer to, a foreign trust by a U.S. person requires the filing of Form 3520.

G. Information returns are required in connection with foreign investment in U.S. real property interests.

TEST FOR SELF-EVALUATION

True or False

T F 1. With respect to foreign corporations, one of the factors that can be considered in establishing whether fixed or determinable annual or periodic income and similar amounts from U.S. sources are effectively connected with a U.S. trade or business, is whether the business activities were a material factor in the realization of the income.
(IRS 97 3A-9)

T F 2. A domestic corporation must withhold tax on cash distributions made on its stock in the ordinary course of its business to foreign shareholders. (IRS 97 3A-10)

T F 3. For a foreign tax levy to qualify for the foreign tax credit, it must resemble U.S. income tax.

T F 4. Unused excess foreign taxes can be carried back 2 years and carried over 5 years subject to limitations in the same basket for the carryover year.

T F 5. One of the factors that is considered in establishing whether a foreign corporation's fixed or determinable annual or periodic income from U.S. sources is effectively connected with a U.S. trade or business is whether the income is from assets used in the conduct of that trade or business. (IRS 94 3A-18)

T F 6. A purchaser of U.S. real property is required to withhold 10% of the amount realized on purchases from foreign persons.

T F 7. The Foreign Personal Holding Company Tax is levied on the corporation's U.S. shareholders rather than the corporation.

T F 8. The de minimis rule applies to all Subpart F income.

T F 9. The foreign earned income exclusion is more beneficial than the foreign tax credit if the foreign country's tax rate is higher than the U.S. income tax rate.

T F 10. Interest expense must always be apportioned and allocated between U.S. and foreign sourced income components.

Fill in the Blanks

1. The Foreign Tax Credit is _____ for any particular year.

2. Issuance of a _____ and physical presence in the U.S. establishes residency for U.S. income taxes.

3. Foreign currency is treated as property other than _____.

4. For FTC purposes, foreign taxes are translated at the exchange rate in effect when _____.

5. Functional currency is translated at _____ exchange rate for the _____.

6. An _____ is an individual who is not a citizen or resident of the U.S.

7. A foreign corporation is a FPHC if _____% or more of gross income is FPHC income and,

8. more than _____% of the total voting power or the total value of the stock is held by _____ or fewer U.S. persons.

Multiple Choice

_____ 1. Which one of the following factors has to be considered in establishing whether fixed or determinable annual or periodic income and similar amounts from U.S. sources are effectively connected with a U.S. trade or business?
(IRS 92 3B-44)
- a. Whether the income is from assets used in, or held for use in, the conduct of that trade or business.
- b. Whether the activities in the U.S. were a material factor in the realization of income and whether a certain percent of its employees were U.S. citizens.
- c. Whether the trade or business sold a majority of its products to other businesses in the United States.
- d. Whether a majority of the principal suppliers to the trade or business were in the United States.

_____ 2. Foreign tax credits are:

- a. elective
- b. subject to basket limitations only
- c. based on a weighted average exchange rate
- d. all of the above
- e. none of the above

_____ 3.   Eric, a nonresident alien, employed by a foreign manufacturing company, spent 5 weeks in the U.S. arranging equipment purchases. His salary for the 5 weeks was $4,000.

a. This will be considered U.S. source income.
b. This will not be considered U.S. source income.

_____ 4.   Which of the following statements is not correct in respect to withholding on nonresident aliens and foreign corporations?   (IRS 92 3B-45)

a. Generally, fixed or determinable annual or periodic income from within the United States is subject to withholding unless specifically exempted under the Internal Revenue Code or a tax treaty.
b. Generally, income is from United States sources if it is paid by any domestic or foreign businesses located in the United States.
c. Income effectively connected with the conduct of a trade or business in the United States is generally not subject to withholding if certain conditions are met.
d. Winnings from wagers or blackjack, baccarat, craps, roulette, or big-6 wheel are not subject to income tax withholding or 30 percent withholding tax.

_____ 5.   The foreign earned income exclusion is:

a. elective
b. limited in amount
c. available to self-employed individuals
d. all of the above
e. a and b only

_____ 6.   For this year, Bill, a U.S. resident, has worldwide taxable income of $180,000, $150,000 in salary from a U.S. employer and $30,000 from investments in foreign securities. Foreign tax authorities withheld $9,000 of tax on the dividend income. If Bill's U.S. income tax before FTC is $48,540, his FTC is:

a. $9,000
b. $8,090
c. $8,292
d. $7,200

7. A, a U.S. corporation, incurred $100,000 of interest expense during the year. None of this interest expense can be attributed to a specific purpose. Based on the following information, how should this interest be allocated and apportioned?

Asset Value:	Fair Market	Tax/Book
U.S. Source Income	$3,500,000	$2,300,000
Foreign Source Income	2,000,000	1,500,000

    a. $63,636, U.S. sourced
    b. $60,526, foreign sourced
    c. $52,632, foreign sourced
    d. $41,818, U.S. sourced

8. D, a domestic corporation, began operation of a QBU in 1993 with an initial capitalization of 900K, (1K:$1). Determine the income taxed to D in each year based on the following:

Income in Ks		Exchange Rate
1993	200K	1K = $1
1994	200K	1.25K = $1
1995	200K	1.6K = $1

    a. 125, 160, 200
    b. 200, 160, 125
    c. 200, 125, 160
    d. 160, 125, 200

9. In 1995 the QBU from question 8 above distributes 300 K to D when the exchange rate is 1.6K to $1. Does D have a foreign currency loss and if so, how much?

    a. No, -0-
    b. Yes, $55.50
    c. Yes, $77.50
    d. Yes, $89.50

_____ 10. Corporation R, a domestic corporation, distributed the following dividends to its shareholders in 1989.

$5,000 to Shareholder A, a foreign partnership
$4,000 to Shareholder B, an unrelated foreign corporation
$3,000 to Shareholder C, a resident alien
$2,000 to Shareholder D, a nonresident alien

All of the income of Corporation R was from sources within the U.S. On what amount of dividends must R withhold tax? (IRS 90 3B-43)

a. $-0-
b. $7,000
c. $9,000
d. $11,000

_____ 11. All of the following items of gross income earned by a foreign corporation in the United States are subject to 30% withholding except: (IRS 90 3B-55)

a. Rents
b. Sale of real property
c. Interest
d. Dividends

SOLUTIONS
True or False

1. T (p. 9-20)
2. T (p. 9-19)
3. T (p. 9-9)
4. T (p. 9-6)
5. F (p. 9-20)
6. T (p. 9-25)
7. T (p. 9-32)
8. F (p. 9-31)
9. F (p. 9-44)
10. F (p. 9-16)

Fill in the Blanks

1. elective (p. 9-3)
2. green card (p. 9-18)
3. money (p. 9-40)
4. foreign taxes are paid (p. 9-44)
5. weighted average; taxable year (p. 9-41)
6. NRA nonresident alien (p. 9-18)
7. 60 (p. 9-32)
8. 50, 5 (p. 9-32)

Multiple Choice

1. a (p. 9-20)
2. a (p. 9-3)
3. a (p. 9-13)
4. b (p. 9-20)
5. d (p. 9-27, 28)
6. b (p, 9-4; 48,540 X 30,000/180,000)
7. a (using fair market: US = 63636, foreign =36364; using tax book: US = 60526, foreign = 39474)
8. b (p. 9-41)
9. d (equity in K's: 900+200+200+200=1500; basis in $s: 900+200+160+125=1385 distribution 300K of 1500K total equity = 20%; 20% of 1385 basis = 277; 277 - (300K@1.6) or $187.50 = $89.50 loss)
10. d (p. 9-20)
11. b (p. 9-20, 24)

CHAPTER 10

PARTNERSHIPS: FORMATION, OPERATIONS, AND BASIS

LEARNING OBJECTIVES

After completing Chapter 10, you should be able to:

1. Discuss governing principles and theories of partnership taxation.

2. Describe the tax effects of forming a partnership with cash and property contributions.

3. Examine the tax treatment of expenditures of a newly formed partnership and identify elections available to the partnership.

4. Specify the methods of determining a partnership's tax year.

5. Calculate partnership taxable income and describe how partnership items affect a partner's income tax return.

6. Determine a partner's basis in the partnership interest.

7. Explain how liabilities affect a partner's basis.

8. Describe the limitations on deducting partnership losses.

9. Review the treatment of transactions between a partner and the partnership.

10. Provide insights regarding advantageous use of a partnership.

KEY TERMS

Aggregate concept
Basis in partnership interest
Capital account
Capital interest
Capital sharing ratio
Constructive liquidation scenario
Disguised sale
Economic effect test
Electing large partnership
Entity concept
General partnership
Guaranteed payment
Inside basis
Least aggregate deferral rule
Limited liability company
Limited liability partnership
Limited partnership
Nonrecourse debt
Outside basis
Precontribution gain or loss
Profit and loss sharing ratio
Profits (loss) interest
Qualified nonrecourse debt
Recourse debt
Separately stated items
Special allocation
Syndication costs

OUTLINE

I. OVERVIEW OF PARTNERSHIP TAXATION

   A. What is a Partnership?
      1. A partnership is an association of two or more persons to carry on a trade or business, with each contributing money, property, labor, or skill, and with all expecting to share in profits and losses.
      2. For Federal tax purposes, a partnership includes a syndicate, group, pool, joint venture, or other unincorporated organization through which any business, financial operation, or venture is carried on, and which is not classified as a corporation, trust, or estate.
      3. Four types of entities taxed as partnerships are:
         a. general partnerships
         b. limited partnerships
         c. limited liability partnerships
         d. limited liability companies
      4. Liability of partners
         a. general partners are personally liable for partnership debt.
         b. limited partners are liable for partnership debt only to the extent of their investment in the partnership.
         c. limited liability partners are not liable for malpractice committed by their partner(s).
         d. limited liability company members are provided liability protection similar to corporate shareholders.
      5. Certain unincorporated organizations may elect to be excluded from treatment as partnerships for purposes of Federal income tax. This exclusion applies in situations where:
         a. the organization's purpose is for investment, rather than the active conduct of a trade or business,
         b. the organization's purpose is for the joint production, extraction, or use of property, or
         c. for purposes of underwriting, selling, or distributing a particular security issue.

   B. Partnership Taxation and Reporting
      1. Partnership are not taxable entities; the taxable income or loss of the partnership flows through to the partners.
      2. Each partner reports his allocable share of partnership income or loss on his personal tax return.
      3. A partnership must report the results of its activities on Form 1065. Each partner receives a Form 1065, Schedule K-1 which shows his share of all partnership items.

C. Partner's Ownership Interest in a Partnership
1. A capital interest is a partner's percentage ownership of partnership capital usually measured as the percentage of net assets a partner would receive on immediate liquidation of the partnership.
2. A profits interest is the partner's percentage allocation of current operating results.

D. Conceptual Basis for Partnership Taxation
1. The conduit concept treats the partnership as a channel through which income, credits and deductions flow to the partners.
2. The entity concept treats partners and the partnership as distinct, separate units. The nature and amount of entity gains and losses are determined at the partnership level.

II. FORMATION OF A PARTNERSHIP: TAX EFFECTS

A. Gain or Loss on Contributions the Partnership
1. The formation of a partnership requires a contribution of assets to the partnership by the partners. Section 721 permits these contributions to, generally, be tax free, gain or loss recognition is deferred.
2. Exceptions to the nonrecognition provisions occur when:
   a. the transfer consists of appreciated stock or securities and the partnership is an investment partnership.
   b. the transaction is a disguised sale of properties.
   c. the transaction is essentially an exchange of properties.
   d. the partner receives his interest in the partnership in exchange for services.

B. Tax Issues Relative to Contributed Property
1. Basis
   a. the partnership uses a carryover basis, the contributing partner's basis in the property becomes the partnership's basis in that property.
   b. the partner uses a substitute basis, the adjusted basis of the property contributed becomes the basis of that partner's partnership interest.
2. Holding Period
   a. the holding period of an interest acquired by a cash contribution begins on the day the interest is acquired.
   b. the holding period of an interest acquired by a contribution of property that was a §1231 or capital asset carries over to the holding period of the partnership interest.
   c. the partnership's holding period for contributions of property includes the period during which the partner owned the property individually.

3. The transferring partner's method and remaining recovery period of depreciable property contributed to the partnership carries over, the partnership continues the same cost recovery calculations.
4. Gain or loss is treated as ordinary when the partnership disposes of either:
   1. contributed receivables
   2. contributed inventory, if disposed of within 5 years of the contribution.

C. Tax Accounting Elections
1. Most tax elections are made by the partnership, these elections decide how particular transactions and tax attributes will be handled.
2. Each partner is bound by the elections made by the partnership.
3. The only elections made by individual partners concern:
   a. discharge of indebtedness,
   b. depletion method for oil and gas wells,
   c. foreign tax deductions and credits.

D. Initial Costs of a Partnership
1. Organization costs
   a. are costs incident to the creation of the partnership.
   b. may be amortized over 60 months or more.
2. Start up costs
   a. are operating costs incurred after formation but before the entity begins business.
   b. may be amortized over 60 months or more.
3. Syndication costs
   a. are costs incurred in promoting and marketing partnership interests.
   b. are capitalized with no amortization allowed.

E. Taxable year of the Partnership
1. A partnership's tax year is, generally, determined in the following order:
   a. the tax year of the majority partners having the same tax year,
   b. the tax year of all the principal partners,
   c. the least aggregate deferral year.
2. Exceptions are allowed:
   a. if the existence of a business purpose can be established to IRS satisfaction, i.e., if a partnership recognizes 25% or more of gross receipts in the last two months of a 12 month period.
   b. taxes are deferred for not more than 3 months from the required year and deposits of estimated deferred taxes are made.

III. OPERATION OF THE PARTNERSHIP

A. Measuring and Reporting Income

1. Form 1065 is an informational return which organizes and reports the year's activities.
2. A partnership must file a return, Form 1065, by the 15th day of the fourth month following the close of the partnership's tax year.
3. Income measurement:
    a. First, under the conduit concept, items which affect exclusions, deductions and credits at the partner level are reported separately.
    b. Second, under the entity concept, all items not required to be stated separately are netted at the partnership level to determine the partnership's ordinary income or loss.

B. Partnership Allocations
1. The partnership agreement can provide for any partner to share capital, profits and losses in different ratios.
2. Special allocations must follow the rules and regulations of §704(b). One of these is the Economic Effect Test.
3. The economic effect test requires that:
    a. income allocations increase a partner's capital account.
    b. deduction or loss allocations decrease a partner's capital account balance.
    c. when a partner's interest is liquidated he must:
        1. receive assets having a FMV equal to his capital account, or
        2. restore his capital account if it is negative.
4. Precontribution gain or loss
    a. precontribution gain or loss must be allocated among the partners taking into account variations between the basis and the FMV of the property on the contribution date.
    b. built-in gain or loss is allocated to the contributing partner when the partnership disposes of nondepreciable property.
    c. Regulations describe allowable methods of allocating depreciation deductions if the property is depreciable.

C. Basis of Partnership Interest
1. The original basis of a contributing partner's interest is:
    FMV of any services performed
    + money contributed
    + adjusted basis of property contributed
    - liabilities transferred
    + share of partnership debt
2. For partnership interests acquired after the partnership has been formed, the method of acquisition determines how the partner's adjusted basis is computed.
    a. purchased from another partner = cost
    b. acquired by gift = donor's basis + some, or all, of the gift tax paid by the donor

        c.   acquired by inheritance = FMV on date of partner's death
3. Basis can never be less than zero.
4. A partner's basis in the partnership interest is subject to continuous fluctuations. Events and transactions which will have an effect on the partnership interest are:
    a. Increases:
        1. additional contributions and debt increases
        2. taxable income of the partnership, including capital gains
        3. tax-exempt income of the partnership
    b. Decreases:
        1. distribution of partnership property and debt decreases
        2. partnership expenditures which are not deductible in computing taxable income or loss and which are not capital expenditures
        3. partnership losses, including capital losses.
5. Liability sharing
    a. recourse debt is partnership debt for which the partnership or at least one partner is personally liable.
    b. nonrecourse debt is debt for which no partner is personally liable.
    c. debts created before January 29, 1989:
        1. recourse debt is shared according to the partners' loss sharing ratio.
        2. nonrecourse debt is shared according to the partners' profit sharing ratio.
    d. debts created after January 29, 1989:
        1. recourse debt is shared according to "constructive liquidation scenario."
        2. Nonrecourse debt is allocated in three stages:
            a. minimum gain, (liability in excess of book basis)
            b. remaining precontribution gain
            c. remainder is allocated according to profit sharing or the manner in which future nonrecourse deductions are expected to be shared.

D. Loss Limitations
1. The overall limitation allows losses only to the extent of the partner's adjusted basis in the partnership interest.
2. The "at-risk" limitation allows losses only to the extent of the partner's economic investment basis.
3. Passive loss limitations, generally, allow losses only to the extent of passive income.
4. These three loss limitations are applied in the order listed: overall, at-risk, passive.

IV. TRANSACTIONS BETWEEN PARTNER AND PARTNERSHIP

    A. Fixed or guaranteed payments made by the partnership to a partner for services rendered or use of the partner's capital are deductible by the partnership as ordinary business expenses, as long as the payments are not based on the income of the partnership.

    B. When a partner engages in certain transaction with the partnership, he or she can be treated as a nonpartner, thus recognizing any gain or loss that might be incurred. Two exceptions to this rule are:
1. Any loss is disallowed on a transaction between a partner and the partnership if the partner has more than a 50% interest in the capital or profits of the partnership.
2. A gain on a sale or exchange of property between a partner and the partnership shall be treated as ordinary income if he/she has more than an 50% interest in the capital or profits of the partnership unless the asset is a capital asset to both the seller and the purchaser.

TEST FOR SELF-EVALUATION

True or False

T F 1. A partner in a partnership can be an individual, a corporation, an estate, a trust, or another partnership. (IRS 96 2A-13)

T F 2. A partnership liability affects a partner's basis in a cash basis partnership if, and to the extent that, the liability increases the partnership's basis in any of its assets. (IRS 96 2A-14)

T F 3. The partnership agreement can be modified for a particular tax year after the close of the year, but NOT later than the date for filing the partnership return for that year, not including extensions. (IRS 97 2A-9)

T F 4. Syndication fees for issuing and marketing interests in the partnership, such as commissions and professional fees, can be deducted as a current expense. (IRS 97 2A-11)

T F 5. A joint undertaking merely to share expenses or a mere co-ownership of property that is maintained and rented is NOT a partnership. But, if the co-owners provide services to the tenants, a partnership exists. (IRS 97 2A-10)

T F 6. A partnership is the relationship between two or more persons who join together to carry on a trade or business. Persons, when used to describe a partner, means only an individual. (IRS 92 2A-14)

T F 7. In determining a partner's income tax for the year, a partner must take into account separately his or her distributive share of all of the following partnership items whether or not they are actually distributed. (IRS 92 3A-15)

   1. Net income from rental real estate
   2. Charitable contributions
   3. Gains and losses from sales or exchanges of capital assets
   4. Ordinary income or loss from trade or business activities

T F 8. On March 10, 1990, Daniel contributed land in exchange for a partnership interest in Parr Company. The fair market value of the land at that time was $40,000 and Daniel's adjusted basis was $25,000. On December 2, 1991, Parr distributed that land to another partner. The fair market value at that time was $40,000. These transactions would not require a gain to be recognized by Daniel. (IRS 92 2A-16)

T F 9. Mr. Diaz and Mr. Garcia are both dentists who maintain separate practices, but they share the same office space. They equally divide the expenses, such as receptionist salary, rent, and utilities. This arrangement is a partnership for federal income tax purposes. (IRS 92 2A-13)

T F 10. The character of partner's distributive share of a partnership item of income, gain, loss, credit or deduction that the partner must take into account separately, is determined as if the partner had realized it directly from the same source or incurred it in the same manner as it was realized or incurred by the partnership. (IRS 90 2A-23)

Fill in the Blanks

1. Two legal concepts which have had a significant influence on the tax treatment of partners and partnerships are known as the _____ concept and the _____ concept.

2. According to Section 704(a), a partner's share of any partnership item is to be determined by _____.

3. Under Section 707(b) a loss from the sale or exchange of property will be disallowed if the partner has _____ percent interest in the partnership.

4. The measurement of partnership income requires a two step approach: the first step is the _____ and _____ of specific items on the partnership return; the second step is the measurement and reporting of the partnership's _____ income.

5. The partnership return is filed on Form _____.

6. The individual's copy of the partnership return is known as Schedule _____.

7. A partner's share of a distributive loss in the partnership is limited to his _____ in the partnership.

Multiple Choice

_____ 1. DCS Partnership, formed on September 15, 1996, elected to use a fiscal year ending November 30. DCS is required to file its return by which of the following dates? (IRS 97 2B-21)

    a. December 31, 1996
    b. January 15, 1997
    c. March 17, 1997
    d. April 15, 1997

_____ 2. Tri-State Partnership has a fiscal year ending June 30. The partnership's four partners have the following fiscal years:

Boulder	40% Owner	March 31
Granite	30% Owner	December 31
Shale	20% Owner	June 30
Slate	10% Owner	June 30

Assuming the partnership does NOT make a Section 444 election and does NOT establish a business purpose for a different period, what tax year must Tri-State use to file its tax return? (IRS 97 2B-31)

a. March 31
b. June 30
c. September 30
d. December 31

_____ 3. With regard to a partnership computing its income, which of the following is determined by the individual partners and NOT by the partnership?
(IRS 97 2B-32)

a. Accounting methods.
b. Amortization of certain organization fees and start-up costs.
c. Income from cancellation of debt.
d. Depreciation methods.

_____ 4. In which one of the following ownership combinations of Prescott Partnership would Pete be treated as owning more than 50% of the partnership?
(IRS 97 2B-33)

a. Pete   30 percent
   Wife   10 percent
   Pete's Aunt   60 percent
b. Pete   45 percent
   His Uncle's trust   55 percent
c. Pete   10 percent
   Pete's wife's corporation   90 percent
d. Pete   30 percent
   Pete's Father   10 percent
   Pete's Nephew   60 percent

_____ 5. Ken and Liz each have a 50% interest in KeLi Partnership. The partnership and the individuals file on a calendar year basis. For its 1995 tax year, KeLi had a $30,000 loss. Ken's adjusted basis in his partnership interest on January 1, 1995 was $8,000. In 1996, KeLi Partnership had a profit of $28,000. Assuming there were NO other adjustments to Ken's basis in the partnership in 1995 and 1996, what amount of partnership income (loss) would Ken show on his 1995 and 1996 individual income tax returns? (IRS 97 2C-62)

        1995   1996
- a. ($ 8,000) $ 0
- b. ($ 8,000) $ 7,000
- c. ($15,000) $ 7,000
- d. ($15,000) $ 14,000

_____ 6. The DKC Partnership, which is NOT a publicly traded partnership or a rental real estate partnership, was formed on January 1, 1996. DKC incurred a $24,000 loss for the year ending December 31, 1996 and had no income. The three partners share profits and losses equally. Ms. K is a passive investor in DKC. She contributed $3000 to the partnership on January 1, 1996, and an additional $5000 during 1996. Ms. K had draws totaling $1000 during 1996. What is Ms. K's deductible loss from DKC for 1996, if she had $4500 in income from other passive investments? (IRS 97 2C-63)
- a. $8,000
- b. $7,000
- c. $6,000
- d. $4,500

_____ 7. Gerard has a 60% interest in the capital and profits of Sly Partnership. He also owns a 65% interest in the capital and profits of Brice Partnership. On February 5, 1996, Sly Partnership sold land to Brice Partnership for $35,000. At the time of the sale, the land had an adjusted basis to Sly Partnership of $40,000. What is the amount of loss that Sly Partnership can recognize in 1996? (IRS 97 2C-64)

- a. $6,500
- b. $5,000
- c. $3,250
- d. $0

_____ 8. Under the terms of a partnership agreement, Annabelle is entitled to a fixed annual payment of $10,000 without regard to the income of the partnership. Her distributive share of the partnership income is 10 percent. The partnership has $50,000 of ordinary income after deducting the guaranteed payment. Which of the following states the amount and character of Annabelle's income from the partnership? (IRS 97 2C-65)

- a. $15,000 of ordinary income.
- b. $10,000 capital gain and $5,000 of ordinary income.
- c. $15,000 of capital gain.
- d. $10,000 of ordinary income and $5,000 capital gain.

____ 9. At-risk rules apply to most trade or business activities, including activities conducted through a partnership. The at-risk rules limit a partner's deductible loss to the amounts for which that partner is considered at risk in the activity. Select the statement below that is INCORRECT. (IRS 97 2C-66)

A partner is considered at risk for:
a. The money and adjusted basis of any property he or she contributed to the activity.
b. The partner's share of net income retained by the partnership.
c. Certain amounts borrowed by the partnership for use in the activity if the partner is personally liable for repayment or the amounts borrowed are secured by the partner's property(other than property used in the activity).
d. 90% of the total expected tax for the current year.

____ 10. Josephine acquired a 20 percent interest in a partnership by contributing property that had an adjusted basis to her of $8,000 and a $4,000 mortgage. The partnership assumed payment of the mortgage. What is the basis of Josephine's interest? (IRS 97 2C-71)

a. $1,600
b. $2,400
c. $3,600
d. $4,800

SOLUTIONS

True or False

1. T (p. 10-20)
2. T (p. 10-28)
3. T (p. 10-7)
4. F (p. 10-18)
5. T (p. 10-5; active conduct of trade or business)
6. F (p. 10-4, 20)
7. T (p. 10-21)
8. F (p. 10-25)
9. F (p. 10-4)
10. T (P. 10-21)

Fill in the Blanks

1. entity; conduit (p. 10-8)
2. partnership agreement (p. 10-7)
3. more than 50% (p. 10-39)
4. segregation; reporting; ordinary (p. 10-21)
5. 1065 (p. 10-6)
6. K-1 (p. 10-6)
7. adjusted basis (p. 10-33)

Multiple Choice

1. c (p. 10-21; 15th day of fourth month)
2. d (p. 10-20; lease aggregate deferral)
3. c (p. 10-15)
4. c (a. = 40%, b. = 45%, d. = 40%)
5. b (p. 10-33; 1995, limited to basis, 1996, 14,000 - 7,000 loss carryover)
6. d (p. 10-36; passive income limitation)
7. d (p. 10-40; Gerard is a more than 50% owner, related party loss)
8. a (guaranteed payment, 10,000 +10%(50,000))
9. d (p. 10-35)
10. d (p. 10-27; 8,000 - 4,000 + 20%(4,000))

CHAPTER 11

PARTNERSHIPS: DISTRIBUTIONS, TRANSFER OF INTERESTS, AND TERMINATIONS

LEARNING OBJECTIVES

After completing Chapter 11, you should be able to:

1. Determine the tax treatment of proportionate nonliquidating distributions from a partnership to a partner.

2. Determine the tax treatment of proportionate distributions that liquidate a partnership.

3. Describe the general concepts governing the tax treatment of disproportionate distributions.

4. Determine the tax treatment under §736 of payments from a partnership to a retiring or deceased partner.

5. Calculate the selling partner's amount and character of gain or loss on the sale or exchange of a partnership interest.

6. Calculate the optional adjustments to basis under §754.

7. Outline the methods of terminating a partnership.

8. Describe the special considerations of a family partnership.

9. Describe the application of partnership provisions to limited liability companies (LLCs) and limited liability partnerships (LLPs).

KEY TERMS

Appreciated inventory
Disproportionate distribution
Hot assets
Liquidating distribution
Nonliquidating distribution
Optional adjustment election
Proportionate distribution
Section 754 election
Technical termination of partnership
Unrealized receivables

OUTLINE

I. **DISTRIBUTIONS FROM A PARTNERSHIP**

   A. Nonliquidating distributions are draws or partial liquidations.
      1. Draws are distributions of a partner's share of partnership profits that have been taxed to that partner.
      2. Partial liquidations reduce the partner's interest in partnership capital and are a return OF investment in a partnership interest.

   B. Generally, no gain or loss is recognized by either the partnership or partner on a nonliquidating distribution.
      1. The partner takes a carryover basis in the assets distributed.
      2. The partner's outside basis is reduced by the amount of cash and the adjusted basis of property distributed. The partner's outside basis cannot be reduced below $0.
      3. If the cash distributed exceeds the partner's outside basis, the partner recognizes capital gain.
      4. Losses are not recognized on nonliquidating distributions.
      5. If the inside basis of the assets distributed exceed the partner's outside basis an ordering of the distribution is required
         a. first, cash
         b. second, unrealized receivables and inventory, ordinary income producing property
         c. third, other property
      6. If the partner's outside basis cannot absorb the second and/or third order of distributions, his basis, after the cash distribution, is to be allocated pro rata based on the relative inside bases of the assets distributed first within the second class, then, to the other property.

   C. Liquidating distributions terminate the partner's entire interest in the partnership.

   D. Partnership Liquidates
      1. Distributions reduce the partner's outside basis
         a. cash: dollar for dollar
         b. unrealized receivables and inventory: partnership (inside) adjusted basis
         c. other property: inside basis.
      2. No gain or loss is recognized by the partnership.
      3. The partner recognizes gain if the cash received exceeds his outside basis.
      4. The partner recognizes loss if:
         a. ONLY money, unrealized receivables or inventory are received, and
         b. the partner's outside basis exceeds the inside basis of the assets distributed.

        c.   if any other property is received, loss recognition is postponed.

    E.   Property Distributions with Special Tax Treatment
        1.   In a "disguised sale", the partner is treated as having sold the property and must report a gain on the sale.
        2.   Marketable securities are treated as cash distributions, unless:
            a.   they were originally contributed by the partner to whom they are now distributed.
            b.   the property was not a marketable security when acquired by the partnership.
            c.   the partner is an eligible partner of an investment partnership.
        3.   Precontribution Gain
            a.   if a partner contributes appreciated property to a partnership, that partner recognizes gain if:
                1.   the contributed property is distributed to another partner within seven years of the contribution date.
                2.   the partnership distributes any property other than cash to that partner within seven years after the partner contributed the appreciated property.
            b.   the partner's basis in the partnership interest is increased by the amount of gain recognized.
                1.   for property distributed to another partner, the basis of the distributed property is increased by the amount of gain recognized.
                2.   for property other than cash distributed to the contributing partner, the partnership increases its basis in the precontribution gain property remaining in the partnership.

    F.   Disproportionate Distributions
        1.   A disproportionate distribution occurs when a partnership makes a distribution that increases or decreases a partner's proportionate interest in certain ordinary income producing property.
        2.   The transaction is recast so that each partner recognizes and reports his proportionate share of ordinary income based on his proportionate share of the underlying assets of the partnership.

II.   LIQUIDATING DISTRIBUTIONS TO RETIRING OR DECEASED PARTNER

    A.   Payments made by an ongoing partnership in complete liquidation of a partner's interest are classified as either property or income payments.

    B.   Property payments are made in exchange for the partner's pro rata share of each partnership asset, §736(b).

1. In general, §736(b) payments are considered a return of the partner's outside basis in the partnership.
2. Cash payments in excess of that outside basis will be taxed as capital gains.
3. Cash payments insufficient to cover that outside basis will be taxed as capital losses.

C. Income payments, §736(a), are all payments not classified as §736(b) payments including:
1. Payments made for a partner's pro rata share of unrealized receivables.
2. Payments made for the partner's pro rata share of partnership goodwill if such payments are not provided for in the partnership agreement.
3. Certain annuity and lump sum payments.
4. Income payments are classified as guaranteed payments or distributive shares.
   a. guaranteed payments are NOT determined by reference to partnership income and are fully deductible by the partnership, taxed as ordinary income to the recipient partner.
   b. distributive share payments are determined by reference to partnership income and retain their character when distributed to the recipient partner.

D. Series of Payments
1. If the partners have specifically agreed to the allocation and timing of property and income payments, the agreement normally controls.
2. If no agreement is made, regulations specify the classification rules for each payment.

III. SALE OF A PARTNERSHIP INTEREST

A. As a general rule, capital gain or loss results from the sale or exchange of a partnership interest. The gain or loss recognized is the difference between the amount realized and the partner's adjusted basis, including liability effects.

B. The partnership's tax year closes as of the date of sale for the partner disposing of his entire interest.

C. Major exceptions to the general rule arise when a partner sells his or her interest in a partnership and there are unrealized receivables or appreciated inventory. Under Section 751 of the Code, these items, when included in the sale of a partnership interest, generate ordinary income.
1. "Unrealized receivables" includes:
   a. accounts receivable of a cash basis partnership, and,
   b. for sale or exchange purposes, depreciation recapture potential.

PARTNERSHIPS: DISTRIBUTIONS, TRANSFER OF INTERESTS, TERMINATIONS

2. "Appreciated inventory" includes essentially all partnership property except money, capital assets and §1231 property. Receivables are included in this definition.
3. Inventory is appreciated when its aggregate FMV exceeds its adjusted basis to the partnership.

IV. OTHER TRANSACTIONS WITH PARTNERSHIP INTERESTS

A. The transfer of a partnership interest to a controlled corporation will be treated as a nontaxable exchange if the conditions of Section 351 are satisfied.

B. The incorporation method used should be carefully chosen when §1244 stock is to be issued and/or an S corporation election is planned. The partnership should distribute all assets and liabilities to the partners who then transfer their interests to the corporation.

C. Like-kind exchange rules do not apply to the exchange of different partnerships' interests but, can apply to exchanges of interests in the same partnership.

V. OPTIONAL ADJUSTMENTS TO PROPERTY BASIS

A. A partnership may elect to adjust the basis of its property when a partner's interest is sold or exchanged, a partner dies, or an interest is distributed.

B. The adjustment to the property is the difference between what the transferee paid for the property and his share of the inside basis of the property.

C. The purpose of this optional adjustment is to equalize the inside and outside bases of the partner's interest.

D. If a step-up of depreciable property is involved, the optional adjustment is depreciated by the transferee partner, as if a newly acquired asset.

E. Once made, the election remains in effect until the IRS consents to its revocation.

VI. TERMINATION OF A PARTNERSHIP

A. The partnership incorporates.

B. In a two partner partnership, when one partner buys out the other, creating a sole proprietorship.

C. The partnership ceases operations and liquidates - a sale or exchange of partnership interest(s) result.

D. A technical termination occurs if more than 50% of the partnerships' capital and profits are transferred within a 12 month period.

VII. OTHER ISSUES

A. Family partnerships require special consideration. Because of the close relationship between family members, there is the possibility of channeling income from high tax-bracket members to low tax-bracket members.

B. A family member will be recognized as a partner if:
1. He performs substantial or vital services and capital is not a material consideration in the operation of the business;
2. The family member acquired his capital interest in a bona fide transaction, actually owns the partnership interest, is vested with control over it, and capital is a material income-producing factor.

C. When the partner is a child, under 14 years of age, a substantial portion of the child's distributive income may be taxed at the parent/partner's marginal rate. If the minor child is 14 or older, these taxing restrictions might be avoided.

D. Limited Liability Companies
1. Generally, none of the owners of a LLC are personally liable for LLC debt.
2. All owners can participate in management of the LLC.
3. Transfers of property to the LLC in exchange for an ownership interest are governed by partnership tax provisions.
4. An owner's basis in an LLC includes the owner's share of the LLC's liabilities under §752; all liabilities are treated as nonrecourse.
5. Special allocations under §704(b) are permitted.
6. Optional adjustments to basis election can be made.

E. Limited Liability Partnerships
1. Partners in a registered LLP are jointly and severally liable for contractual liability.
2. Partners are liable for their own malpractice or other torts, but are not liable for their partners' malpractice or torts.

TEST FOR SELF-EVALUATION

True or False

T F 1. Joanie received a gift from her father of a capital interest in a family partnership. There are NO limits on the amount that can be allocated Joannie as a distributive share of partnership income because capital is a material income producing factor.
(IRS 97 2A-4)

T F 2. Payments made in liquidation of the interest of a retiring or deceased partner in exchange for his or her interest in partnership property are considered a distribution, not a distributive share or guaranteed payment that could give rise to a deduction (or its equivalent) for the partnership.   (IRS 97 2A-20)

T F 3. During 1995, Sergio contributed property to his partnership. Sergio must recognize gain or loss on the distribution of the property to another partner within 7 years of the contribution.   (IRS 96 2A-15)

T F 4. When there is a sale or liquidation of a partner's interest in a partnership, the adjusted basis of the partner's partnership interest is determined on the date of the sale or liquidation.   (IRS 96 2A-16)

T F 5. Mr. Clysdale is a partner in Clysdale and Associates Partnership. The other two partners are his sister and his 17-year old son, Gregory. The partnership's income consists mostly of compensation for services performed by Mr. Clysdale and his sister. Gregory is a high school student and acquired his one-third interest by gift. Gregory is recognized as a partner in the firm for tax purposes. (IRS 95 2A-14)

T F 6. On December 31, 1994, Kay-Ann's adjusted basis in GEM Partnership was zero and her share of partnership liabilities was $30,000. The partnership had no unrealized receivables or substantially appreciated inventory items. Kay-Ann withdrew from the partnership on December 31, 1994, and was relieved of any partnership liabilities. As a result she has a $30,000 capital LOSS.
(IRS 95 2A-15)

T F 7. Chad's interest in BCD Partnership had an adjusted basis of $80,000. In complete liquidation of his interest, he received $30,000 cash, inventory items having a basis to the partnership of $44,000, and a company automobile having an adjusted basis to the partnership of $12,000. The basis of the automobile in Chad's hands is $12,000.   (IRS 95 2A-17)

T F 8. In a liquidating distribution a loss is recognized if the sum of the cash received plus the basis of distributed unrealized receivables and inventory is less than the adjusted basis of the partner's interest prior to the liquidating distribution and no other property is distributed.

T F 9. Recognition of gain will not occur in the liquidating distribution of property unless cash is received in excess of interest.

T F 10. The Code permits a partnership to increase or decrease the basis of partnership assets in the event of a death of one of the partners or if a partner's interest is sold or exchanged.

T F 11. An optional basis adjustment is binding only for the year in which it is made unless consent is received from the IRS to make it continuous.

Fill in the Blanks

1. Under the general rule of section 741, a partnership interest is a _____ asset, the sale or exchange of which will result in the recognition of _____.

2. Section 751 provides that amount realized from the sale of a partnership interest which are attributable to _____ or _____ must be treated as the sale of a noncapital asset.

3. Partnership liabilities forgiven or assumed by another partner are treated as _____ distributions.

Multiple Choice

_____ 1. All of the following statements with respect to property contributed to a partnership are correct except: (IRS 97 2B-34)

    a. Usually, NEITHER the partners NOR the partnership recognizes a gain or loss when property is contributed to the partnership in exchange for a partnership interest.
    b. The contributing partner must recognize gain or loss on a distribution of the property to another partner within 5 years of the contribution.
    c. Exchanges of partnership interests generally qualify for NONTAXABLE treatment as exchanges of like-kind property.
    d. The exchange of limited partnership interests in one partnership for limited partnership interests in another partnership may qualify as a tax-free contribution of property to the second partnership if the transaction is made for business purposes.

_____ 2. All of the following statements with respect to a partner's sale or exchange of a partnership interest are correct except: (IRS 97 2B-35)

a. The sale or exchange of a partner's interest in a partnership usually results in a capital gain or loss.
   b. Gain or loss recognized by the selling partner is the difference between the amount realized and the adjusted basis of the partner's interest in the partnership.
   c. The selling partner must include as part of the amount realized, any partnership liability he or she is relieved of.
   d. The installment method of reporting CANNOT be used by the partner who sells a partnership interest at a gain.

_____ 3. A partnership terminates when: (IRS 97 2C-61)

   (1) All of its operations are discontinued and no part of any business, financial operations, or venture is continued by any of its partners in a partnership or a limited liability company classified as a partnership, or
   (2) At least 50% of the total interest in partnership capital and profits is sold or exchanged within a 12 month period, including a sale or exchange to another partner.

   a. The above statement is true in its entirety.
   b. The above statement is fase in its entirety.
   c. Only item (1) above is true.
   d. Only item (2) above is true.

_____ 4. Walter is a limited partner in Cat Partnership. He contributed $30,000 in cash on the formation of the partnership. His adjusted basis in the partnership is $40,000, which includes his share of partnership liabilities of $10,000. In 1996, Walter sold his interest in the partnership for $60,000 in cash. He had been paid his share of partnership income for the tax year. The partnership has no other liabilities or receivables or substantially appreciated inventory. What is the amount and character of Walter's gain? (IRS 97 2C-67)

   a. $20,000 capital gain
   b. $20,000 ordinary gain
   c. $30,000 capital gain
   d. $30,000 ordinary gain

_____ 5. The adjusted basis of Ted's partnership interest is $30,000. In complete liquidation of his interest, he receives $10,000 in cash, his share of the inventory items having a basis to the partnership of $12,000, and two parcels of land having adjusted bases to the partnership of $12,000 and $4,000. What is Ted's basis in the two parcels of land? (IRS 97 2C-68)

a. $8,000 and $4,000
b. $5,000 and $3,000
c. $6,000 and $2,000
d. $8,000 and $0

_____ 6. Rick's interest in ATP Partnership has an adjusted basis of $300,000. In a complete liquidation of his interest, he received the following:

	ATP's Adjusted Basis	Fair Market Value
Cash	$140,000	$140,000
Building	160,000	180,000
Computer	40,000	20,000
Inventory	60,000	60,000

What is Rick's basis in the building and computer, respectively? (IRS 97 2C-69)

	Building	Computer
a.	$ 80,000	$20,000
b.	$ 90,000	$10,000
c.	$120,000	$30,000
d.	$135,000	$30,000

_____ 7. Fred became a limited partner in the Happy Partnership by contributing $10,000 in cash on the formation of the partnership. The adjusted basis of his partnership interest at the end of the current year is $20,000, which includes his $15,000 share of partnership liabilities. The partnership has no unrealized receivables or substantially appreciated inventory items. Fred sells his interest in the partnership for $10,000 in cash. He had been paid his share of the partnership income for the tax year.

Fred realized $25,000 from the sale of partnership interest ($10,000 cash payment plus $15,000 liability relief). How much should he report as a capital gain?
(IRS 97 2C-70)

a. $2,500
b. $5,000
c. $7,500
d. $10,000

_____ 8. Cynthia is a partner in CF Partnership. The adjusted basis of her partnership interest is $19,000, of which $15,000 represents her share of partnership liabilities. Cynthia's share of the partnership's unrealized receivables is $6,000. The partnership has NO substantially appreciated inventory items. Cynthia sold her partnership interest for $28,000 cash. What is the amount and character of her gain? (IRS 97 2C-72)

a. $6,000 capital gain
b. $6,000 ordinary income; $18,000 capital gain
c. $18,000 capital gain
d. $18,000 ordinary income; $6,000 capital gain

_____ 9. You are a partner in ABC Partnership. The adjusted basis of your partnership interest at the end of the current year is zero. Your share of potential ordinary income from partnership depreciable property is $5,000. The partnership has no other unrealized receivables or substantially appreciated inventory items. You sell your interest in the partnership for $11,000 in cash. Which of the following statements is accurate: (IRS 97 2C-73)

(1) You report the entire amount as a gain since your adjusted basis in the partnership is zero.
(2) You report $5,000 as ordinary income from the partnership's depreciable property.
(3) You report the remaining $6,000 gain as capital gain.

a. 2 and 3 are correct, but 1 is incorrect.
b. All of the statements are incorrect.
c. All of the statements are correct.
d. 1 is correct, but 2 and 3 are incorrect.

SOLUTIONS

True or False

1. F (p. 11-37; father is allocated reasonable compensation first)
2. T (p. 11-19; property payments)
3. T (p. 11-14; pre-contribution gain)
4. T (p. 11-24; partnership tax year closes for that partner)
5. F (p. 11-36; Gregory would need to provide services)
6. F (p. 11-5; reduction in share of debt in excess of basis is capital gain)
7. F (Chad's basis in the auto would be 6,000)
8. T (p. 11-11)
9. T (p. 11-9)
10. T (p. 11-30)
11. F (p. 11-34)

Fill in the Blanks

1. capital; capital gain; loss (p. 11-28)
2. unrealized receivables; inventory (p. 11-25)
3. cash (p. 11-5)

Multiple Choice

1. c (p. 11-30)
2. d (p. 11-23)
3. a (p. 11-34)
4. c (p. 11-23; 60,000 + 10,000 - 40,000)
5. c (30,000 - 10,000 - 12,000 = 8,000 to allocate; 8,000(12,000/16,000) + 8,000(4,000/16,000)
6. a (300,000 - 140,000 - 60,000 = 100,000 to allocate; 100,000(160,000/200,000) + 100,000(40,000/200,000)
7. b (25,000 realized - 20,000 basis)
8. b (15,000 + 28,000 realized - 6,000 ordinary - 19,000 basis = 18,000 capital gain)
9. c

Return Problem 2

Jan and Dee formed a partnership on January 1, 1998. Jan contributed land and a building with an adjusted basis of $180,000, the land was originally valued at $30,000. This property had been used in Jan's sole proprietorship for the past eight years and depreciated using the straight line method over 40 years. The fair market value of the property at the date of formation was $300,000, at which time the land was valued at $50,000. Dee contributed $150,000 cash, which was immediately used to buy new equipment. The equipment had a useful life of six years and zero salvage value. Because of the unequal investment, Jan and Dee agree that Jan should receive a guaranteed payment in the form of salary of $15,000, and all remaining items should be split 60% for Jan and 40% for Dee. Jan and Dee each made a cash withdrawal of $7,500 during the year.

Given the following data, you are to prepare Form 1065, U.S. Partnership Return including Jan's Schedule K-1, plus other related forms as required.

1. Name of partnership: Jan & Dee's
   Employer identification number: 36-1234567
   Address: 951 South Ravine, Chicago, IL 60632
   Method of accounting: Accrual

2. Partners:

Jan Such	Dee Notch
825 North Hopenstead	581 South Marigold
Chicago, IL 60421	Suberian, IL 60600
SSN 362-19-3801	SSN 358-33-0001

3. Revenue: $400,000
   Beginning inventory: -0-
   Purchases: 190,000
   Ending inventory at cost: 15,000
   Ending cash balance: 3,000
   Ending accounts receivable: 84,400
   Ending accounts payable: 15,000

Other expenses:
   Wages (not including Jan's) $ 40,000
   Insurance 5,000
   Taxes 3,600
   Advertising 22,000
   Legal and professional 18,000
   Promotion 17,000
   Telephone 2,000

11-14 2000/CORPORATIONS, PARTNERSHIPS, ESTATES, AND TRUSTS

Form **1065**		**U. S. Partnership Return of Income**		OMB No. 1545-0099
Department of the Treasury Internal Revenue Service		For calendar year 1998, or tax year beginning _____, 1998, and ending _____, 19 ___ ▶ See separate instructions.		**1998**

A	Principal business activity	Use the IRS label. Otherwise, please print or type.		D	Employer identification number
B	Principal product or service			E	Date business started
C	New business code no. (see pages 25-27 of instructions)			F	Total assets (see page 10 of the instructions) $

G Check applicable boxes: (1) ☐ Initial return   (2) ☐ Final return   (3) ☐ Change in address   (4) ☐ Amended return
H Check accounting method: (1) ☐ Cash   (2) ☐ Accrual   (3) ☐ Other (specify) ▶
I Number of Schedules K-1. Attach one for each person who was a partner at any time during the tax year .... ▶

Caution: Include **only** trade or business income and expenses on lines 1a through 22 below. See the instructions for more information.

INCOME

1a	Gross receipts or sales	1a		
	b Less returns and allowances	1b		1c
2	Cost of goods sold (Schedule A, line 8)			2
3	Gross profit. Subtract line 2 from line 1c			3
4	Ordinary income (loss) from other partnerships, estates and trusts (attach schedule)			4
5	Net farm profit (loss) (attach Schedule F (Form 1040))			5
6	Net gain (loss) from Form 4797, Part II, line 18			6
7	Other income (loss) (attach schedule)			7
8	**Total income (loss).** Combine lines 3 through 7			8

DEDUCTIONS (SEE INSTRUCTIONS FOR LIMITATIONS)

9	Salaries and wages (other than to partners) (less employment credits)			9
10	Guaranteed payments to partners			10
11	Repairs and maintenance			11
12	Bad debts			12
13	Rent			13
14	Taxes and licenses			14
15	Interest			15
16a	Depreciation (if required, attach Form 4562)	16a		
	b Less depreciation reported on Schedule A and elsewhere on return	16b		16c
17	Depletion **(Do not deduct oil and gas depletion.)**			17
18	Retirement plans, etc			18
19	Employee benefit programs			19
20	Other deductions (attach schedule)			20
21	**Total deductions.** Add the amounts shown in the far right column for lines 9 through 20			21
22	**Ordinary income (loss)** from trade or business activities. Subtract line 21 from line 8			22

Please Sign Here

Under penalties of perjury, I declare that I have examined this return, including accompanying schedules and statements, and to the best of my knowledge and belief, it is true, correct, and complete. Declaration of preparer (other than general partner or limited liability company member) is based on all information of which preparer has any knowledge.

▶ _____   ▶ _____
Signature of general partner or limited liability company member   Date

Paid Preparer's Use Only

| Preparer's signature | ▶ | | Date | | Check if self-employed ▶ ☐ | Preparer's social security no. |
| Firm's name (or yours if self-employed) and address | ▶ | | | | EIN ▶
ZIP code ▶ | |

For Paperwork Reduction Act Notice, see page 1 of separate instructions.   Form **1065** (1998)

KFA

PARTNERSHIPS: DISTRIBUTIONS, TRANSFER OF INTERESTS, TERMINATIONS 11-15

Form 1065 (1998) Page **2**

Schedule A — Cost of Goods Sold (see page 14 of the instructions)

1	Inventory at beginning of year	1
2	Purchases less cost of items withdrawn for personal use	2
3	Cost of labor	3
4	Additional section 263A costs (attach schedule)	4
5	Other costs (attach schedule)	5
6	**Total.** Add lines 1 through 5	6
7	Inventory at end of year	7
8	**Cost of goods sold.** Subtract line 7 from line 6. Enter here and on page 1, line 2	8

9a Check all methods used for valuing closing inventory:
  (i) ☐ Cost as described in Regulations section 1.471-3
  (ii) ☐ Lower of cost or market as described in Regulations section 1.471-4
  (iii) ☐ Other (specify method used and attach explanation) ▶
 b Check this box if there was a writedown of "subnormal" goods as described in Regulations section 1.471-2(c) ▶ ☐
 c Check this box if the LIFO inventory method was adopted this tax year for any goods (if checked, attach Form 970) ▶ ☐
 d Do the rules of section 263A (for property produced or acquired for resale) apply to the partnership? ☐ Yes ☐ No
 e Was there any change in determining quantities, cost, or valuations between opening and closing inventory? ☐ Yes ☐ No
   If "Yes," attach explanation.

Schedule B — Other Information

		Yes	No
1	What type of entity is filing this return? Check the applicable box:		
	a ☐ General partnership b ☐ Limited partnership c ☐ Limited liability company		
	d ☐ Limited liability partnership e ☐ Other ▶		
2	Are any partners in this partnership also partnerships?		
3	Is this partnership a partner in another partnership?		
4	Is this partnership subject to the consolidated audit procedures of sections 6221 through 6233? If "Yes," see **Designation of Tax Matters Partner** below		
5	Does this partnership meet **ALL THREE** of the following requirements?		
a	The partnership's total receipts for the tax year were less than $250,000;		
b	The partnership's total assets at the end of the tax year were less than $600,000; **AND**		
c	Schedules K-1 are filed with the return and furnished to the partners on or before the due date (including extensions) for the partnership return.		
	If "Yes," the partnership is not required to complete Schedules L, M-1, and M-2; Item F on page 1 of Form 1065; or Item J on Schedule K-1		
6	Does this partnership have any foreign partners?		
7	Is this partnership a publicly traded partnership as defined in section 469(k)(2)?		
8	Has this partnership filed, or is it required to file, **Form 8264**, Application for Registration of a Tax Shelter?		
9	At any time during calendar year 1998, did the partnership have an interest in or a signature or other authority over a financial account in a foreign country (such as a bank account, securities account, or other financial account)? (See page 14 of the instructions for exceptions and filing requirements for Form TD 90-22.1.) If "Yes," enter the name of the foreign country. ▶		
10	During the tax year, did the partnership receive a distribution from, or was it the grantor of, or transferor to, a foreign trust? If "Yes," the partnership may have to file Form 3520. See page 14 of the instructions		
11	Was there a distribution of property or a transfer (e.g., by sale or death) of a partnership interest during the tax year? If "Yes," you may elect to adjust the basis of the partnership's assets under section 754 by attaching the statement described under **Elections Made By the Partnership** on page 5 of the instructions		

Designation of Tax Matters Partner (see page 15 of the instructions)
Enter below the general partner designated as the tax matters partner (TMP) for the tax year of this return:

Name of designated TMP ▶   Identifying number of TMP ▶

Address of designated TMP ▶

Form 1065 (1998) Page **3**

Schedule K — Partners' Shares of Income, Credits, Deductions, etc.

		(a) Distributive share items		(b) Total amount
Income (Loss)	1	Ordinary income (loss) from trade or business activities (page 1, line 22)	1	
	2	Net income (loss) from rental real estate activities (attach Form 8825)	2	
	3a	Gross income from other rental activities 3a		
	b	Exp. from other rental activities 3b		
	c	Net income (loss) from other rental activities. Subtract line 3b from line 3a	3c	
	4	Portfolio income (loss):		
	a	Interest income	4a	
	b	Ordinary dividends	4b	
	c	Royalty income	4c	
	d	Net short-term capital gain (loss) (attach Schedule D (Form 1065))	4d	
	e	Net long-term capital gain (loss) (attach Schedule D (Form 1065)):		
		(1) 28% rate gain (loss) ▶ _____ (2) Total for year .... ▶	4e(2)	
	f	Other portfolio income (loss) (attach schedule)	4f	
	5	Guaranteed payments to partners	5	
	6	Net section 1231 gain (loss) (other than due to casualty or theft) (attach Form 4797)	6	
	7	Other income (loss) (attach schedule)	7	
Deductions	8	Charitable contributions (attach schedule)	8	
	9	Section 179 expense deduction (attach Form 4562)	9	
	10	Deductions related to portfolio income (itemize)	10	
	11	Other deductions (attach schedule)	11	
Credits	12a	Low-income housing credit:		
		(1) From partnerships to which section 42(j)(5) applies for property placed in service before 1990	12a(1)	
		(2) Other than on line 12a(1) for property placed in service before 1990	12a(2)	
		(3) From partnerships to which section 42(j)(5) applies for property placed in service after 1989	12a(3)	
		(4) Other than on line 12a(3) for property placed in service after 1989	12a(4)	
	b	Qual. rehabilitation expenditures related to rental real estate activities	12b	
	c	Credits (other than credits on lines 12a & 12b) related to rental real estate activities	12c	
	d	Credits related to other rental activities	12d	
	13	Other credits	13	
Investment Interest	14	Interest expense on investment debts	14a	
	a	(1) Investment income included on lines 4a, 4b, 4c, and 4f above	14b(1)	
	b	(2) Investment expenses included on line 10 above	14b(2)	
Self-Employment	15a	Net earnings (loss) from self-employment	15a	
	b	Gross farming or fishing income	15b	
	c	Gross nonfarm income	15c	
Adjustments and Tax Preference Items	16a	Depreciation adjustment on property placed in service after 1986	16a	
	b	Adjusted gain or loss	16b	
	c	Depletion (other than oil and gas)	16c	
	d	(1) Gross income from oil, gas, and geothermal properties	16d(1)	
		(2) Deductions allocable to oil, gas, and geothermal properties	16d(2)	
	e	Other adjustments and tax preference items (attach schedule)	16e	
Foreign Taxes	17a	Type of income ▶ _____		
	b	Name of foreign country or U.S. possession ▶ _____		
	c	Total gross income from sources outside the U.S. (attach schedule)	17c	
	d	Total applicable deductions and losses (attach schedule)	17d	
	e	Total foreign taxes (check one): ▶ ☐ Paid ☐ Accrued	17e	
	f	Reduction in taxes available for credit (attach schedule)	17f	
	g	Other foreign tax information (attach schedule)	17g	
Other	18	Section 59(e)(2) expenditures: a Type ▶ _____ b Amount ▶	18b	
	19	Tax-exempt interest income	19	
	20	Other tax-exempt income	20	
	21	Nondeductible expenses	21	
	22	Distributions of money (cash and marketable securities)	22	
	23	Distributions of property other than money	23	
	24	Other items & amounts required to be rptd. separately to partners		

PARTNERSHIPS: DISTRIBUTIONS, TRANSFER OF INTERESTS, TERMINATIONS 11-17

Form 1065 (1998) Page **4**

Analysis of Net Income (Loss)

1 Net income (loss). Combine Schedule K, lines 1 through 7 in column (b). From the result, subtract the sum of Schedule K, lines 8 through 11, 14a, 17e and 18b **1**

2 Analysis by partner type:	(i) Corporate	(ii) Individual (active)	(iii) Individual (passive)	(iv) Partnership	(v) Exempt organization	(vi) Nominee/Other
a Gen. partners						
b Lim. partners						

Schedule L Balance Sheets per Books (Not required if Question 5 on Schedule B is answered "Yes.")

Assets	Beginning of tax year (a)	(b)	End of tax year (c)	(d)
1 Cash..				
2a Trade notes and accounts receivable.................				
b Less allowance for bad debts......................				
3 Inventories.....................................				
4 U.S. government obligations......................				
5 Tax-exempt securities...........................				
6 Other current assets (attach schedule)................				
7 Mortgage and real estate loans.....................				
8 Other investments (attach schedule).................				
9a Buildings and other depreciable assets...............				
b Less accumulated depreciation.....................				
10a Depletable assets..............................				
b Less accumulated depletion.......................				
11 Land (net of any amortization)......................				
12a Intangible assets (amortizable only).................				
b Less accumulated amortization.....................				
13 Other assets (attach schedule).....................				
14 Total assets....................................				
Liabilities and Capital				
15 Accounts payable...............................				
16 Mortgages, notes, bonds payable in less than 1 year......				
17 Other current liabilities (attach schedule).............				
18 All nonrecourse loans............................				
19 Mortgages, notes, bonds payable in 1 year or more.......				
20 Other liabilities (attach schedule)....................				
21 Partners' capital accounts.........................				
22 Total liabilities and capital........................				

Schedule M–1 Reconciliation of Income (Loss) per Books With Income (Loss) per Return
(Not required if Question 5 on Schedule B is answered "Yes." See page 23 of the instructions.)

1 Net income (loss) per books...................		6 Income recorded on books this year not included on Schedule K, lines 1 through 7 (itemize):	
2 Income included on Schedule K, lines 1 through 4, 6, and 7, not recorded on books this year (itemize):		**a** Tax-exempt interest $ _____	
3 Guaranteed payments (other than health insurance)...............................		7 Deductions included on Schedule K, lines 1 through 11, 14a, 17e, and 18b not charged against book income this year (itemize):	
4 Expenses recorded on books this year not included on Schedule K, lines 1 through 11, 14a, 17e, & 18b (itemize): _____		**a** Depreciation $ _____	
a Depreciation $ _____			
b Travel and entertainment $ _____		8 Add lines 6 and 7........................	
5 Add lines 1 through 4........................		9 Income (loss) (Analysis of Net Income (Loss), line 1). Subtract line 8 from line 5...........	

Schedule M–2 Analysis of Partners' Capital Accounts (Not required if Question 5 on Schedule B is answered "Yes.")

1 Balance at beginning of year..................		6 Distributions: **a** Cash...................	
2 Capital contributed during year.................		**b** Property...............	
3 Net income (loss) per books...................		7 Other decreases (itemize):	
4 Other increases (itemize):			
		8 Add lines 6 and 7........................	
5 Add lines 1 through 4........................		9 Balance at end of year. Subtract line 8 from line 5	

11-18 2000/CORPORATIONS, PARTNERSHIPS, ESTATES, AND TRUSTS

SCHEDULE K-1 (Form 1065)	Partner's Share of Income, Credits, Deductions, etc. ▶ See separate instructions.	OMB No. 1545-0099
Department of the Treasury Internal Revenue Service	For calendar year 1998 or tax year beginning ____ , 1998, and ending ____ , 19 ____	**1998**

Partner's identifying number ▶
Partner's name, address, and ZIP code

Partnership's identifying number ▶
Partnership's name, address, and ZIP code

A This partner is a ☐ general partner ☐ limited partner
☐ limited liability company member

B What type of entity is this partner? . . ▶ _____

C Is this partner a ☐ domestic or a ☐ foreign partner?

D Enter partner's percentage of: (i) Before change or termination (ii) End of year
Profit sharing . . . . ____% ____%
Loss sharing . . . . ____% ____%
Ownership of capital . . . . . . ____% ____%

E IRS Center where partnership filed return: _____

F Partner's share of liabilities (see instructions):
Nonrecourse . . . . $ _____
Qualified nonrecourse financing . . . . $ _____
Other . . . . $ _____

G Tax shelter registration number . . . . ▶ _____

H Check here if this partnership is a publicly traded partnership as defined in section 469(k)(2) . . . . ☐

I Check applicable boxes: (1) ☐ Final K-1   (2) ☐ Amended K-1

J Analysis of partner's capital account:

(a) Capital account at beginning of year	(b) Capital contributed during year	(c) Partner's share of lines 3, 4, and 7, Form 1065, Schedule M-2	(d) Withdrawals and distributions	(e) Capital account at end of year (combine columns (a) through (d)
			( )	

	(a) Distributive share item		(b) Amount	(c) 1040 filers enter the amount in column (b) on:
INCOME/LOSS	1	Ordinary income (loss) from trade or business activities	1		} See page 6 of Partner's Instructions for Schedule K-1 (Form 1065).
	2	Net income (loss) from rental real estate activities	2		
	3	Net income (loss) from other rental activities	3		
	4	Portfolio income (loss):			
	a	Interest	4a		Sch. B, Part I, line 1
	b	Ordinary dividends	4b		Sch. B, Part II, line 5
	c	Royalties	4c		Sch. E, Part I, line 4
	d	Net short-term capital gain (loss)	4d		Sch. D, line 5, col. (f)
	e	Net long-term capital gain (loss):			
		(1) 28% rate gain (loss)	e(1)		Sch. D, line 12, col. (g)
		(2) Total for year	e(2)		Sch. D, line 12, col. (f)
	f	Other portfolio income (loss) (attach schedule)	4f		Enter on applicable line of your return.
	5	Guaranteed payments to partner	5		} See page 6 of Partner's Instructions for Schedule K-1 (Form 1065).
	6	Net section 1231 gain (loss) (other than due to casualty or theft)	6		
	7	Other income (loss) (attach schedule)	7		Enter on applicable line of your return.
DEDUCTIONS	8	Charitable contributions (see instructions)	8		Sch. A, line 15 or 16
	9	Section 179 expense deduction	9		} See page 7 and 8 of Partner's Instructions for Schedule K-1 (Form 1065).
	10	Deductions related to portfolio income	10		
	11	Other deductions (attach schedule)	11		
CREDITS	12 a	Low-income housing credit:			
		(1) From section 42(j)(5) partnerships for property placed in service before 1990	a(1)		} Form 8586, line 5
		(2) Other than on line 12a(1) for property placed in service before 1990	a(2)		
		(3) From section 42(j)(5) partnerships for property placed in service after 1989	a(3)		
		(4) Other than on line 12a(3) for property placed in service after 1989	a(4)		
	b	Qualified rehabilitation expenditures related to rental real estate activities	12b		} See page 8 of Partner's Instructions for Schedule K-1 (Form 1065).
	c	Credits (other than credits shown on lines 12a and 12b) related to rental real estate activities	12c		
	d	Credits related to other rental activities	12d		
	13	Other credits	13		

For Paperwork Reduction Act Notice, see instructions for Form 1065.

Schedule K-1 (Form 1065) 1998

KFA

PARTNERSHIPS: DISTRIBUTIONS, TRANSFER OF INTERESTS, TERMINATIONS   11-19

Schedule K-1 (Form 1065) 1998   Page **2**

	(a) Distributive share item	(b) Amount	(c) 1040 filers enter the amount in column (b) on:
INVESTMENT INTEREST	**14a** Interest expense on investment debts 14a		Form 4952, line 1
	b (1) Investment income included on lines 4a, 4b, 4c, and 4f .... b(1)		} See page 9 of Partner's Instructions for Schedule K-1 (Form 1065).
	(2) Investment expenses included on line 10 .... b(2)		
SELF-EMPLOYMENT	**15a** Net earnings (loss) from self-employment................................ 15a		Sch. SE, Section A or B
	b Gross farming or fishing income 15b		} See page 9 of Partner's Instructions for Schedule K-1 (Form 1065).
	c Gross nonfarm income 15c		
ADJUSTMENTS AND TAX PREFERENCE ITEMS	**16a** Depreciation adjustment on property placed in service after 1986........... 16a		
	b Adjusted gain or loss.. 16b		See page 9 of Partner's Instructions for Schedule K-1 (Form 1065 and Instructions for Form 6251.
	c Depletion (other than oil and gas) 16c		
	d (1) Gross income from oil, gas, and geothermal properties .... d(1)		
	(2) Deductions allocable to oil, gas, and geothermal properties .... d(2)		
	e Other adjustments and tax preference items 16e		
FOREIGN TAXES	**17a** Type of income ▶ _____		Form 1116, check boxes
	b Name of foreign country or U.S. possession ▶ _____		
	c Total gross income from sources outside the U.S......................... 17c		} Form 1116, Part I
	d Total applicable deductions and losses (attach sch.)..................... 17d		
	e Total foreign taxes (check one): ▶ ☐ Paid ☐ Accrued 17e		Form 1116, Part II
	f Reduction in taxes available for credit (att. schedule) 17f		Form 1116, Part III
	g Other foreign tax information (attach schedule) 17g		See Instructions for Form 1116.
OTHER	**18** Section 59(e)(2) expenditures: a Type ▶ _____		} See page 9 of Partner's Instructions for Schedule K-1 (Form 1065).
	b Amount 18b		
	19 Tax-exempt interest income 19		Form 1040, line 8b
	20 Other tax-exempt income 20		} See page 9 and 10 of Partner's Instructions for Schedule K-1 (Form 1065).
	21 Nondeductible expenses.. 21		
	22 Distributions of money (cash and marketable securities) 22		
	23 Distributions of property other than money 23		
	24 Recapture of low-income housing credit:		
	a From section 42(j)(5) partnerships.................................... 24a		} Form 8611, line 8
	b Other than on line 24a.. 24b		

25 Supplemental information required to be reported separately to each partner (attach additional schedules if more space is needed):

11-20 2000/CORPORATIONS, PARTNERSHIPS, ESTATES, AND TRUSTS

Form **4562**	**Depreciation and Amortization** (Including Information on Listed Property)	OMB No. 1545-0172 **1998**
Department of the Treasury Internal Revenue Service (99)	▶ See separate instructions. ▶ Attach this form to your return.	Attachment Sequence No. **67**

Name(s) shown on return | Identifying number

Business or activity to which this form relates

Part I — Election To Expense Certain Tangible Property (Section 179) (Note: If you have any "listed property," complete Part V before you complete Part I.)

1	Maximum dollar limitation. If an enterprise zone business, see page 2 of the instructions	1	$18,500
2	Total cost of section 179 property placed in service. See page 2 of the instructions	2	
3	Threshold cost of section 179 property before reduction in limitation	3	$200,000
4	Reduction in limitation. Subtract line 3 from line 2. If zero or less, enter –0–	4	
5	Dollar limitation for tax year. Subtract line 4 from line 1. If zero or less, enter –0–. If married filing separately, see page 2 of the instructions	5	

6	(a) Description of property	(b) Cost (business use only)	(c) Elected cost

7	Listed property. Enter amount from line 27	7	
8	Total elected cost of section 179 property. Add amounts in column (c), lines 6 and 7	8	
9	Tentative deduction. Enter the smaller of line 5 or line 8	9	
10	Carryover of disallowed deduction from 1997. See page 3 of the instructions	10	
11	Business income limitation. Enter the smaller of business income (not less than zero) or line 5 (see instructions)	11	
12	Section 179 expense deduction. Add lines 9 and 10, but do not enter more than line 11	12	
13	Carryover of disallowed deduction to 1999. Add lines 9 and 10, less line 12 ▶	13	

Note: Do not use Part II or Part III below for listed property (automobiles, certain other vehicles, cellular telephones, certain computers, or property used for entertainment, recreation, or amusement). Instead, use Part V for listed property.

Part II — MACRS Depreciation For Assets Placed in Service ONLY During Your 1998 Tax Year (Do Not Include Listed Property.)

Section A – General Asset Account Election

14 If you are making the election under section 168(i)(4) to group any assets placed in service during the tax year into one or more general asset accounts, check this box. See page 3 of the instructions .... ▶ ☐

Section B – General Depreciation System (GDS) (See page 3 of the instructions.)

(a) Classification of property	(b) Month and year placed in service	(c) Basis for depreciation (business/investment use only – see instructions)	(d) Recovery period	(e) Convention	(f) Method	(g) Depreciation deduction
15a 3-year property						
b 5-year property						
c 7-year property						
d 10-year property						
e 15-year property						
f 20-year property						
g 25-year property			25 yrs		S/L	
h Residential rental property			27.5 yrs	MM	S/L	
			27.5 yrs	MM	S/L	
i Nonresidential real property			39 yrs	MM	S/L	
				MM	S/L	

Section C – Alternative Depreciation System (ADS): (See page 5 of the instructions.)

16a Class life					S/L	
b 12-year			12 yrs		S/L	
c 40-year			40 yrs	MM	S/L	

Part III — Other Depreciation (Do Not Include Listed Property.) (See page 6 of the instructions.)

17	GDS and ADS deductions for assets placed in service in tax years beginning before 1998	17	
18	Property subject to section 168(f)(1) election	18	
19	ACRS and other depreciation	19	

Part IV — Summary (See page 6 of the instructions.)

20	Listed property. Enter amount from line 26	20	
21	**Total.** Add deductions on line 12, lines 15 and 16 in column (g), and lines 17 through 20. Enter here and on the appropriate lines of your return. Partnerships & S corporations - see instructions	21	
22	For assets shown above and placed in service during the current year, enter the portion of the basis attributable to section 263A costs	22	

KFA For Paperwork Reduction Act Notice, see of the separate instructions. Form **4562** (1998)

PARTNERSHIPS: DISTRIBUTIONS, TRANSFER OF INTERESTS, TERMINATIONS   11-21

Form 4562 (1998)   Page **2**

Part V — Listed Property – Automobiles, Certain Other Vehicles, Cellular Telephones, Certain Computers, and Property Used for Entertainment, Recreation, or Amusement

Note: For any vehicle for which you are using the standard mileage rate or deducting lease expense, complete **only** 23a, 23b, columns (a) through (c) of Section A, all of Section B, and Section C if applicable.

Section A – Depreciation and Other Information (Caution: See page 8 of the instructions for limits for passenger automobiles.)

23a Do you have evidence to support the business/investment use claimed? ☐ Yes ☐ No   23b If "Yes," is the evidence written? ☐ Yes ☐ No

(a) Type of property (list vehicles first)	(b) Date placed in service	(c) Business/investment use percentage	(d) Cost or other basis	(e) Basis for depreciation (business/investment use only)	(f) Recovery period	(g) Method/Convention	(h) Depreciation deduction	(i) Elected section 179 cost

24 Property used more than 50% in a qualified business use (See page 7 of the instructions.):

25 Property used 50% or less in a qualified business use (See page 7 of the instructions.):

26 Add amounts in column (h). Enter the total here and on line 20, page 1 .... | 26 |

27 Add amounts in column (i). Enter the total here and on line 7, page 1 .... | 27 |

Section B – Information on Use of Vehicles

Complete this section for vehicles used by a sole proprietor, partner, or other "more than 5% owner," or related person.
If you provided vehicles to your employees, first answer questions in Section C to see if you meet an exception to completing this section for those vehicles.

	(a) Vehicle 1	(b) Vehicle 2	(c) Vehicle 3	(d) Vehicle 4	(e) Vehicle 5	(f) Vehicle 6
28 Total business/investment miles driven during the year (DO NOT include commuting miles)						
29 Total commuting miles driven during the year						
30 Total other personal (noncommuting) miles driven						
31 Total miles driven during the year. Add lines 28 to 30						
32 Was the vehicle available for personal use during off-duty hours?	Yes No	Yes No	Yes No	Yes No	Yes No	Yes No
33 Was the vehicle used primarily by a more than 5% owner or related person?						
34 Is another vehicle available for personal use?						

Section C – Questions for Employers Who Provide Vehicles for Use by Their Employees

Answer these questions to determine if you meet an exception to completing Section B for vehicles used by employees who **are not** more than 5% owners or related persons.

	Yes	No
35 Do you maintain a written policy statement that prohibits all personal use of vehicles, including commuting, by your employees?		
36 Do you maintain a written policy statement that prohibits personal use of vehicles, except commuting, by your employees? See page 9 of the instructions for vehicles used by corporate officers, directors, or 1% or more owners		
37 Do you treat all use of vehicles by employees as personal use?		
38 Do you provide more than five vehicles to your employees, obtain information from your employees about the use of the vehicles, and retain the information received?		
39 Do you meet the requirements concerning qualified automobile demonstration use? See page 9 of the instructions		

Note: If your answer to 35, 36, 37, 38 or 39 is "Yes," you need not complete Section B for the covered vehicles.

Part VI — Amortization

(a) Description of costs	(b) Date amortization begins	(c) Amortizable amount	(d) Code section	(e) Amortization period or percentage	(f) Amortization for this year

40 Amortization of costs that begins during your 1998 tax year:

41 Amortization of costs that began before 1998 .... | 41 |

42 Total. Enter here and on "Other Deductions" or "Other Expenses" line of your return .... | 42 |

11-22 2000/CORPORATIONS, PARTNERSHIPS, ESTATES, AND TRUSTS

Form **1065** Department of the Treasury Internal Revenue Service
U.S. Partnership Return of Income **1998**
▶ See separate instructions.
IRS use only — Do not write or staple in this space.

For calendar year 1998, or tax year beginning , 1998, & ending , 19 .
OMB No.1545-0099

A Principal Business Activity	Name of Partnership: **Jan & Dee's**	**D** Employer ID Number: **36-1234567**
B Principal Product or Service	Number, Street, and Room or Suite No. If a P.O. box, see instructions. **951 South Ravine**	**E** Date Business Started: **01/01/98**
C New Business Code Number (see instructions)	City or Town: **Chicago** State **IL** ZIP Code **60632**	**F** Total Assets (see instr) $ **406,278.**

Use the IRS label. Otherwise please print or type.

G Check applicable boxes: (1) [X] Initial return (2) [ ] Final return (3) [ ] Change in address (4) [ ] Amended return
H Check accounting method: (1) [ ] Cash (2) [X] Accrual (3) [ ] Other (specify) ▶ _____
I Number of Schedules K-1. Attach one for each person who was a partner at any time during the tax year ....▶ **2**

Caution: *Include only trade or business income and expenses on lines 1a through 22 below. See the instructions for more information.*

INCOME

1a	Gross receipts or sales	1a 400,000.	
b	Less returns and allowances	1b	1c 400,000.
2	Cost of goods sold (Schedule A, line 8)		2 175,000.
3	Gross profit. Subtract line 2 from line 1c		3 225,000.
4	Ordinary income (loss) from other partnerships, estates, and trusts (attach schedule)		4
5	Net farm profit (loss) (attach Schedule F (Form 1040))		5
6	Net gain (loss) from Form 4797, Part II, line 18		6
7	Other income (loss) (attach schedule)		7
8	**Total income (loss).** Combine lines 3 through 7		8 225,000.

DEDUCTIONS (SEE INSTRUCTIONS FOR LIMITATIONS)

9	Salaries and wages (other than to partners) (less employment credits)		9 40,000.
10	Guaranteed payments to partners		10 15,000.
11	Repairs and maintenance		11
12	Bad debts		12
13	Rent		13
14	Taxes and licenses		14 3,600.
15	Interest		15
16a	Depreciation (if required, attach Form 4562)	16a 26,122.	
b	Less depreciation reported on Schedule A & elsewhere on return	16b	16c 26,122.
17	Depletion (**Do not deduct oil and gas depletion.**)		17
18	Retirement plans, etc		18
19	Employee benefit programs		19
20	Other deductions (attach schedule) .... See.Other.deductions		20 64,000.
21	**Total deductions.** Add the amounts shown in the far right column for lines 9 through 20		21 148,722.
22	**Ordinary income (loss)** from trade or business activities. Subtract line 21 from line 8		22 76,278.

Please Sign Here
Under penalties of perjury, I declare that I have examined this return, including accompanying schedules and statements, and to the best of my knowledge and belief, it is true, correct, and complete. Declaration of preparer (other than general partner or limited liability company member) is based on all information of which preparer has any knowledge.

▶ Signature of General Partner or Limited Liability Company Member   Date

Paid Preparer's Use Only
Preparer's Signature ▶   Date   Check if self-employed [ ]   Preparer's Social Security Number
Firm's Name (or yours if self-employed) and Address ▶ **Self Prepared**
EIN ▶
ZIP Code ▶

BAA For Paperwork Reduction Act Notice, see separate instructions.   Form **1065** (1998)

PTPA0112 12/01/98

PARTNERSHIPS: DISTRIBUTIONS, TRANSFER OF INTERESTS, TERMINATIONS 11-23

Form **1065** (1998) Jan & Dee's   36-1234567   Page 2

Schedule A — Cost of Goods Sold

1	Inventory at beginning of year	
2	Purchases less cost of items withdrawn for personal use	190,000.
3	Cost of labor	
4	Additional section 263A costs (attach schedule)	
5	Other costs (attach schedule)	
6	**Total.** Add lines 1 through 5	190,000.
7	Inventory at end of year	15,000.
8	**Cost of goods sold.** Subtract line 7 from line 6. Enter here and on page 1, line 2	175,000.

9a Check all methods used for valuing closing inventory:
  (i) [X] Cost as described in Regulations section 1.471-3
  (ii) [ ] Lower of cost or market as described in Regulations section 1.471-4
  (iii) [ ] Other (specify method used and attach explanation) ▶ _____

b Check this box if there was a writedown of 'subnormal' goods as described in Regulations section 1.471-2(c) ▶ [ ]
c Check this box if the LIFO inventory method was adopted this tax year for any goods (if checked, attach Form 970) ▶ [ ]
d Do the rules of section 263A (for property produced or acquired for resale) apply to the partnership? .... Yes [ ] No [ ]
e Was there any change in determining quantities, cost, or valuations between opening and closing inventory? .. Yes [ ] No [X]
  If 'yes', attach explanation.

Schedule B — Other Information

		Yes	No
1	What type of entity is filing this return? Check the applicable box: a [X] General partnership b [ ] Limited partnership c [ ] Limited liability company d [ ] Limited liability partnership e [ ] Other ▶ _____		
2	Are any partners in this partnership also partnerships?		X
3	Is this partnership a partner in another partnership?		X
4	Is this partnership subject to the consolidated audit procedures of sections 6221 through 6233? If 'Yes,' see **Designation of Tax Matters Partner** below		X
5	Does this partnership meet **All Three** of the following requirements?		
	a The partnership's total receipts for the tax year were less than $250,000;		
	b The partnership's total assets at the end of the tax year were less than $600,000; **and**		
	c Schedules K-1 are filed with the return and furnished to the partners on or before the due date (including extensions) for the partnership return.		
	If 'Yes,' the partnership is not required to complete Schedules L, M-1, and M-2; item F on page 1 of Form 1065; or item J on Schedule K-1		X
6	Does this partnership have any foreign partners?		X
7	Is this partnership a publicly traded partnership as defined in section 469(k)(2)?		X
8	Has this partnership filed, or is it required to file, **Form 8264**, Application for Registration of a Tax Shelter?		X
9	At any time during calendar year 1998, did the partnership have an interest in or a signature or other authority over a financial account in a foreign country (such as a bank account, securities account, or other financial account)? See the instructions for exceptions and filing requirements for Form TD F 90-22.1. If 'Yes,' enter the name of the foreign country. ▶ _____		X
10	During the tax year, did the partnership receive a distribution from, or was it the grantor of, or transferor to, a foreign trust? If 'Yes,' the partnership may have to file Form 3520. See instructions		X
11	Was there a distribution of property or a transfer (e.g., by sale or death) of a partnership interest during the tax year? If 'Yes,' you may elect to adjust the basis of the partnership's assets under section 754 by attaching the statement described in the instructions under **Elections Made by the Partnership**		X

Designation of Tax Matters Partner

Enter below the general partner designated as the tax matters partner (TMP) for the tax year of this return:

Name of Designated TMP ▶ Jan Such   Identifying Number of TMP ▶ 362-19-3801

Address of Designated TMP ▶ 825 North Hopenstead
Chicago, IL 60421

BAA   PTPA0112 12/01/98

Form 1065 (1998)   Jan & Dee's   36-1234567   Page 3

Schedule K — Partners' Shares of Income, Credits, Deductions, etc

	(a) Distributive share items		(b) Total amount
Income (Loss)	1 Ordinary income (loss) from trade or business activities (page 1, line 22)	1	76,278.
	2 Net income (loss) from rental real estate activities *(attach Form 8825)*	2	
	3a Gross income from other rental activities 3a		
	b Expenses from other rental activities *(attach schedule)* 3b		
	c Net income (loss) from other rental activities. Subtract line 3b from line 3a	3c	
	4 Portfolio income (loss):		
	a Interest income	4a	
	b Dividend income	4b	
	c Royalty income	4c	
	d Net short-term capital gain (loss) *(attach Schedule D (Form 1065))*	4d	
	e Net long-term capital gain (loss) *(attach Schedule D (Form 1065))*:		
	(1) 28% rate gain (loss) ▶ _____ (2) Total for year ▶	4e (2)	
	f Other portfolio income (loss) *(attach schedule)*	4f	
	5 Guaranteed payments to partners	5	15,000.
	6 Net Section 1231 gain (loss) (other than due to casualty or theft) *(attach Form 4797)*	6	
	7 Other income (loss)	7	
Deductions	8 Charitable contributions *(attach schedule)*	8	
	9 Section 179 expense deduction *(attach Form 4562)*	9	
	10 Deductions related to portfolio income (itemize)	10	
	11 Other deductions	11	
Credits	12a Low-income housing credit:		
	(1) From partnerships to which Section 42(j)(5) applies for property placed in service before 1990	12a (1)	
	(2) Other than on line 12a(1) for property placed in service before 1990	12a (2)	
	(3) From partnerships to which Section 42(j)(5) applies for property placed in service after 1989	12a (3)	
	(4) Other than on line 12a(3) for property placed in service after 1989	12a (4)	
	b Qualified rehabilitation expenditures related to rental real estate activities *(attach Form 3468)*	12b	
	c Credits (other than credits shown on lines 12a and 12b) related to rental real estate activities	12c	
	d Credits related to other rental activities	12d	
	13 Other credits	13	
Investment Interest	14a Interest expense on investment debts	14a	
	b(1) Investment income included on lines 4a, 4b, 4c, and 4f above	14b (1)	
	(2) Investment expenses included on line 10 above	14b (2)	
Self-Employment	15a Net earnings (loss) from self-employment	15a	91,278.
	b Gross farming or fishing income	15b	
	c Gross nonfarm income	15c	225,000.
Adjustments and Tax Preference Items	16a Depreciation adjustment on property placed in service after 1986	16a	12,060.
	b Adjusted gain or loss	16b	
	c Depletion (other than oil and gas)	16c	
	d (1) Gross income from oil, gas, and geothermal properties	16d (1)	
	(2) Deductions allocable to oil, gas, and geothermal properties	16d (2)	
	e Other adjmnts & tax pref items	16e	
Foreign Taxes	17a Type of income ▶ _____		
	b Name of foreign country or U.S. possession ▶ _____		
	c Total gross income from sources outside the United States *(attach schedule)*	17c	
	d Total applicable deductions and losses *(attach schedule)*	17d	
	e Total foreign taxes (check one): ▶ ☐ Paid ☐ Accrued	17e	
	f Reduction in taxes available for credit *(attach schedule)*	17f	
	g Other foreign tax information *(attach schedule)*	17g	
Other	18 Section 59(e)(2) expenditures: a Type ... ▶ _____ b Amount ... ▶	18b	
	19 Tax-exempt interest income	19	
	20 Other tax-exempt income	20	
	21 Nondeductible expenses	21	
	22 Distributions of money (cash and marketable securities)	22	15,000.
	23 Distributions of property other than money	23	
	24 Other items and amounts required to be reported separately to partners *(attach schedule)*		

BAA   PTPA0134 11/17/98

Form 1065 (1998) Jan & Dee's 36-1234567 Page 4

Analysis of Net Income (Loss)

1	Net income (loss). Combine Schedule K, lines 1 through 7 in column (b). From the result, subtract the sum of Schedule K, lines 8 through 11, 14a, 17e, and 18b	1	91,278.

2 Analysis by partner type:	(i) Corporate	(ii) Individual (active)	(iii) Individual (passive)	(iv) Partnership	(v) Exempt organization	(vi) Nominee/Other
a General partners		91,278.				
b Limited partners						

Schedule L — Balance Sheets per Books (Not required if question 5 on Schedule B is answered 'Yes.')

Assets	Beginning of tax year (a)	(b)	End of tax year (c)	(d)
1 Cash				3,000.
2a Trade notes and accounts receivable			84,400.	
b Less allowance for bad debts				84,400.
3 Inventories				15,000.
4 U.S. government obligations				
5 Tax-exempt securities				
6 Other current assets (attach schedule)				
7 Mortgage and real estate loans				
8 Other investments (attach schedule)				
9a Buildings and other depreciable assets			337,500.	
b Less accumulated depreciation			63,622.	273,878.
10a Depletable assets				
b Less accumulated depletion				
11 Land (net of any amortization)				30,000.
12a Intangible assets (amortizable only)				
b Less accumulated amortization				
13 Other assets (attach schedule)				
14 Total assets				406,278.
Liabilities and Capital				
15 Accounts payable				15,000.
16 Mortgages, notes, bonds payable in less than 1 year				
17 Other current liabilities (attach sch)				
18 All nonrecourse loans				
19 Mortgages, notes, bonds payable in 1 year or more				
20 Other liabilities (attach schedule)				
21 Partners' capital accounts			0.	391,278.
22 Total liabilities and capital			0.	406,278.

Schedule M-1 — Reconciliation of Income (Loss) per Books With Income (Loss) per Return
(Not required if question 5 on Schedule B is answered 'Yes.' See instructions.)

1	Net income (loss) per books	76,278.	6	Income recorded on books this year not included on Schedule K, lines 1 though 7 (itemize):	
2	Income included on Schedule K, lines 1 through 4, 6, and 7, not recorded on books this year (itemize): _____ _____		a	Tax-exempt interest ... $ _____	
3	Guaranteed pmts (other than health insurance)	15,000.	7	Deductions included on Schedule K, lines 1 through 11, 14a, 17e, and 18b, not charged against book income this year (itemize):	
4	Expenses recorded on books this year not included on Schedule K, lines 1 through 11, 14a, 17e, and 18b (itemize):		a	Depreciation ...... $ _____ _____	
a	Depreciation ... $ _____				
b	Travel and entertainment .. $ _____		8	Add lines 6 and 7	
			9	Income (loss) (Analysis of net income (loss), line 1). Subtract line 8 from line 5	91,278.
5	Add lines 1 through 4	91,278.			

Schedule M-2 — Analysis of Partners' Capital Accounts (Not required if question 5 on Schedule B is answered 'Yes.')

1	Balance at beginning of year	0.	6	Distributions: a Cash	15,000.
2	Capital contributed during year	330,000.		b Property	
3	Net income (loss) per books	76,278.	7	Other decreases (itemize): _____ _____	
4	Other increases (itemize): _____ _____				
			8	Add lines 6 and 7	15,000.
5	Add lines 1 through 4	406,278.	9	Balance at end of year. Subtract line 8 from line 5	391,278.

11-26 2000/CORPORATIONS, PARTNERSHIPS, ESTATES, AND TRUSTS

Schedule K-1 (Form 1065) Department of the Treasury Internal Revenue Service	Partner's Share of Income, Credits, Deductions, Etc For calendar year 1998 or tax year beginning , 1998, and ending , 19	OMB No. 1545-0099 **1998**
Partner's identifying number ▶ 362-19-3801	Partnership's identifying number ▶ 36-1234567	

Partner's Name, Address, and ZIP Code:
Jan Such
825 North Hopenstead
Chicago, IL 60421

Partnership's Name, Address, and ZIP Code:
Jan & Dee's
951 South Ravine
Chicago, IL 60632

A This partner is a [X] general partner [ ] limited partner
[ ] limited liability company member
B What type of entity is this partner? ▶ Individual
C Is this partner a [X] domestic or a [ ] foreign partner?
D Enter partner's % of: (i) Before change or termination   (ii) End of year
Profit sharing ..... _____% 60.00000%
Loss sharing ..... _____% 60.00000%
Ownership of capital .. _____% 56.00000%
E IRS Center where partnership filed return: Kansas City, MO

F Partner's share of liabilities:
Nonrecourse .... $ _____
Qualified nonrecourse financing ... $ _____
Other .... $ 9,000.
G Tax shelter registration number ▶ _____
H Check here if this partnership is a publicly traded partnership as defined in section 469(k)(2) .... [ ]
I Check applicable boxes: (1) [ ] Final K-1 (2) [ ] Amended K-1

J Analysis of partner's capital account:

(a) Capital account at beginning of year	(b) Capital contributed during year	(c) Partner's share of lines 3, 4, and 7, Form 1065, Schedule M-2	(d) Withdrawals and distributions	(e) Capital account at end of year (combine columns (a) through (d))
0.	180,000.	45,767.	7,500.	218,267.

	(a) Distributive share item		(b) Amount	(c) 1040 filers enter the amount in column (b) on:
Income (Loss)	1 Ordinary income (loss) from trade or business activities	1	45,767.	See Partner's Instructions for Schedule K-1 (Form 1065).
	2 Net income (loss) from rental real estate activities	2		
	3 Net income (loss) from other rental activities	3		
	4 Portfolio income (loss):			
	a Interest	4a		Schedule B, Part I, line 1
	b Ordinary dividends	4b		Schedule B, Part II, line 5
	c Royalties	4c		Schedule E, Part I, line 4
	d Net short-term capital gain (loss)	4d		Schedule D, line 5, column (f)
	e Net long-term capital gain (loss):			
	(1) 28% rate gain (loss)	e(1)		Schedule D, line 12, column (g)
	(2) Total for year	e(2)		Schedule D, line 12, column (f)
	f Other portfolio income (loss) (attach schedule)	4f		Enter on applicable ln of your return
	5 Guaranteed payments to partner	5	9,000.	See Partner's Instructions for Schedule K-1 (Form 1065).
	6 Net section 1231 gain (loss) (other than due to casualty or theft)	6		
	7 Other income (loss) (attach schedule)	7		Enter on applicable ln of your return
Deductions	8 Charitable contributions (attach schedule)	8		Schedule A, line 15 or 16
	9 Section 179 expense deduction	9		See Partner's Instructions for Schedule K-1 (Form 1065).
	10 Deductions related to portfolio income (attach schedule)	10		
	11 Other deductions (attach schedule)	11		
Credits	12a Low-income housing credit:			
	(1) From section 42(j)(5) p'ships for property placed in service before 1990	a(1)		Form 8586, line 5
	(2) Other than on line 12a(1) for property placed in service before 1990	a(2)		
	(3) From section 42(j)(5) partnerships for property placed in service after 1989	a(3)		
	(4) Other than on line 12a(3) for property placed in service after 1989	a(4)		
	b Qualified rehabilitation expenditures related to rental real estate activities	12b		See Partner's Instructions for Schedule K-1 (Form 1065).
	c Credits (other than credits shown on lines 12a and 12b) related to rental real estate activities	12c		
	d Credits related to other rental activities	12d		
	13 Other credits	13		

BAA For Paperwork Reduction Act Notice, see instructions for Form 1065.   Schedule K-1 (Form 1065) 1998

PTPA0312 11/17/98

PARTNERSHIPS: DISTRIBUTIONS, TRANSFER OF INTERESTS, TERMINATIONS 11-27

Schedule **K-1** (Form 1065) 1998   Jan Such   362-19-3801   Page **2**

	(a) Distributive share item		(b) Amount	(c) 1040 filers enter the amount in column (b) on:
Investment Interest	**14a** Interest expense on investment debts	14a		Form 4952, line 1
	b (1) Investment income included on lines 4a, 4b, 4c, and 4f	b(1)		See Partner's Instructions for Schedule K-1 (Form 1065).
	(2) Investment expenses included on line 10	b(2)		
Self-employment	**15a** Net earnings (loss) from self-employment	15a	54,767.	Schedule SE, Section A or B
	b Gross farming or fishing income	15b		See Partner's Instructions for Schedule K-1 (Form 1065).
	c Gross nonfarm income	15c	135,000.	
Adjustments and Tax Preference Items	**16a** Depreciation adjustment on property placed in service after 1986	16a	7,236.	See Partner's Instructions for Schedule K-1 (Form 1065) and instructions for Form 6251.
	b Adjusted gain or loss	16b		
	c Depletion (other than oil and gas)	16c		
	d (1) Gross income from oil, gas, and geothermal properties	d(1)		
	(2) Deductions allocable to oil, gas, and geothermal properties	d(2)		
	e Other adjustments & tax preference items *(attach schedule)*	16e		
Foreign Taxes	**17a** Type of income ▶ _____			Form 1116, check boxes
	b Name of foreign country or possession ▶ _____			
	c Total gross income from sources outside the United States *(attach schedule)*	17c		Form 1116, Part I
	d Total applicable deductions and losses *(attach schedule)*	17d		
	e Total foreign taxes (check one): ▶ ☐ Paid ☐ Accrued	17e		Form 1116, Part II
	f Reduction in taxes available for credit *(attach schedule)*	17f		Form 1116, Part III
	g Other foreign tax information *(attach schedule)*	17g		See instructions for Form 1116.
Other	**18a** Section 59(e)(2) expenditures: **a** Type ▶ _____			See Partner's Instructions for Schedule K-1 (Form 1065).
	b Amount	18b		
	19 Tax-exempt interest income	19		Form 1040, line 8b
	20 Other tax-exempt income	20		See Partner's Instructions for Schedule K-1 (Form 1065).
	21 Nondeductible expenses	21		
	22 Distributions of money (cash and marketable securities)	22	7,500.	
	23 Distributions of property other than money	23		
	24 Recapture of low-income housing credit:			
	a From section 42(j)(5) partnerships	24a		Form 8611, line 8
	b Other than on line 24a	24b		

Supplemental Information

25 Supplemental information required to be reported separately to each partner *(attach additional schedules if more space is needed)*:

```
Item J (c) - Capital account adjustments:
  Ordinary income (loss)                                        45,767.
    Total                                                       45,767.
```

Schedule **K-1** (Form 1065) 1998

11-28 2000/CORPORATIONS, PARTNERSHIPS, ESTATES, AND TRUSTS

Form 4562
Department of the Treasury
Internal Revenue Service (99)

Depreciation and Amortization
(Including Information on Listed Property)
► See instructions.
► Attach this form to your return.

OMB No. 1545-0172
1998
67

Name(s) Shown on Return: Jan & Dee's
Business or Activity to Which This Form Relates: Form 1065 Line 22
Identifying Number: 36-1234567

Part I — Election to Expense Certain Tangible Property (Section 179)
(Note: If you have any 'listed property,' complete Part V before you complete Part I.)

1	Maximum dollar limitation. If an enterprise zone business, see instructions	$18,500.
2	Total cost of Section 179 property placed in service. See instructions	
3	Threshold cost of Section 179 property before reduction in limitation	$200,000.
4	Reduction in limitation. Subtract line 3 from line 2. If zero or less, enter -0-	
5	Dollar limitation for tax year. Subtract line 4 from line 1. If zero or less, enter -0-. If married filing separately, see instructions	

6

(a) Description of property	(b) Cost (business use only)	(c) Elected cost

7	Listed property. Enter amount from line 27	
8	Total elected cost of Section 179 property. Add amounts in column (c), lines 6 and 7	
9	Tentative deduction. Enter the smaller of line 5 or line 8	
10	Carryover of disallowed deduction from 1997. See instructions	
11	Business income limitation. Enter the smaller of business income (not less than zero) or line 5 (see instrs)	
12	Section 179 expense deduction. Add lines 9 and 10, but do not enter more than line 11	
13	Carryover of disallowed deduction to 1999. Add lines 9 and 10, less line 12 ► 13	

Note: *Do not use Part II or Part III below for listed property (automobiles, certain other vehicles, cellular telephones, certain computers, or property used for entertainment, recreation, or amusement). Instead, use Part V for listed property.*

Part II — MACRS Depreciation for Assets Placed in Service Only During Your 1998 Tax Year
(Do Not Include Listed Property)

Section A — General Asset Account Election

14 If you are making the election under Section 168(i)(4) to group any assets placed in service during the tax year into one or more general asset accounts, check this box. See instructions ► ☐

Section B — General Depreciation System (GDS) (See instructions)

(a) Classification of property	(b) Month and year placed in service	(c) Basis for depreciation (business/investment use only — see instructions)	(d) Recovery period	(e) Convention	(f) Method	(g) Depreciation deduction
15a 3-year property						
b 5-year property						
c 7-year property		150,000.	7.0 yrs	HY	200DB	21,435.
d 10-year property						
e 15-year property						
f 20-year property						
g 25-year property			25 yrs		S/L	
h Residential rental property			27.5 yrs	MM	S/L	
			27.5 yrs	MM	S/L	
i Nonresidential real property			39 yrs	MM	S/L	
				MM	S/L	

Section C — Alternative Depreciation System (ADS) (See instructions)

16a Class life					S/L	
b 12-year			12 yrs		S/L	
c 40-year			40 yrs	MM	S/L	

Part III — Other Depreciation (Do Not Include Listed Property) (See instructions)

17	GDS and ADS deductions for assets placed in service in tax years beginning before 1998	4,687.
18	Property subject to Section 168(f)(1) election	
19	ACRS and other depreciation	

Part IV — Summary (See instructions)

20	Listed property. Enter amount from line 26	
21	**Total.** Add deductions on line 12, lines 15 and 16 in column (g), and lines 17 through 20. Enter here and on the appropriate lines of your return. Partnerships and S corporations — see instructions	26,122.
22	For assets shown above and placed in service during the current year, enter the portion of the basis attributable to Section 263A costs	

BAA For Paperwork Reduction Act Notice, see the separate instructions.   FDIZ0812 07/23/98   Form **4562** (1998)

PARTNERSHIPS: DISTRIBUTIONS, TRANSFER OF INTERESTS, TERMINATIONS   11-29

Form **4562** (1998)   Jan & Dee's   36-1234567   Page 2

Part V — Listed Property — Automobiles, Certain Other Vehicles, Cellular Telephones, Certain Computers, and Property Used for Entertainment, Recreation, or Amusement

Note: *For any vehicle for which you are using the standard mileage rate or deducting lease expense, complete **only** 23a, 23b, columns (a) through (c) of Section A, all of Section B, and Section C if applicable.*

Section A — Depreciation and Other Information (Caution: See instructions for limits for passenger automobiles.)

23a Do you have evidence to support the business/investment use claimed? .... Yes ☐ No ☐   **23b** If 'Yes,' is the evidence written? ...... Yes ☐ No ☐

(a) Type of property (list vehicles first)	(b) Date placed in service	(c) Business/ investment use percentage	(d) Cost or other basis	(e) Basis for depreciation (business/investment use only)	(f) Recovery period	(g) Method/ Convention	(h) Depreciation deduction	(i) Elected Section 179 cost

24 Property used more than 50% in a qualified business use (see instructions):

25 Property used 50% or less in a qualified business use (see instructions):

26 Add amounts in column (h). Enter the total here and on line 20, page 1 .... **26**

27 Add amounts in column (i). Enter the total here and on line 7, page 1 .... **27**

Section B — Information on Use of Vehicles

Complete this section for vehicles used by a sole proprietor, partner, or other 'more than 5% owner,' or related person.
If you provided vehicles to your employees, first answer the questions in Section C to see if you meet an exception to completing this section for those vehicles.

	(a) Vehicle 1	(b) Vehicle 2	(c) Vehicle 3	(d) Vehicle 4	(e) Vehicle 5	(f) Vehicle 6
28 Total business/investment miles driven during the year (**Do not** include commuting miles)						
29 Total commuting miles driven during the year						
30 Total other personal (noncommuting) miles driven						
31 Total miles driven during the year. Add lines 28 through 30						
	Yes No	Yes No	Yes No	Yes No	Yes No	Yes No
32 Was the vehicle available for personal use during off-duty hours?						
33 Was the vehicle used primarily by a more than 5% owner or related person?						
34 Is another vehicle available for personal use?						

Section C — Questions for Employers Who Provide Vehicles for Use by Their Employees

*Answer these questions to determine if you meet an exception to completing Section B for vehicles used by employees who **are not** more than 5% owners or related persons.*

	Yes	No
35 Do you maintain a written policy statement that prohibits all personal use of vehicles, including commuting, by your employees?		
36 Do you maintain a written policy statement that prohibits personal use of vehicles, except commuting, by your employees? See instructions for vehicles used by corporate officers, directors, or 1% or more owners		
37 Do you treat all use of vehicles by employees as personal use?		
38 Do you provide more than five vehicles to your employees, obtain information from your employees about the use of the vehicles, and retain the information received?		
39 Do you meet the requirements concerning qualified automobile demonstration use? See instructions		

Note: *If your answer to 35, 36, 37, 38, or 39 is 'Yes,' you need not complete Section B for the covered vehicles.*

Part VI — Amortization

(a) Description of costs	(b) Date amortization begins	(c) Amortizable amount	(d) Code Section	(e) Amortization period or percentage	(f) Amortization for this year

40 Amortization of costs that begins during your 1998 tax year:

41 Amortization of costs that began before 1998 .... **41**

42 **Total.** Enter here and on 'Other Deductions' or 'Other Expenses' line of your return **42**

FDIZ0812   07/23/98

JAN & DEE'S
Form 1065

36-1234567
12/31/98

Page 1, Line 20, Schedule of Other Expenses:

Advertising	$22,000
Insurance	5,000
Legal and professional	18,000
Promotion	17,000
Telephone	<u>2,000</u>
Total	<u>$64,000</u>

CHAPTER 12

S CORPORATIONS

LEARNING OBJECTIVES

After completing Chapter 12, you should be able to:

1. Explain the tax effects that S corporation status has on shareholders.

2. Identify corporations that qualify for the S election.

3. Understand how to make an S election.

4. Explain how an S election can be terminated.

5. Compute nonseparately stated income and identify separately stated items.

6. Allocate income, deductions, and credits to shareholders.

7. Understand how distributions to S corporation shareholders are taxed.

8. Calculate a shareholder's basis in S corporation stock.

9. Explain the tax effects that losses have on shareholders.

10. Compute the built-in gains tax.

11. Compute the passive investment income penalty tax.

KEY TERMS

Accumulated adjustments account	Passive investment income	Small business corporation
Built-in gains tax	S corporation	Subchapter S

OUTLINE

I. QUALIFYING FOR S CORPORATION STATUS

    A. Definition of a Small Business Corporation
        1. For S corporation status, a small business corporation
            a. is a domestic corporation.
            b. is an eligible corporation
                1. certain banks and insurance companies are ineligible.
                2. Puerto Rico or possessions corporations are ineligible.
                3. foreign corporations are ineligible.
            c. issues only one class of stock.
                1. differences in voting rights are permitted.
                2. distribution or liquidation rights must be identical.
            d. has no more than 75 shareholders.
                1. husband and wife are considered one shareholder.
                2. widowers or widows and their spouse's estate are considered one shareholder.
            e. has as its shareholders only individuals, estates, and certain trusts.
            f. has no nonresident alien shareholder.

    B. Making the Election
        1. The S election is made on Form 2553.
        2. All shareholders must consent to the election in writing.
        3. The election must be made on or before the 15th day of the 3rd month to be effective for the current year.
        4. The election may be made at any time during the current year to be effective for the following year.
        5. No election can be made for a corporation not yet in existence; the first month of a newly created corporation is the earliest of:
            a. when the corporation has shareholders,
            b. when the corporation acquires assets,
            c. when the corporation begins doing business.

    C. Loss of the Election
        1. Violation of one of the eligibility rules causes termination as of the date on which the disqualifying event occurred.
            a. the number of shareholders exceeds the maximum allowed.
            b. a nonresident alien becomes a shareholder.
            c. another class of stock is created.
        2. Voluntary revocation may be made by shareholders owning a majority of shares.
        3. Failing the passive investment income limitation causes termination as of the beginning of the 4th year. This limitation:

a. applies only to S corporations having accumulated E & P from years in which it was a C corporation.
b. applies if the corporation has passive income in excess of 25% of its gross receipts for 3 consecutive years.
c. passive investment income includes dividends, interest, rents, gains and losses from sale of securities, and royalties.

D. Reelection After Termination
1. Generally, 5 years must pass before a new election can be made.
2. Exceptions may be allowed when:
   a. there is a more than 50% change in ownership, or
   b. the event which caused disqualification was not reasonably within the control of the S corporation or its majority shareholders.

II. OPERATIONAL RULES

A. Computation of Taxable Income
1. Nonseparately computed income or losses are allocated pro rata to each shareholder for each day the stock is owned.
2. Each shareholder also receives a pro rata share of separately stated items.
3. Separately stated income, losses, deductions, and credits are items which could uniquely affect the tax liability of a shareholder.
4. Refer to the text, for a listing of separately stated items.

B. Tax Treatment of Distributions to Shareholders
1. The amount of any distribution to an S corporation shareholder is the cash plus the fair market value of any other property distributed.
2. An S corporation should maintain an accumulated adjustments account.
   a. AAA is a cumulative total of undistributed net income items.
   b. AAA is not adjusted for tax-exempt income and related expenses, or for Federal income taxes attributable to C corporation years.
   c. Distributions cannot make the AAA negative or increase a negative balance.
3. A shareholder has a proportionate interest in the AAA.
4. For an S corporation having no accumulated E & P from C corporation years, a distribution is not includible in the shareholders' gross income to the extent that it does not exceed the shareholder's adjusted basis in stock.
5. For an S corporation with accumulated E & P, a distribution is:
   a. tax-free up to the amount in AAA, limited to stock basis,
   b. if cash, tax-free up to the amount of PTI, previously taxed income, pre 1983,
   c. a taxable dividend to the extent of accumulated E & P,
   d. return of capital,

e. capital gain.
C. Tax Treatment of Property Distributions by the Corporation
1. Property is distributed at fair market value.
2. Gains, not losses, are recognized.

D. Shareholder's Tax Basis
1. Initial stock basis is determined similar to that of basis in a C corporation.
2. Basis is increased by further stock purchases and capital contributions.
3. Corporate operations during the year increase and decrease stock basis.
4. Basis is reduced by distributions of AAA or PTI.
5. Basis can never be negative.
6. Once stock basis is zero, any additional basis reductions from losses or deductions, NOT distributions, decrease the shareholder's basis in loans made to the S corporation.
7. The basis for loans is established by actual advances to the corporation, not by indirect loans.

E. Treatment of Losses
1. Net operating losses are passed through to the shareholders and are deductible to the extent of stock and loan bases.
2. An NOL which exceeds the shareholder's basis may be carried forward and deducted by the same shareholder, if and when, basis is restored.
3. Passively activity losses and credits flow through to shareholders and decrease the shareholders' basis, whether or not deductible under the passive loss limitation rules.

F. Tax on Preelection Built-In Gains
1. A C corporation electing S status, after 1986, may incur a corporate level tax on gains attributable to asset appreciation during C corporation years.
2. The total amount of gain recognized is limited to the aggregate, net built-in gains at the time of conversion to S status.
3. The tax applies when the S corporation disposes of such an asset, in a taxable disposition, within 10 years of the conversion to S status.
4. For purposes of the tax on built-in gains, certain C corporation carryovers are allowed as offsets.
   a. Unexpired NOLs or capital losses
   b. AMT credit carryovers and business credit carryovers

G. Passive Investment Income Penalty Tax
1. An S corporation having accumulated E & P from C corporation years is taxed on its excess passive income.
2. Excess Net Passive Income is:

$$\frac{\text{passive investment income - 25\% of gross receipts}}{\text{total passive investment for the year}} * \text{net passive investment income for the year}$$

       3. The amount subject to tax cannot exceed the corporations taxable income for the year.
       4. The applicable tax rate is the highest corporate tax rate in effect for that year.

  H. Other Operational Rules
       1. S corporations must make estimated tax payments for any recognized built-in gain and excess passive investment income.
       2. An S corporation may own stock in another corporation but, is not eligible for a dividend received deduction.
       3. An S corporation is not subject to the 10 percent of taxable income limitation applicable to charitable contributions made by a Subchapter C corporation.
       4. Any family member who renders services or furnishes capital to the electing corporation must be reasonably compensated to avoid adjustments by the IRS to reflect the value of such services or capital.
       5. A shareholder's portion of S income is not self-employment income. Compensation for services rendered to an S corporation are subject to FICA taxes.

III. TAX PLANNING CONSIDERATIONS

  A. In determining when the S election is advisable, it is necessary to consider all of the provisions that will affect the owners.

  B. Because Subchapter S is an elective provision, strict compliance with the Code is required in making and preserving the election and operating the corporation. Shareholders and management should be made aware of the various transactions that could cause involuntary termination.

Section 1361 - Definition of a Small Business Corporation

```
                    Start
                      │
                      ▼
          ┌──────────────────────┐    NO
          │ Is it a domestic     ├─────────────────┐
          │ corporation?         │                 │
          └──────────┬───────────┘                 │
                   YES                             │
                     │                             │
          ┌──────────▼───────────┐    YES          │
          │ Is it an ineligible  ├─────────────┐   │
          │ corporation?         │             │   │
          └──────────┬───────────┘             │   │
                    NO                         │   │
                     │                         │   │
          ┌──────────▼───────────┐    YES      │   │
          │ Does it have more    ├─────────┐   │   │
          │ than one class       │         │   │   │
          │ of stock?            │         │   │   │
          └──────────┬───────────┘         │   │   │         ◇
                    NO                     ├───┴───┴──▶  Does NOT
                     │                     │             Qualify To
          ┌──────────▼───────────┐    YES  │              Elect S
          │ Does it have a       ├─────────┤             Corporation
          │ nonresident alien    │         │               Status
          │ as a shareholder?    │         │                 ◇
          └──────────┬───────────┘         │                 ▲
                    NO                     │                 │
                     │                     │                 │
          ┌──────────▼───────────┐    YES  │                 │
          │ Does it have, as     ├─────────┘                 │
          │ shareholders,        │                           │
          │ entities other than  │                           │
          │ individuals, estates │                           │
          │ and certain trusts?  │                           │
          └──────────┬───────────┘                           │
                    NO                                       │
                     │                                       │
          ┌──────────▼───────────┐  YES  ┌───────────────────┴──┐
          │ Does it have more    ├──────▶│ Is any stock owned by│
          │ than 75 shareholders?│       │ husband and wife?    │
          └──────────┬───────────┘       └──────────┬───────────┘
                    NO                              │
                     │                              ▼
                     ▼                  ┌──────────────────────┐
                  ◇                     │ Treat as one          │
              Qualifies                 │ shareholder          │
               To Elect  ◀──────NO──────┴──────────┬───────────┘
               S Status                            │
                  ◇                                ▼
                                       ┌──────────────────────┐  YES
                                       │ NOW does it have     ├──────▶
                                       │ more than 75         │
                                       │ shareholders?        │
                                       └──────────────────────┘
```

S CORPORATION
DISTRIBUTIONS TO SHAREHOLDERS

Does corporation have any accumulated E&P?

- **No** → Tax free to extent of shareholder's basis → Gain from sale of property - capital gain
- **Yes** → Did all shareholders consent to AAA Bypass Elections?
  - **No** → Tax free up to amount in AAA - limited to basis → Tax free up to amount of PTI - under pre 83 rules → Dividend to extent of accumulated E&P → Return of capital → Gain from sale of property - capital gain

Shareholder's Basis Cannot Be Less Than Zero

TEST FOR SELF-EVALUATION

True or False

T F 1. A corporation's election of S corporation status is valid if a majority of its shareholders consent to the election. (IRS 97 3A-18)

T F 2. Both separately stated items and the nonseparately stated income or loss are passed through to the shareholders of an S corporation in proportion to their shareholdings. (IRS 97 3A-19)

T F 3. Blue, an S Corporation, has no earnings and profits. In 1996, Blue distributed cash of $40,000 to Sunny, its sole shareholder. Sunny's basis in Blue's stock on December 31, 1996 (before considering the distribution) was $35,000. On January 1, 1997, Sunny's basis in Blue's stock would be ($5,000). (IRS 97 3A-20)

T F 4. A loss on the sale or exchange of property is NOT deductible if the transaction is directly or indirectly between two S corporations and the same persons own more than 50% in value of the outstanding stock of each corporation. (IRS 96 3A-7)

T F 5. If an S corporation is subject to the tax on excess net passive investment income, it must reduce the items of passive income passed through to the shareholders. (IRS 96 3A-10)

T F 6. If an S corporation's passive investment income is more than 25% of gross receipts for two consecutive tax years and the corporation has pre-S corporation earnings and profits at the end of each of those years, the corporation's S corporation status will be terminated. (IRS 95 3A-13)

T F 7. Omega Corporation, an S corporation, has 10 shareholders on January 1, 1993. During the year, 8 of the existing shareholders, owning 51% of the stock, sold their interests to one new individual shareholder. Omega will automatically terminate its S corporation status on the day over 50% of Omega's stock was transferred. (IRS 94 3A-9)

T F 8. Exodus Corporation, a calendar year corporation, has 35 shareholders on January 1, 1993. On June 30, 1993, a shareholder sold her stock to Interferon Corporation. On July 1, 1993, Interferon sold the stock to its sole shareholder, Anthony. Exodus Corporation will file TWO short period returns for 1993. (IRS 94 3A-10)

T F 9. For any tax year, an S corporation can elect its distributions as coming first from earnings and profits if ALL shareholders who receive a distribution during the tax year consent to the election. This election remains in effect for ALL tax years thereafter. (IRS 93 3A-12)

T F 10. For 1991, the books and records of Clover, Inc., a cash basis S corporation, reflected the following: (IRS 92 3A-11)

Salary to Dad Clover, President and 50% shareholder	$22,000
Salary to Son Clover, Janitor and 50% shareholder	$60,000
Loans to Dad Clover during 1991, no repayments	$30,000

Dad Clover worked 40 hour weeks for the entire year but said that the business could not afford to pay him a salary more than $22,000. The IRS could reclassify the $30,000 and/or part of the son's salary to Dad Clover, and assess income tax withholding as well as employment taxes on those amounts.

Fill in the Blanks

1. Generally an S corporation is a tax _____ rather than a tax _____ entity.

2. A distribution by an S corporation having no earnings and profits is _____ in gross income to the extent that it does not exceed the shareholder's adjusted basis in stock.

3. An S corporation's net operating loss pass through cannot exceed a shareholder's adjusted basis in the _____ plus the basis of any _____ made to the corporation.

4. The term "small" for purposes of the S election refers to the _____.

5. The long-term capital gain from the sale of securities would generally be treated as _____ investment income.

6. Distributions that exceed the shareholder's tax basis for the stock are taxable as _____.

7. The _____ of stock in an S corporation is calculated similarly to the basis of stock in a regular corporation.

8. Net operating losses which exceed the shareholder's stock basis are used to reduce _____ the shareholder.

Multiple Choice

_____ 1. All of the following factors serve to determine whether an S corporation may be subject to the tax on excess net passive income except: (IRS 97 3B-45)

a. The S corporation has been an S corporation from the date of its incorporation.
b. The S corporation has Subchapter C earnings and profits at the end of the year.
c. Passive investment income is more than 25% of its gross receipts.
d. More than 50% of loans payable are NOT at-risk.

_____ 2. What is the nonseparately stated income amount of an accrual basis, calendar year S corporation with the following items? (IRS 97 3C-78)

Gross receipts	200,000
Interest income	12,000
Rental income	25,000
Cost of goods sold and commissions	127,000
Net long-term capital gain	17,000
Compensation paid to shareholder	10,000

a. $63,000
b. $73,000
c. $117,000
d. $127,000

_____ 3. Twister, an S corporation, has no earnings and profits. In 1996, Twister distributed property with a fair market value of $65,000 and an adjusted basis of $52,000 to Carlos, its sole shareholder. After recognizing his share of any corporate gain or loss, his adjusted basis in Twister's stock at year end was $50,000. How should the distribution be handled by Carlos? (IRS 97 3C-79)

a. $50,000 as return of capital and $15,000 as nontaxable distribution.
b. $50,000 as return of capital and $15,000 as taxable capital gain.
c. $50,000 as return of capital and $2,000 as taxable capital gain.
d. $50,000 as nontaxable distribution.

_____ 4. On January 1, 1996, Jon purchased 50% of Waite, an S corporation, for $75,000. At the end of 1996, Waite incurred an ordinary loss of $160,000. How much of the loss can Jon deduct on his personal income tax return for 1996?
(IRS 97 3C-80)

a. $37,500
b. $75,000
c. $80,000
d. $160,000

_____ 5. To qualify for S corporation status, a corporation must meet all of the following requirements except: (IRS 96 3B-27)

a. Must be a domestic corporation.
b. Must have no more than 75 shareholders.
c. Must have as shareholders only individuals, certain trusts or other corporations.
d. Must have shareholders who are citizens or residents of the U.S.

_____ 6. All of the following would reduce the basis of a shareholder's stock in an S corporation except: (IRS 96 3B-28)
a. A shareholder's pro rata share of nontaxable distributions by the S corporation to its shareholders.
b. A shareholder's share of all loss and deduction items of the S corporation that are separately stated and passed through to the shareholder.
c. A shareholder's pro rata share of any nonseparately stated loss of the S corporation.
d. A shareholder's pro rata share of any nonseparately stated income of the S corporation.

_____ 7. On December 31, 1995, Valor, a calendar year S corporation since 1981, made a $100,000 distribution to its sole shareholder, Bryant. Valor's books and records reflect the following for 1995.

Accumulated adjustments account - 1/1/95	$ 5,000
Ordinary income for 1995	50,000
Previously taxed income account at the time of the distribution	10,000
Accumulated earnings and profits at the time of the distribution	5,000

Bryant's basis in Valor's stock on January 1, 1995 was $40,000. How much income will Bryant report from this S corporation investment in 1995 and what is its character? (IRS 96 3C-67)

	Ordinary Income	*Capital Gain*
a.	$50,000	$10,000
b.	$55,000	$5,000
c.	$60,000	$-0-
d.	$50,000	$60,000

_____ 8. Magnolia Corporation, a calendar year S corporation, was formed on January 1, 1994. Kathy owns 25 percent of Magnolia's outstanding stock which she purchased for $20,000. In 1994, Kathy guaranteed a corporate loan for $40,000. In 1995, Kathy made payments on the loan totaling $10,000. Magnolia had losses of $90,000 and $60,000 in 1994 and 1995 respectively. What is the amount of the unallowed loss that Kathy can carry over to 1996? (IRS 96 3C-68)

a. $0
b. $7,500
c. $10,000
d. $17,500

_____ 9. On January 1, 1995, Mr. Wise purchased 50 percent of S Corporation Cobra's only class of stock outstanding for $150,000. On December 1, 1995, he purchased the other 50% of Cobra's stock for $150,000. For 1995 Cobra incurred a net operating loss of $237,250. How much of the loss can Mr. Wise deduct on his individual income tax return for 1995? (IRS 96 3C-69)

a. $118,625
b. $128,700
c. $150,000
d. $237,250

_____ 10. In 1994, Lisa acquired 100% of the stock of Computers Inc. for $50,000 cash. Computers incurred a loss of $15,600 for 1994. On January 1, 1995, Computers properly elected S corporation status. Its net income for 1995 was $20,000. A dividend of $5,000 was declared and paid in 1995. What is Lisa's basis in Computers Inc. as of December 31, 1995? (IRS 96 3C-70)

a. $70,000
b. $65,000
c. $51,000
d. $50,000

_____ 11. In the context of the tax on excess net passive income paid by S corporations, net passive income does NOT include: (IRS 95 3B-33)

a. interest and dividends.
b. annuities.
c. net operating losses.
d. sales or exchanges of stock.

_____ 12. Mr. Oliver received a distribution from an S corporation that was in excess of the basis of his stock in the corporation. The S corporation had NO earnings and profits. Mr. Oliver should treat the distribution in excess of his basis as
(IRS 95 3B-34)

a. a return of capital.
b. previously taxed income.
c. a capital gain.
d. a reduction in the basis of his stock.

_____ 13. With regard to an S corporation and its shareholders, the at-risk rules applicable to losses (IRS 95 3B-35)

a. take into consideration the S corporation's ratio of debt to equity.
b. apply at the shareholder level rather than at the corporate level.
c. are subject to the elections made by the S corporation's shareholders.
d. depend on the type of income reported by the S corporation.

_____ 14. All of the following would reduce the basis of a shareholder's stock in an S corporation except: (IRS 95 3B-36)

a. A shareholder's pro rata share of any nonseparately stated loss of the S corporation.
b. A shareholder's share of all loss and deduction items of the S corporation that are separately stated.
c. A shareholder's pro rata share of any nondeductible expenses of the S corporation that are not properly chargeable to capital account.
d. A shareholder's pro rata share of any nonseparately stated income of the S corporation.

_____ 15. Which of the following events would cause an S corporation to cease to qualify as an S corporation: (IRS 95 3B-37)

a. A 25% shareholder sells her shares to an individual who wants to revoke the S corporation status.
b. The corporation is liable for tax on excess net passive investment income for two consecutive years.
c. A shareholder has zero basis in his stock.
d. The S corporation issues its stock to another corporation.

_____ 16. The books and records of May Inc., a calendar year S corporation since 1982, reflect the following information for 1994:

  Accumulated adjustments account 1/1/94 $ 60,000
  Accumulated earnings & profits 1/1/94   150,000
  Ordinary income for 1994   204,000

May Inc. has one shareholder, Paula, whose basis in May's stock was $100,000 on January 1, 1994. During 1994, May distributed $300,000 to Paula. What is the amount of the distribution that would be treated as a dividend by Paula?
(IRS 95 3C-73)

a. $0
b. $36,000
c. $264,000
d. $300,000

SOLUTIONS

True or False
1. F (p. 12-8; all shareholders must consent)
2. T (p. 12-13)
3. F (p. 12-20)
4. T (related party)
5. T (p. 12-29; passive income reported by each shareholder is reduced by their allocable portion of the tax)
6. F (p. 12-10; three years)
7. F (p. 12-9; only if a voluntary revocation is filed)
8. T (p. 12-10; termination of S on date event occurred)
9. F (p. 12-18; election is made for a particular distribution)
10. T (p. 12-33)

Fill in the Blanks
1. reporting; paying (p. 12-2)
2. not included (p. 12-15)
3. stock; loans (p. 12-24)
4. number of shareholders (p. 12-6)
5. passive (p. 12-29)
6. capital gains (p. 12-15)
7. initial tax basis (p. 12-20)
8. loans from (p. 12-24)

Multiple Choice
1. d (p. 12-29)
2. a (p. 12-12; 200,000 - 127,000 - 10,000)
3. b (p. 12-15; 65,000 - 50,000)
4. b (p. 12-22; limited to basis)
5. c (corporations are ineligible)
6. d (income increases basis)
7. b (50,000 + 5,000 dividend; 100,000 - 5,000 dividend = 95,000 S distribution; 95,000 - 55,000 AAA - 10,000 PTI = 30,000 - basis of 25,000 = 5,000 capital)
8. b ((20,000 - 25%(90,000) + (10,000 - 25%(60,000) = 7,500)
9. b (50%(237,250)(31/365) + 50%(237,250) = 128,700)
10. a (50,000 + 20,000 - 5,000)
11. c (p. 12-29)
12. c (p. 12-15)
13. b (p. 12-25)
14. d (income increases basis)
15. d (p. 12-6)
16. b ($300,000 - 264,000 = 36,000)

Return Problem 3

Given the following data, prepare Form 1120S-U.S. Income Tax Return for an S Corporation, other related forms as required and Schedules K-1 for Gerri Glad and Debbie Black.

Name: Glad's Flower Shop, Inc.
E.I.N.: 37-4536271
Address: 311 Main Street, Superior, IL 60654
Business Activity: Selling freshcut flowers and plants

Shareholders:

Gerri Glad, President	Terri Glad, Secretary	Debbie Black
922 Main Street	922 Main Street	38 Madison Street
Superior, IL 60654	Superior, IL 60654	Chicago, IL 60499
354-24-8833	354-42-3257	354-98-7667

The flower shop was formed and incorporated on May 2, 1998. A timely and proper S election was filed and become effective on the same date. Gerri, Terri and Debbie are sisters, each contributed $10,500 to the corporation for a one-third interest. Gerri and Terri received a salary of $8,000 each for operating the flower shop during 1998. The corporation uses the accrual method of accounting and files its returns on the calendar year basis. Balances on the corporation books as of December 31, 1998 were:

Gross Sales	$128,000	Store Equipment & Fixtures	9,750
Returns & Allowances	395	Rent	6,400
Purchases	74,240	Truck	11,250
Delivery Wages	1,200	Interest Income	942
Delivery Truck Expenses	838	Common Stock, $100 par	3,000
Advertising	2,500	Contributions	930
Insurance, Store	800	Taxes, Payroll	2,022
Insurance, Truck	645	Taxes, Sales	7,405
Supplies	3,898	Telephone	4,324
Office Supplies	480	Bank Service Charges	87
Organizational Expense	700	Accounts Payable	2,395
Accounts Receivable	3,790	Cash	12,183
*Land	18,000	Interest Expense	1,000

*The land was purchased as a future building site with a cash down payment of $2,000 and a mortgage of $16,000 on October 31, 1998.

A physical count of inventory, valued at $2,010, was done December 31.

12-16 2000/CORPORATIONS, PARTNERSHIPS, ESTATES, AND TRUSTS

Form 1120S
Department of the Treasury
Internal Revenue Service

U.S. Income Tax Return for an S Corporation
▶ Do not file this form unless the corporation has timely filed Form 2553 to elect to be an S corporation.
▶ See separate instructions.

OMB No. 1545-0130

1998

For calendar year 1998, or tax year beginning   , and ending

A Effective date of election as an S corporation	Use IRS label. Otherwise, please print or type.	Name / Number, street, and room or suite no. (If a P.O. box, see page 10 of the instr.)	**C** Employer identification no.
B NEW bus. code no. (see pages 26–28)		City or town, state, and ZIP code	**D** Date incorporated
			E Total assets (see page 10) $

F Check applicable boxes: (1) ☐ Initial return (2) ☐ Final return (3) ☐ Change in address (4) ☐ Amended return
G Enter number of shareholders in the corporation at end of the tax year ▶

Caution: Include **only** trade or business income and expenses on lines 1a through 21. See the instructions for more information.

Income
- 1a Gross receipts/sales _____ b Less returns & allowances _____ c Bal ▶ **1c**
- 2 Cost of goods sold (Schedule A, line 8) **2**
- 3 Gross profit. Subtract line 2 from line 1c **3**
- 4 Net gain (loss) from Form 4797, Part II, line 18 (attach Form 4797) **4**
- 5 Other income (loss) (attach schedule) **5**
- 6 **Total income (loss).** Combine lines 3 through 5 ▶ **6**

Deductions
(see page 11 of the instructions for limitations)
- 7 Compensation of officers **7**
- 8 Salaries and wages (less employment credits) **8**
- 9 Repairs and maintenance **9**
- 10 Bad debts **10**
- 11 Rents **11**
- 12 Taxes and licenses **12**
- 13 Interest **13**
- 14a Depreciation (if required, attach Form 4562) **14a**
-   b Depreciation claimed on Schedule A and elsewhere on return **14b**
-   c Subtract line 14b from line 14a **14c**
- 15 Depletion **(Do not deduct oil and gas depletion.)** **15**
- 16 Advertising **16**
- 17 Pension, profit-sharing, etc., plans **17**
- 18 Employee benefit programs **18**
- 19 Other deductions (attach schedule) **19**
- 20 **Total deductions.** Add the amounts shown in the far right column for lines 7 through 19 ▶ **20**
- 21 Ordinary income (loss) from trade or business activities. Subtract line 20 from line 6 **21**

Tax and Payments
- 22 Tax: a Excess net passive income tax (attach sch.) **22a**
-   b Tax from Schedule D (Form 1120S) **22b**
-   c Add lines 22a and 22b (see page 14 of the instructions for additional taxes) **22c**
- 23 Payments: a 1998 estimated tax payments & amount applied from 1997 return **23a**
-   b Tax deposited with Form 7004 **23b**
-   c Credit for Federal tax paid on fuels (attach Form 4136) **23c**
-   d Add lines 23a through 23c **23d**
- 24 Estimated tax penalty. Check if Form 2220 is attached ▶ ☐ **24**
- 25 **Tax due.** If the total of lines 22c and 24 is larger than line 23d, enter amount owed. See page 4 of the instructions for depository method of payment ▶ **25**
- 26 **Overpayment.** If line 23d is larger than the total of lines 22c and 24, enter amount overpaid ▶ **26**
- 27 Enter amount of ln. 26 you want: Credited to 1999 estimated tax ▶ _____ Refunded ▶ **27**

Please Sign Here
Under penalties of perjury, I declare that I have examined this return, including accompanying schedules and statements, and to the best of my knowledge and belief, it is true, correct, and complete. Declaration of preparer (other than taxpayer) is based on all information of which preparer has any knowledge.

▶ Signature of officer / Date / ▶ Title

Paid Preparer's Use Only

Preparer's signature	Date	Check if self-employed ▶ ☐	Preparer's social security number
Firm's name (or yours if self-employed) and address			EIN ▶
			ZIP code ▶

For Paperwork Reduction Act Notice, see the separate instructions.
DAA

Form **1120S** (1998)

Form 1120S (1998) Page **2**

Schedule A — Cost of Goods Sold (see page 15 of the instructions)

1	Inventory at beginning of year	1
2	Purchases	2
3	Cost of labor	3
4	Additional section 263A costs (attach schedule)	4
5	Other costs (attach schedule)	5
6	**Total.** Add lines 1 through 5	6
7	Inventory at end of year	7
8	**Cost of goods sold.** Subtract line 7 from line 6. Enter here and on page 1, line 2	8

9a Check all methods used for valuing closing inventory:
  (i) ☐ Cost as described in Regulations section 1.471–3
  (ii) ☐ Lower of cost or market as described in Regulations section 1.471–4
  (iii) ☐ Other (specify method used and attach explanation) ▶
 b Check if there was a writedown of "subnormal" goods as described in Regulations section 1.471–2(c) ▶ ☐
 c Check if the LIFO inventory method was adopted this tax year for any goods (if checked, attach Form 970) ▶ ☐
 d If the LIFO inventory method was used for this tax year, enter percentage (or amounts) of closing inventory computed under LIFO | 9d |
 e Do the rules of section 263A (for property produced or acquired for resale) apply to the corporation? ☐ Yes ☐ No
 f Was there any change in determining quantities, cost, or valuations between opening and closing inventory? ☐ Yes ☐ No
   If "Yes," attach explanation.

Schedule B — Other Information

		Yes	No
1	Check method of accounting: (a) ☐ Cash (b) ☐ Accrual (c) ☐ Other (specify) ▶		
2	Refer to the list on pages 26 through 28 of the instructions and state the corporation's principal: (a) Business activity ▶ (b) Product or service ▶		
3	Did the corporation at the end of the tax year own, directly or indirectly, 50% or more of the voting stock of a domestic corporation? (For rules of attribution, see section 267(c).) If "Yes," attach a schedule showing: **(a)** name, address, and employer identification number and **(b)** percentage owned		
4	Was the corporation a member of a controlled group subject to the provisions of section 1561?		
5	At any time during calendar year 1998, did the corporation have an interest in or a signature or other authority over a financial account in a foreign country (such as a bank account, securities account, or other financial account)? (See page 15 of the instructions for exceptions and filing requirements for Form TD F 90–22.1.) If "Yes," enter the name of the foreign country ▶		
6	During the tax year, did the corporation receive a distribution from, or was it the grantor of, or transferor to, a foreign trust? If "Yes," the corporation may have to file Form 3520. See page 15 of the instructions		
7	Check this box if the corporation has filed or is required to file **Form 8264**, Application for Registration of a Tax Shelter ▶ ☐		
8	Check this box if the corporation issued publicly offered debt instruments with original issue discount ▶ ☐ If so, the corporation may have to file **Form 8281**, Information Return for Publicly Offered Original Issue Discount Instruments.		
9	If the corporation: **(a)** filed its election to be an S corporation after 1986, **(b)** was a C corporation before it elected to be an S corporation **or** the corporation acquired an asset with a basis determined by reference to its basis (or the basis of any other property) in the hands of a C corporation, and **(c)** has net unrealized built-in gain (defined in section 1374(d)(1)) in excess of the net recognized built-in gain from prior years, enter the net unrealized built-in gain reduced by net recognized built-in gain from prior years (see page 16 of the instructions) ▶ $		
10	Check this box if the corporation had accumulated earnings and profits at the close of the tax year (see page 16 of the instructions) ▶ ☐		

DAA

Form 1120S (1998)   Page 3

Schedule K   Shareholders' Shares of Income, Credits, Deductions, etc.

		(a) Pro rata share items		(b) Total amount
Income (Loss)	1	Ordinary income (loss) from trade or business activities (page 1, line 21)	1	
	2	Net income (loss) from rental real estate activities (attach Form 8825)	2	
	3a	Gross income from other rental activities ... 3a		
	b	Expenses from other rental activities (attach schedule) ... 3b		
	c	Net income (loss) from other rental activities. Subtract line 3b from line 3a	3c	
	4	Portfolio income (loss):		
	a	Interest income	4a	
	b	Ordinary dividends	4b	
	c	Royalty income	4c	
	d	Net short–term capital gain (loss) (attach Schedule D (Form 1120S))	4d	
	e	Net long–term capital gain (loss) (attach Schedule D (Form 1120S)):		
		(1) 28% rate gain (loss) ▶ (2) Total for year ▶	4e(2)	
	f	Other portfolio income (loss) (attach schedule)	4f	
	5	Net section 1231 gain (loss) (other than due to casualty or theft) (attach Form 4797)	5	
	6	Other income (loss) (attach schedule)	6	
Deductions	7	Charitable contributions (attach schedule)	7	
	8	Section 179 expense deduction (attach Form 4562)	8	
	9	Deductions related to portfolio income (loss) (itemize)	9	
	10	Other deductions (attach schedule)	10	
Investment Interest	11a	Interest expense on investment debts	11a	
	b	(1) Investment income included on lines 4a, 4b, 4c, and 4f above	11b(1)	
		(2) Investment expenses included on line 9 above	11b(2)	
Credits	12a	Credit for alcohol used as a fuel (attach Form 6478)	12a	
	b	Low–income housing credit:		
		(1) From partnerships to which section 42(j)(5) applies for property placed in service before 1990	12b(1)	
		(2) Other than on line 12b(1) for property placed in service before 1990	12b(2)	
		(3) From partnerships to which section 42(j)(5) applies for property placed in service after 1989	12b(3)	
		(4) Other than on line 12b(3) for property placed in service after 1989	12b(4)	
	c	Qualified rehabilitation expenditures related to rental real estate activities (attach Form 3468)	12c	
	d	Credits (other than credits shown on lines 12b and 12c) related to rental real estate activities	12d	
	e	Credits related to other rental activities	12e	
	13	Other credits	13	
Adjustments and Tax Preference Items	14a	Depreciation adjustment on property placed in service after 1986	14a	
	b	Adjusted gain or loss	14b	
	c	Depletion (other than oil and gas)	14c	
	d	(1) Gross income from oil, gas, or geothermal properties	14d(1)	
		(2) Deductions allocable to oil, gas, or geothermal properties	14d(2)	
	e	Other adjustments and tax preference items (attach schedule)	14e	
Foreign Taxes	15a	Type of income ▶		
	b	Name of foreign country or U.S. possession		
	c	Total gross income from sources outside the United States (attach schedule)	15c	
	d	Total applicable deductions and losses (attach schedule)	15d	
	e	Total foreign taxes (check one): ▶ ☐ Paid ☐ Accrued	15e	
	f	Reduction in taxes available for credit (attach schedule)	15f	
	g	Other foreign tax information (attach schedule)	15g	
Other	16	Section 59(e)(2) expenditures: a Type ▶		
	b	Amount ▶	16b	
	17	Tax–exempt interest income	17	
	18	Other tax–exempt income	18	
	19	Nondeductible expenses	19	
	20	Total property distributions (including cash) other than dividends reported on line 22 below	20	
	21	Other items and amounts required to be reported separately to shareholders (attach schedule)		
	22	Total dividend distributions paid from accumulated earnings and profits	22	
	23	**Income (loss).** (Required only if Schedule M–1 must be completed.) Combine lines 1 through 6 in column (b). From the result, subtract the sum of lines 7 through 11a, 15e, and 16b	23	

DAA

S CORPORATIONS 12-19

Form 1120S (1998) Page 4

Schedule L — Balance Sheets per Books

	Assets	Beginning of tax year (a)	(b)	End of tax year (c)	(d)
1	Cash				
2a	Trade notes and accounts receivable				
b	Less allowance for bad debts				
3	Inventories				
4	U.S. Government obligations				
5	Tax-exempt securities				
6	Other current assets				
7	Loans to shareholders				
8	Mortgage and real estate loans				
9	Other investments				
10a	Buildings and other depreciable assets				
b	Less accumulated depreciation				
11a	Depletable assets				
b	Less accumulated depletion				
12	Land (net of any amortization)				
13a	Intangible assets (amortizable only)				
b	Less accumulated amortization				
14	Other assets (attach sch.)				
15	Total assets				
	Liabilities and Shareholders' Equity				
16	Accounts payable				
17	Mortgages, notes, bonds payable in less than 1 year				
18	Other current liabilities				
19	Loans from shareholders				
20	Mortgages, notes, bonds payable in 1 year or more				
21	Other liabilities (att. sch.)				
22	Capital stock				
23	Additional paid-in capital				
24	Retained earnings				
25	Adjustments to S/H equity				
26	Less cost of treasury stock				
27	Total liabilities and shareholders' equity				

Schedule M-1 — Reconciliation of Income (Loss) per Books With Income (Loss) per Return
(You are not required to complete this schedule if the total assets on line 15, column (d), of Schedule L are less than $25,000.)

1 Net income (loss) per books
2 Income included on Schedule K, lines 1 through 6, not recorded on books this year (itemize):

3 Expenses recorded on books this year not included on Schedule K, lines 1 through 11a, 15e, and 16b (itemize):
 a Depreciation $
 b Travel and entertainment $

4 Add lines 1 through 3

5 Income recorded on books this year not included on Schedule K, lines 1 through 6 (itemize):
 a Tax-exempt interest $

6 Deductions included on Schedule K, lines 1 through 11a, 15e, and 16b, not charged against book income this year (itemize):
 a Depreciation $

7 Add lines 5 and 6
8 Income (loss) (Sch. K, line 23). Line 4 less line 7

Schedule M-2 — Analysis of Accumulated Adjustments Account, Other Adjustments Account, and Shareholders' Undistributed Taxable Income Previously Taxed (see page 24 of the instructions)

		(a) Accumulated adjustments account	(b) Other adjustments account	(c) Shareholders' undistributed taxable income previously taxed
1	Balance at beginning of tax year			
2	Ordinary income from page 1, line 21			
3	Other additions			
4	Loss from page 1, line 21			
5	Other reductions			
6	Combine lines 1 through 5			
7	Distributions other than divd. distributions			
8	Balance at end of tax year. Subtract ln. 7 from ln. 6			

DAA

12-20 2000/CORPORATIONS, PARTNERSHIPS, ESTATES, AND TRUSTS

0308

SCHEDULE K-1 (Form 1120S) Department of the Treasury Internal Revenue Service	Shareholder's Share of Income, Credits, Deductions, etc. ▶ See separate instructions. For calendar year 1998 or tax year beginning , and ending	OMB No. 1545-0130 **1998**

Shareholder's identifying number ▶   Corporation's identifying number ▶

Shareholder's name, address, and ZIP code   Corporation's name, address, and ZIP code

- **A** Shareholder's percentage of stock ownership for tax year (see instructions for Schedule K-1) ▶ %
- **B** Internal Revenue Service Center where corporation filed its return ▶
- **C** Tax shelter registration number (see instructions for Schedule K-1) ▶
- **D** Check applicable boxes: (1) ☐ Final K-1   (2) ☐ Amended K-1

	(a) Pro rata share items		(b) Amount	(c) Form 1040 filers enter the amount in column (b) on:
Income (Loss)	1 Ordinary income (loss) from trade or business activities	1		See pages 4 and 5 of the Shareholder's Instructions for Schedule K-1 (Form 1120S).
	2 Net income (loss) from rental real estate activities	2		
	3 Net income (loss) from other rental activities	3		
	4 Portfolio income (loss):			
	a Interest	4a		Sch. B, Part I, line 1
	b Ordinary dividends	4b		Sch. B, Part II, line 5
	c Royalties	4c		Sch. E, Part I, line 4
	d Net short-term capital gain (loss)	4d		Sch. D, line 5, col. (f)
	e Net long-term capital gain (loss):			
	(1) 28% rate gain (loss)	e(1)		Sch. D, line 12, col. (g)
	(2) Total for year	e(2)		Sch. D, line 12, col. (f)
	f Other portfolio income (loss) (attach schedule)	4f		(Enter on appl. ln. of your return.)
	5 Net section 1231 gain (loss) (other than due to casualty or theft)	5		See Shareholder's Instructions for Schedule K-1 (Form 1120S).
	6 Other income (loss) (attach schedule)	6		(Enter on appl. ln. of your return.)
Deductions	7 Charitable contributions (attach schedule)	7		Sch. A, line 15 or 16
	8 Section 179 expense deduction	8		See page 6 of the Shareholder's Instructions for Schedule K-1 (Form 1120S).
	9 Deductions related to portfolio income (loss)	9		
	10 Other deductions (attach schedule)	10		
Investment Interest	11a Interest expense on investment debts	11a		Form 4952, line 1
	b (1) Investment income included on lines 4a, 4b, 4c, and 4f above	b(1)		See Shareholder's Instructions for Schedule K-1 (Form 1120S).
	(2) Investment expenses included on line 9 above	b(2)		
Credits	12a Credit for alcohol used as fuel	12a		Form 6478, line 10
	b Low-income housing credit:			
	(1) From section 42(j)(5) partnerships for property placed in service before 1990	b(1)		▶ Form 8586, line 5
	(2) Other than on line 12b(1) for property placed in service before 1990	b(2)		
	(3) From section 42(j)(5) partnerships for property placed in service after 1989	b(3)		
	(4) Other than on line 12b(3) for property placed in service after 1989	b(4)		
	c Qualified rehabilitation expenditures related to rental real estate activities	12c		See page 7 of the Shareholder's Instructions for Schedule K-1 (Form 1120S).
	d Credits (other than credits shown on lines 12b and 12c) related to rental real estate activities	12d		
	e Credits related to other rental activities	12e		
	13 Other credits	13		

For Paperwork Reduction Act Notice, see the Instructions for Form 1120S.   Schedule K-1 (Form 1120S) 1998

DAA

Schedule K-1 (Form 1120S) (1998) Page 2

		(a) Pro rata share items		(b) Amount	(c) Form 1040 filers enter the amount in column (b) on:
Adjust-ments and Tax Prefer-ence Items	14a	Depreciation adjustment on property placed in service after 1986	14a		See page 7 of the Shareholder's Instructions for Schedule K-1 (Form 1120S) and Instructions for Form 6251
	b	Adjusted gain or loss	14b		
	c	Depletion (other than oil and gas)	14c		
	d	(1) Gross income from oil, gas, or geothermal properties	d(1)		
		(2) Deductions allocable to oil, gas, or geothermal properties	d(2)		
	e	Other adjustments and tax preference items	14e		
Foreign Taxes	15a	Type of income ▶			Form 1116, Check boxes
	b	Name of foreign country or U.S. possession ▶			
	c	Total gross income from sources outside the United States (attach schedule)	15c		Form 1116, Part I
	d	Total applicable deductions and losses (att. schedule)	15d		
	e	Total foreign taxes (check one): ▶ ☐ Paid ☐ Accrued	15e		Form 1116, Part II
	f	Reduction in taxes available for credit (attach sch.)	15f		Form 1116, Part III
	g	Other foreign tax information (attach schedule)	15g		See Instructions for Form 1116
Other	16	Section 59(e)(2) expenditures:			See Shareholder's Instructions for Schedule K-1 (Form 1120S).
	a	Type ▶			
	b	Amount	16b		
	17	Tax-exempt interest income	17		Form 1040, line 8b
	18	Other tax-exempt income	18		See pages 7 and 8 of the Shareholder's Instructions for Schedule K-1 (Form 1120S)
	19	Nondeductible expenses	19		
	20	Property distributions (including cash) other than dividend distributions reported to you on Form 1099-DIV	20		
	21	Amount of loan repayments for "Loans From Shareholders"	21		
	22	Recapture of low-income housing credit:			
	a	From section 42(j)(5) partnerships	22a		Form 8611, line 8
	b	Other than on line 22a	22b		
Supplemental Information	23	Supplemental information required to be reported separately to each shareholder (attach additional schedules if more space is needed):			

SCHEDULE K–1 (Form 1120S) Department of the Treasury Internal Revenue Service	Shareholder's Share of Income, Credits, Deductions, etc. ▶ See separate instructions. For calendar year 1998 or tax year beginning , and ending	OMB No. 1545-0130 **1998**
Shareholder's identifying number ▶	Corporation's identifying number ▶	
Shareholder's name, address, and ZIP code	Corporation's name, address, and ZIP code	

A Shareholder's percentage of stock ownership for tax year (see instructions for Schedule K–1) .... ▶ .... %
B Internal Revenue Service Center where corporation filed its return ▶ .... ▶
C Tax shelter registration number (see instructions for Schedule K–1) .... ▶
D Check applicable boxes: (1) ☐ Final K–1 (2) ☐ Amended K–1

		(a) Pro rata share items		(b) Amount	(c) Form 1040 filers enter the amount in column (b) on:
Income (Loss)	1	Ordinary income (loss) from trade or business activities	1		See pages 4 and 5 of the Shareholder's Instructions for Schedule K–1 (Form 1120S).
	2	Net income (loss) from rental real estate activities	2		
	3	Net income (loss) from other rental activities	3		
	4	Portfolio income (loss):			
	a	Interest	4a		Sch. B, Part I, line 1
	b	Ordinary dividends	4b		Sch. B, Part II, line 5
	c	Royalties	4c		Sch. E, Part I, line 4
	d	Net short–term capital gain (loss)	4d		Sch. D, line 5, col. (f)
	e	Net long–term capital gain (loss):			
		(1) 28% rate gain (loss)	e(1)		Sch. D, line 12, col. (g)
		(2) Total for year	e(2)		Sch. D, line 12, col. (f)
	f	Other portfolio income (loss) (attach schedule)	4f		(Enter on appl. ln. of your return.)
	5	Net section 1231 gain (loss) (other than due to casualty or theft)	5		See Shareholder's Instructions for Schedule K–1 (Form 1120S).
	6	Other income (loss) (attach schedule)	6		(Enter on appl. ln. of your return.)
Deductions	7	Charitable contributions (attach schedule)	7		Sch. A, line 15 or 16
	8	Section 179 expense deduction	8		See page 6 of the Shareholder's Instructions for Schedule K–1 (Form 1120S)
	9	Deductions related to portfolio income (loss)	9		
	10	Other deductions (attach schedule)	10		
Investment Interest	11a	Interest expense on investment debts	11a		Form 4952, line 1
	b	(1) Investment income included on lines 4a, 4b, 4c, and 4f above	b(1)		See Shareholder's Instructions for Schedule K–1 (Form 1120S).
		(2) Investment expenses included on line 9 above	b(2)		
Credits	12a	Credit for alcohol used as fuel	12a		Form 6478, line 10
	b	Low–income housing credit:			
		(1) From section 42(j)(5) partnerships for property placed in service before 1990	b(1)		▶ Form 8586, line 5
		(2) Other than on line 12b(1) for property placed in service before 1990	b(2)		
		(3) From section 42(j)(5) partnerships for property placed in service after 1989	b(3)		
		(4) Other than on line 12b(3) for property placed in service after 1989	b(4)		
	c	Qualified rehabilitation expenditures related to rental real estate activities	12c		See page 7 of the Shareholder's Instructions for Schedule K–1 (Form 1120S).
	d	Credits (other than credits shown on lines 12b and 12c) related to rental real estate activities	12d		
	e	Credits related to other rental activities	12e		
	13	Other credits	13		

For Paperwork Reduction Act Notice, see the Instructions for Form 1120S.   Schedule K–1 (Form 1120S) 1998

DAA

Schedule K-1 (Form 1120S) (1998) Page 2

		(a) Pro rata share items		(b) Amount	(c) Form 1040 filers enter the amount in column (b) on:
Adjustments and Tax Preference Items	14a	Depreciation adjustment on property placed in service after 1986	14a		See page 7 of the Shareholder's Instructions for Schedule K-1 (Form 1120S) and Instructions for Form 6251
	b	Adjusted gain or loss	14b		
	c	Depletion (other than oil and gas)	14c		
	d	(1) Gross income from oil, gas, or geothermal properties	d(1)		
		(2) Deductions allocable to oil, gas, or geothermal properties	d(2)		
	e	Other adjustments and tax preference items	14e		
Foreign Taxes	15a	Type of income ▶			Form 1116, Check boxes
	b	Name of foreign country or U.S. possession ▶			
	c	Total gross income from sources outside the United States (attach schedule)	15c		Form 1116, Part I
	d	Total applicable deductions and losses (att. schedule)	15d		
	e	Total foreign taxes (check one): ▶ ☐ Paid ☐ Accrued	15e		Form 1116, Part II
	f	Reduction in taxes available for credit (attach sch.)	15f		Form 1116, Part III
	g	Other foreign tax information (attach schedule)	15g		See Instructions for Form 1116
Other	16	Section 59(e)(2) expenditures:			See Shareholder's Instructions for Schedule K-1 (Form 1120S).
	a	Type ▶			
	b	Amount	16b		
	17	Tax-exempt interest income	17		Form 1040, line 8b
	18	Other tax-exempt income	18		See pages 7 and 8 of the Shareholder's Instructions for Schedule K-1 (Form 1120S).
	19	Nondeductible expenses	19		
	20	Property distributions (including cash) other than dividend distributions reported to you on Form 1099-DIV	20		
	21	Amount of loan repayments for "Loans From Shareholders"	21		
	22	Recapture of low-income housing credit:			
	a	From section 42(j)(5) partnerships	22a		Form 8611, line 8
	b	Other than on line 22a	22b		
Supplemental Information	23	Supplemental information required to be reported separately to each shareholder (attach additional schedules if more space is needed):			

12-24 2000/CORPORATIONS, PARTNERSHIPS, ESTATES, AND TRUSTS

0308

Form **4562**	**Depreciation and Amortization**	OMB No. 1545-0172
Department of the Treasury Internal Revenue Service (99)	(Including Information on Listed Property) ▶ See separate instructions. ▶ Attach this form to your return.	**1998** Attachment Sequence No. **67**

Name(s) shown on return | Identifying number

Business or activity to which this form relates

Part I — Election To Expense Certain Tangible Property (Section 179) (Note: If you have any "listed property," complete Pt. V before Pt. I.)

1	Maximum dollar limitation. If an enterprise zone business, see page 2 of the instructions	1	$18,500
2	Total cost of section 179 property placed in service. See page 2 of the instructions	2	
3	Threshold cost of section 179 property before reduction in limitation	3	$200,000
4	Reduction in limitation. Subtract line 3 from line 2. If zero or less, enter –0–	4	
5	Dollar limitation for tax year. Subtract line 4 from line 1. If zero or less, enter –0–. If married filing separately, see page 2 of the instructions	5	

	(a) Description of property	(b) Cost (business use only)	(c) Elected cost
6			

7	Listed property. Enter amount from line 27	7		
8	Total elected cost of section 179 property. Add amounts in column (c), lines 6 and 7		8	
9	Tentative deduction. Enter the smaller of line 5 or line 8		9	
10	Carryover of disallowed deduction from 1997. See page 3 of the instructions		10	
11	Business income limitation. Enter the smaller of business income (not less than zero) or line 5 (see instructions)		11	
12	Section 179 expense deduction. Add lines 9 and 10, but do not enter more than line 11		12	
13	Carryover of disallowed deduction to 1999. Add lines 9 and 10, less line 12 ▶	13		

Note: Do not use Part II or Part III below for listed property (automobiles, certain other vehicles, cellular telephones, certain computers, or property used for entertainment, recreation, or amusement). Instead, use Part V for listed property.

Part II — MACRS Depreciation For Assets Placed in Service ONLY During Your 1998 Tax Year (Do Not Include Listed Property.)

Section A–General Asset Account Election

14 If you are making the election under section 168(i)(4) to group any assets placed in service during the tax year into one or more general asset accounts, check this box. See page 3 of the instructions ▶ ☐

Section B–General Depreciation System (GDS) (See page 3 of the instructions.)

(a) Classification of property	(b) Month and year placed in service	(c) Basis for depreciation (business/investment use only–see instructions)	(d) Recovery period	(e) Convention	(f) Method	(g) Depreciation deduction
15a 3-year property						
b 5-year property						
c 7-year property						
d 10-year property						
e 15-year property						
f 20-year property						
g 25-year property			25 yrs.		S/L	
h Residential rental property			27.5 yrs.	MM	S/L	
			27.5 yrs.	MM	S/L	
i Nonresidential real property			39 yrs.	MM	S/L	
				MM	S/L	

Section C–Alternative Depreciation System (ADS) (See page 5 of the instructions.)

16a Class life					S/L	
b 12-year			12 yrs.		S/L	
c 40-year			40 yrs.	MM	S/L	

Part III — Other Depreciation (Do Not Include Listed Property.) (See page 6 of the instructions.)

17	GDS and ADS deductions for assets placed in service in tax years beginning before 1998	17	
18	Property subject to section 168(f)(1) election	18	
19	ACRS and other depreciation	19	

Part IV — Summary (See page 6 of the instructions.)

20	Listed property. Enter amount from line 26	20	
21	Total. Add deductions on line 12, lines 15 and 16 in column (g), and lines 17 through 20. Enter here and on the appropriate lines of your return. Partnerships and S corporations–see instructions	21	
22	For assets shown above and placed in service during the current year, enter the portion of the basis attributable to section 263A costs	22	

For Paperwork Reduction Act Notice, see the separate instructions.   Form **4562** (1998)
DAA

Form 4562 (1998) Page 2

Part V — Listed Property–Automobiles, Certain Other Vehicles, Cellular Telephones, Certain Computers, and Property Used for Entertainment, Recreation, or Amusement

Note: For any vehicle for which you are using the standard mileage rate or deducting lease expense, complete only 23a, 23b, columns (a) through (c) of Section A, all of Section B, and Section C if applicable.

Section A–Depreciation and Other Information (Caution: See page 8 of the instructions for limits for passenger automobiles.)

23a Do you have evidence to support the busn./invest. use claimed? ☐ Yes ☐ No 23b If "Yes," is the evidence written? ☐ Yes ☐ No

(a) Type of prop. (list vehicles first)	(b) Date placed in service	(c) Busn./invest. use percentage	(d) Cost or other basis	(e) Basis for depreciation (business/investment use only)	(f) Recovery period	(g) Method/ Convention	(h) Depreciation deduction	(i) Elected section 179 cost

24 Property used more than 50% in a qualified business use (See page 7 of the instructions.):

| | | % | | | | | | |
| | | % | | | | | | |

25 Property used 50% or less in a qualified business use (See page 7 of the instructions.):

| | | % | | | | S/L– | | |
| | | % | | | | S/L– | | |

26 Add amounts in column (h). Enter the total here and on line 20, page 1 26

27 Add amounts in column (i). Enter the total here and on line 7, page 1 27

Section B–Information on Use of Vehicles

Complete this section for vehicles used by a sole proprietor, partner, or other "more than 5% owner," or related person.

If you provided vehicles to your employees, first answer the questions in Section C to see if you meet an exception to completing this section for those vehicles.

	(a) Vehicle 1	(b) Vehicle 2	(c) Vehicle 3	(d) Vehicle 4	(e) Vehicle 5	(f) Vehicle 6
28 Total business/investment miles driven during the year (DO NOT include commuting miles)						
29 Total commuting miles driven during the year						
30 Total other personal (noncommuting) miles driven						
31 Total miles driven during the year. Add lines 28 through 30						

	Yes	No	Yes	No	Yes	No	Yes	No	Yes	No	Yes	No
32 Was the vehicle available for personal use during off–duty hours?												
33 Was the vehicle used primarily by a more than 5% owner or related person?												
34 Is another vehicle available for personal use?												

Section C–Questions for Employers Who Provide Vehicles for Use by Their Employees

Answer these questions to determine if you meet an exception to completing Section B for vehicles used by employees who **are not** more than 5% owners or related persons.

	Yes	No
35 Do you maintain a written policy statement that prohibits all personal use of vehicles, including commuting, by your employees?		
36 Do you maintain a written policy statement that prohibits personal use of vehicles, except commuting, by your employees? See page 9 of the instructions for vehicles used by corporate officers, directors, or 1% or more owners		
37 Do you treat all use of vehicles by employees as personal use?		
38 Do you provide more than five vehicles to your employees, obtain information from your employees about the use of the vehicles, and retain the information received?		
39 Do you meet the requirements concerning qualified automobile demonstration use? See page 9 of the instructions		

Note: If your answer to 35, 36, 37, 38, or 39 is "Yes," you need not complete Section B for the covered vehicles.

Part VI — Amortization

(a) Description of costs	(b) Date amortization begins	(c) Amortizable amount	(d) Code section	(e) Amortization period or percentage	(f) Amortization for this year

40 Amortization of costs that begins during your 1998 tax year:

| | | | | | |
| | | | | | |

41 Amortization of costs that began before 1998 41

42 **Total**. Enter here and on "Other Deductions" or "Other Expenses" line of your return 42

DAA

12-26 2000/CORPORATIONS, PARTNERSHIPS, ESTATES, AND TRUSTS

Form **1120S** Department of the Treasury Internal Revenue Service
U.S. Income Tax Return for an S Corporation **1998** OMB No. 1545-0130 IRS use only — Do not write or staple in this space.

▶ Do not file this form unless the corporation has timely filed Form 2553 to elect to be an S corporation.
▶ See separate instructions.

For calendar year 1998, or tax year beginning **May 2**, 1998, ending **Dec 31**, 19 **98**

A Effective date of Election as an S Corporation **05/02/98**	Use IRS label. Otherwise please print or type.	Name **Glad's Flower Shop, Inc.**	**C** Employer Identification Number **37-4536271**
B New Business Code No. (see instructions) **453110**		Number, Street, and Room or Suite No. (If a P.O. box, see instructions) **311 Main Street**	**D** Date Incorporated **05/02/98**
		City or Town **Superior** State **IL** ZIP Code **60654**	**E** Total Assets (see instructions) $ **55,161.**

F Check applicable boxes: (1) [X] Initial return (2) [ ] Final return (3) [ ] Change in address (4) [ ] Amended return
G Enter number of shareholders in the corporation at end of the tax year .... ▶ **3**

Caution: Include only trade or business income and expenses on lines 1a through 21. See the instructions for more information.

INCOME
1a	Gross receipts or sales .. **128,000.** b Less returns and allowances .. **395.** c Bal ▶	1c	127,605.
2	Cost of goods sold (Schedule A, line 8)	2	76,128.
3	Gross profit. Subtract line 2 from line 1c	3	51,477.
4	Net gain (loss) from Form 4797, Part II, line 18 (attach Form 4797)	4	
5	Other income (loss) (attach schedule)	5	
6	**Total income (loss).** Combine lines 3 through 5 .... ▶	6	51,477.

DEDUCTIONS
7	Compensation of officers	7	16,000.
8	Salaries and wages (less employment credits)	8	1,200.
9	Repairs and maintenance	9	
10	Bad debts	10	
11	Rents	11	6,400.
12	Taxes and licenses	12	9,427.
13	Interest	13	1,000.
14a	Depreciation (if required, attach Form 4562) .... 14a **2,429.**		
b	Depreciation claimed on Schedule A and elsewhere on return 14b		
c	Subtract line 14b from line 14a	14c	2,429.
15	Depletion (**Do not deduct oil and gas depletion.**)	15	
16	Advertising	16	2,500.
17	Pension, profit-sharing, etc, plans	17	
18	Employee benefit programs	18	
19	Other deductions (attach schedule) ..... See Other Deductions	19	7,267.
20	**Total deductions.** Add the amounts shown in the far right column for lines 7 through 19 .... ▶	20	46,223.
21	**Ordinary income (loss) from trade or business activities.** Subtract line 20 from line 6	21	5,254.

TAX AND PAYMENTS
22	Tax: a Excess net passive income tax (att schedule) 22a		
	b Tax from Schedule D (Form 1120S) 22b		
	c Add lines 22a and 22b (see instructions for additional taxes)	22c	
23	Payments: a 1998 estimated tax payments and amount applied from 1997 return 23a		
	b Tax deposited with Form 7004 .... 23b		
	c Credit for federal tax paid on fuels (attach Form 4136) 23c		
	d Add lines 23a through 23c	23d	
24	Estimated tax penalty. Check if Form 2220 is attached .... ▶ [ ]	24	
25	**Tax due.** If the total of lines 22c & 24 is larger than line 23d, enter amount owed. See instrs for depository method of payment ..... ▶	25	
26	**Overpayment.** If line 23d is larger than the total of lines 22c and 24, enter amount overpaid .... ▶	26	
27	Enter amount of line 26 you want: Credited to 1999 estimated tax .... ▶ _____ Refunded ▶	27	

Please Sign Here
Under penalties of perjury, I declare that I have examined this return, including accompanying schedules and statements, and to the best of my knowledge and belief, it is true, correct, and complete. Declaration of preparer (other than taxpayer) is based on all information of which preparer has any knowledge.

▶ _____ _____ ▶ _____
Signature of Officer   Date   Title

Paid Preparer's Use Only
Preparer's Signature ▶	Date	Check if self-employed [ ]	Preparer's Social Security Number
Firm's Name (or yours if self-employed) and Address	Self Prepared	EIN ▶	
		ZIP Code ▶	

BAA For Paperwork Reduction Act Notice, see separate instructions. Form **1120S** (1998)
SPSA0112 11/25/98

Form 1120S (1998)   Glad's Flower Shop, Inc.   37-4536271   Page 2

Schedule A — Cost of Goods Sold (see instructions)

1	Inventory at beginning of year	1	
2	Purchases	2	74,240.
3	Cost of labor	3	
4	Additional Section 263A costs (attach schedule)	4	
5	Other costs (attach schedule) .. See Schedule A, Other Costs	5	3,898.
6	**Total.** Add lines 1 through 5	6	78,138.
7	Inventory at end of year	7	2,010.
8	**Cost of goods sold.** Subtract line 7 from line 6. Enter here and on page 1, line 2	8	76,128.

9a Check all methods used for valuing closing inventory:
   (i) [X] Cost as described in Regulations Section 1.471-3
   (ii) [ ] Lower of cost or market as described in Regulations Section 1.471-4
   (iii) [ ] Other (specify method used and attach explanation) ▶ _____

  b Check if there was a writedown of 'subnormal' goods as described in Regulations Section 1.471-2(c) .... ▶ [ ]
  c Check if the LIFO inventory method was adopted this tax year for any goods (if checked, attach Form 970) ..... ▶ [ ]
  d If the LIFO inventory method was used for this tax year, enter percentage (or amounts) of closing inventory computed under LIFO .... | 9d |
  e Do the rules of Section 263A (for property produced or acquired for resale) apply to the corporation? .... [ ] Yes [X] No
  f Was there any change in determining quantities, cost, or valuations between opening and closing inventory? If 'Yes,' attach explanation .... [ ] Yes [X] No

Schedule B — Other Information

		Yes	No
1	Check method of accounting: (a) [ ] Cash (b) [X] Accrual (c) [ ] Other (specify) ▶ _____		
2	Refer to the list in the instructions and state the corporation's principal: (a) Business activity ▶ Retail Sales (b) Product or service ▶ Flowers		
3	Did the corporation at the end of the tax year own, directly or indirectly, 50% or more of the voting stock of a domestic corporation? (For rules of attribution, see Section 267(c).) If 'Yes,' attach a schedule showing: (a) name, address, and employer identification number and (b) percentage owned		X
4	Was the corporation a member of a controlled group subject to the provisions of Section 1561?		X
5	At any time during calendar year 1998, did the corporation have an interest in or a signature or other authority over a financial account in a foreign country (such as a bank account, securities account, or other financial account)? (See the instructions for exceptions and filing requirements for Form TD F 90-22.1.)		X
	If 'Yes,' enter the name of the foreign country ▶ _____		
6	During the tax year, did the corporation receive a distribution from, or was it the grantor of, or transferor to, a foreign trust? If 'Yes,' the corporation may have to file Form 3520. See instructions		X
7	Check this box if the corporation has filed or is required to file **Form 8264**, Application for Registration of a Tax Shelter .... ▶ [ ]		
8	Check this box if the corporation issued publicly offered debt instruments with original issue discount .... ▶ [ ] If so, the corporation may have to file **Form 8281**, Information Return for Publicly Offered Original Issue Discount Instruments.		
9	If the corporation: (a) filed its election to be an S corporation after 1986, (b) was a C corporation before it elected to be an S corporation **or** the corporation acquired an asset with a basis determined by reference to its basis (or the basis of any other property) in the hands of a C corporation, and (c) has net unrealized built-in gain (defined in Section 1374(d)(1)) in excess of the net recognized built-in gain from prior years, enter the net unrealized built-in gain reduced by net recognized built-in gain from prior years (see instructions) .... ▶ $ _____		
10	Check this box if the corporation had accumulated earnings and profits at the close of the tax year (see instructions) . ▶ [ ]		

12-28 2000/CORPORATIONS, PARTNERSHIPS, ESTATES, AND TRUSTS

Form 1120S (1998) Glad's Flower Shop, Inc.   37-4536271   Page 3

Schedule K — Shareholders' Shares of Income, Credits, Deductions, etc

	(a) Pro rata share items		(b) Total amount
Income (Loss)	1 Ordinary income (loss) from trade or business activities (page 1, line 21)	1	5,254.
	2 Net income (loss) from rental real estate activities (attach Form 8825)	2	
	3a Gross income from other rental activities ... 3a		
	b Expenses from other rental activities (attach schedule) ... 3b		
	c Net income (loss) from other rental activities. Subtract line 3b from line 3a	3c	
	4 Portfolio income (loss):		
	a Interest income	4a	942.
	b Ordinary dividends	4b	
	c Royalty income	4c	
	d Net short-term capital gain (loss) (attach Schedule D (Form 1120S))	4d	
	e Net long-term capital gain (loss) (attach Schedule D (Form 1120S)):		
	(1) 28% rate gain (loss) ▶ _____ (2) Total for year ▶	4e (2)	
	f Other portfolio income (loss) (attach schedule)	4f	
	5 Net section 1231 gain (loss) (other than due to casualty or theft) (attach Form 4797)	5	
	6 Other income (loss) (attach schedule)	6	
Deductions	7 Charitable contributions (attach schedule)	7	930.
	8 Section 179 expense deduction (attach Form 4562)	8	
	9 Deductions related to portfolio income (loss) (itemize)	9	
	10 Other deductions (attach schedule)	10	
Investment Interest	11a Interest expense on investment debts	11a	
	b (1) Investment income included on lines 4a, 4b, 4c, and 4f above	11b (1)	942.
	(2) Investment expenses included on line 9 above	11b (2)	
Credits	12a Credit for alcohol used as a fuel (attach Form 6478)	12a	
	b Low-income housing credit:		
	(1) From partnerships to which section 42(j)(5) applies for property placed in service before 1990	12b (1)	
	(2) Other than on line 12b(1) for property placed in service before 1990	12b (2)	
	(3) From partnerships to which section 42(j)(5) applies for property placed in service after 1989	12b (3)	
	(4) Other than on line 12b(3) for property placed in service after 1989	12b (4)	
	c Qualified rehabilitation expenditures related to rental real estate activities (attach Form 3468)	12c	
	d Credits (other than credits shown on lines 12b and 12c) related to rental real estate activities	12d	
	e Credits related to other rental activities	12e	
	13 Other credits	13	
Adjustments and Tax Preference Items	14a Depreciation adjustment on property placed in service after 1986	14a	898.
	b Adjusted gain or loss	14b	
	c Depletion (other than oil and gas)	14c	
	d (1) Gross income from oil, gas, or geothermal properties	14d (1)	
	(2) Deductions allocable to oil, gas, or geothermal properties	14d (2)	
	e Other adjustments and tax preference items (attach schedule)	14e	
Foreign Taxes	15a Type of income ▶ _____		
	b Name of foreign country or U.S. possession ▶ _____		
	c Total gross income from sources outside the United States (attach schedule)	15c	
	d Total applicable deductions and losses (attach schedule)	15d	
	e Total foreign taxes (check one): ▶ ☐ Paid ☐ Accrued	15e	
	f Reduction in taxes available for credit (attach schedule)	15f	
	g Other foreign tax information (attach schedule)	15g	
Other	16 Section 59(e)(2) expenditures: a Type ▶ _____ b Amount ▶	16b	
	17 Tax-exempt interest income	17	
	18 Other tax-exempt income	18	
	19 Nondeductible expenses	19	
	20 Total property distributions (including cash) other than dividends reported on line 22 below	20	
	21 Other items and amounts required to be reported separately to shareholders (attach schedule)		
	22 Total dividend distributions paid from accumulated earnings and profits	22	
	23 Income (loss). (Required only if Schedule M-1 must be completed.) Combine lines 1 through 6 in column (b). From the result, subtract the sum of lines 7 through 11a, 15e, and 16b	23	5,266.

BAA   SPSA0134 12/01/98

Form 1120S (1998) Glad's Flower Shop, Inc.   37-4536271   Page **4**

Schedule L — Balance Sheets per Books

Assets	Beginning of tax year (a)	(b)	End of tax year (c)	(d)
1 Cash				12,183.
2a Trade notes and accounts receivable			3,790.	
b Less allowance for bad debts				3,790.
3 Inventories				2,010.
4 U.S. government obligations				
5 Tax-exempt securities				
6 Other current assets (attach schedule)				
7 Loans to shareholders				
8 Mortgage and real estate loans				
9 Other investments (attach schedule)				
10a Buildings and other depreciable assets			21,000.	
b Less accumulated depreciation			2,429.	18,571.
11a Depletable assets				
b Less accumulated depletion				
12 Land (net of any amortization)				18,000.
13a Intangible assets (amortizable only)			700.	
b Less accumulated amortization			93.	607.
14 Other assets (attach schedule)				
15 Total assets				55,161.
Liabilities and Shareholders' Equity				
16 Accounts payable				2,395.
17 Mortgages, notes, bonds payable in less than 1 year				16,000.
18 Other current liabilities (attach sch)				
19 Loans from shareholders				
20 Mortgages, notes, bonds payable in 1 year or more				
21 Other liabilities (attach schedule)				
22 Capital stock				3,000.
23 Additional paid-in capital				28,500.
24 Retained earnings				5,266.
25 Adjustments to shareholders' equity (attach schedule)				
26 Less cost of treasury stock				
27 Total liabilities and shareholders' equity				55,161.

Schedule M-1 — Reconciliation of Income (Loss) per Books with Income (Loss) per Return
(You are not required to complete this schedule if the total assets on line 15, column (d), of Schedule L are less than $25,000.)

1 Net income (loss) per books .... 5,266.
2 Income included on Sch K, lines 1 through 6, not recorded on books this year (itemize):
_____
_____
3 Expenses recorded on books this year not included on Schedule K, lines 1 through 11a, 15e, and 16b (itemize):
  a Depreciation .... $ _____
  b Travel and entertainment .... $ _____
_____
4 Add lines 1 through 3 .... 5,266.

5 Income recorded on books this year not included on Schedule K, lines 1 through 6 (itemize):
  a Tax-exempt interest . $ _____
_____
6 Deductions included on Schedule K, lines 1 through 11a, 15e, and 16b, not charged against book income this year (itemize):
  a Depreciation .... $ _____
7 Add lines 5 and 6 ....
8 Income (loss) (Schedule K, ln 23). Ln 4 less ln 7 ... 5,266.

Schedule M-2 — Analysis of Accumulated Adjustments Account, Other Adjustments Account, and Shareholders' Undistributed Taxable Income Previously Taxed (see instructions)

	(a) Accumulated adjustments account	(b) Other adjustments account	(c) Shareholders' undistributed taxable income previously taxed
1 Balance at beginning of tax year			
2 Ordinary income from page 1, line 21	5,254.		
3 Other additions .... See Schedule M-2, Other Additions	942.		
4 Loss from page 1, line 21			
5 Other reductions .... See Schedule M-2, Other Reductions	930.		
6 Combine lines 1 through 5	5,266.		
7 Distributions other than dividend distributions			
8 Balance at end of tax year. Subtract line 7 from line 6	5,266.		

SPSA0134 12/01/98

12-30 2000/CORPORATIONS, PARTNERSHIPS, ESTATES, AND TRUSTS

Schedule K-1 (Form 1120S)
Department of the Treasury
Internal Revenue Service

Shareholder's Share of Income, Credits, Deductions, etc
▶ See separate instructions.
For calendar year 1998 or tax year
beginning May 2, 1998, and ending Dec 31, 19 98

OMB No. 1545-0130

1998

Shareholder's identifying number ▶ 354-24-8833
Corporation's identifying number ▶ 37-4536271

Shareholder's Name, Address, and ZIP Code

Gerri Glad
922 Main Street
Superior, IL 60654

Corporation's Name, Address, and ZIP Code

Glad's Flower Shop, Inc.
311 Main Street
Superior, IL 60654

A Shareholder's percentage of stock ownership for tax year (see instructions for Schedule K-1) .... ▶ 33.33333 %
B Internal Revenue Service Center where corporation filed its return .... ▶ Kansas City, MO 64999-0013
C Tax shelter registration number (see instructions for Schedule K-1) .... ▶
D Check applicable boxes: (1) ☐ Final K-1 (2) ☐ Amended K-1

	(a) Pro rata share items		(b) Amount	(c) Form 1040 filers enter the amount in column (b) on:
Income (Loss)	1 Ordinary income (loss) from trade or business activities	1	1,751.	See Shareholder's Instructions for Schedule K-1 (Form 1120S).
	2 Net income (loss) from rental real estate activities	2		
	3 Net income (loss) from other rental activities	3		
	4 Portfolio income (loss):			
	a Interest	4a	314.	Schedule B, Part I, line 1
	b Ordinary dividends	4b		Schedule B, Part II, line 5
	c Royalties	4c		Schedule E, Part I, line 4
	d Net short-term capital gain (loss)	4d		Schedule D, line 5, col (f)
	e Net long-term capital gain (loss)			
	(1) 28% rate gain (loss)	e(1)		Schedule D, line 12, col (g)
	(2) Total for year	e(2)		Schedule D, line 12, col (f)
	f Other portfolio income (loss) (attach schedule)	4f		(Enter on applicable line of return.) See Shareholder's Instructions for Schedule K-1 (Form 1120S).
	5 Net Section 1231 gain (loss) (other than due to casualty or theft)	5		(Enter on applicable line of return.)
	6 Other income (loss) (attach schedule)	6		
Deductions	7 Charitable contributions (attach schedule)	7	310.	Schedule A, line 15 or 16
	8 Section 179 expense deduction	8		See Shareholder's Instructions for Schedule K-1 (Form 1120S).
	9 Deductions related to portfolio income (loss) (attach schedule)	9		
	10 Other deductions (attach schedule)	10		
Investment Interest	11a Interest expense on investment debts	11a		Form 4952, line 1
	b (1) Investment income included on lines 4a, 4b, 4c, and 4f above	b(1)	314.	See Shareholder's Instructions for Schedule K-1 (Form 1120S).
	(2) Investment expenses included on line 9 above	b(2)		
Credits	12a Credit for alcohol used as fuel	12a		Form 6478, line 10
	b Low-income housing credit:			
	(1) From Section 42(j)(5) partnerships for property placed in service before 1990	b(1)		
	(2) Other than on line 12b(1) for property placed in service before 1990	b(2)		Form 8586, line 5
	(3) From Section 42(j)(5) partnerships for property placed in service after 1989	b(3)		
	(4) Other than on line 12b(3) for property placed in service after 1989	b(4)		
	c Qualified rehabilitation expenditures related to rental real estate activities	12c		See Shareholder's Instructions for Schedule K-1 (Form 1120S).
	d Credits (other than credits shown on lines 12b and 12c) related to rental real estate activities	12d		
	e Credits related to other rental activities	12e		
	13 Other credits	13		

BAA For Paperwork Reduction Act Notice, see the instructions for Form 1120S.

Schedule **K-1** (Form 1120S) 1998

SPSA0412 12/01/98

S CORPORATIONS   12-31

Schedule **K-1** (Form 1120S) (1998)   Gerri Glad   354-24-8833   Page 2

	(a) Pro rata share items		(b) Amount	(c) Form 1040 filers enter the amount in column (b) on:
Adjustments and Tax Preference Items	**14a** Depreciation adjustment on property placed in service after 1986	14a	299.	See Shareholder's Instructions for Schedule K-1 (Form 1120S) and Instructions for Form 6251
	b Adjusted gain or loss	14b		
	c Depletion (other than oil and gas)	14c		
	d (1) Gross income from oil, gas, or geothermal properties	d(1)		
	(2) Deductions allocable to oil, gas, or geothermal properties	d(2)		
	e Other adjustments and tax preference items (attach schedule)	14e		
Foreign Taxes	**15a** Type of income ►			Form 1116, Check boxes
	b Name of foreign country or U.S. possession ►			
	c Total gross income from sources outside the United States (attach schedule)	15c		Form 1116, Part I
	d Total applicable deductions and losses (attach schedule)	15d		
	e Total foreign taxes (check one): ► ☐ Paid ☐ Accrued	15e		Form 1116, Part II
	f Reduction in taxes available for credit (attach schedule)	15f		Form 1116, Part III
	g Other foreign tax information (attach schedule)	15g		See Instructions for Form 1116
Other	**16** Section 59(e)(2) expenditures: **a** Type ►			See Shareholder's Instructions for Schedule K-1 (Form 1120S).
	b Amount	16b		
	17 Tax-exempt interest income	17		Form 1040, line 8b
	18 Other tax-exempt income	18		See Shareholder's Instructions for Schedule K-1 (Form 1120S).
	19 Nondeductible expenses	19		
	20 Property distributions (including cash) other than dividend distributions reported to you on Form 1099-DIV	20		
	21 Amount of loan repayments for 'Loans from Shareholders'	21		
	22 Recapture of low-income housing credit:			
	a From Section 42(j)(5) partnerships	22a		Form 8611, line 8
	b Other than on line 22a	22b		

23 Supplemental information required to be reported separately to each shareholder (attach additional schedules if more space is needed):

Supplemental Information

SPSA0412 12/01/98

Schedule K-1 (Form 1120S)
Shareholder's Share of Income, Credits, Deductions, etc
▶ See separate instructions.

Department of the Treasury — Internal Revenue Service

For calendar year 1998 or tax year beginning **May 2**, 1998, and ending **Dec 31**, 19 **98**

OMB No. 1545-0130

1998

Shareholder's identifying number ▶ 354-98-7667
Corporation's identifying number ▶ 37-4536271

Shareholder's Name, Address, and ZIP Code:
Debbie Black
38 Madison Street
Chicago, IL 60499

Corporation's Name, Address, and ZIP Code:
Glad's Flower Shop, Inc.
311 Main Street
Superior, IL 60654

A Shareholder's percentage of stock ownership for tax year (see instructions for Schedule K-1) ....▶ __33.33333__ %
B Internal Revenue Service Center where corporation filed its return ....▶ Kansas City, MO 64999-0013
C Tax shelter registration number (see instructions for Schedule K-1) ......
D Check applicable boxes: (1) ☐ Final K-1 (2) ☐ Amended K-1

	(a) Pro rata share items		(b) Amount	(c) Form 1040 filers enter the amount in column (b) on:
Income (Loss)	1 Ordinary income (loss) from trade or business activities	1	1,752.	See Shareholder's Instructions for Schedule K-1 (Form 1120S).
	2 Net income (loss) from rental real estate activities	2		
	3 Net income (loss) from other rental activities	3		
	4 Portfolio income (loss):			
	a Interest	4a	314.	Schedule B, Part I, line 1
	b Ordinary dividends	4b		Schedule B, Part II, line 5
	c Royalties	4c		Schedule E, Part I, line 4
	d Net short-term capital gain (loss)	4d		Schedule D, line 5, col (f)
	e Net long-term capital gain (loss)			
	(1) 28% rate gain (loss)	e(1)		Schedule D, line 12, col (g)
	(2) Total for year	e(2)		Schedule D, line 12, col (f)
	f Other portfolio income (loss) (attach schedule)	4f		(Enter on applicable line of return.) See Shareholder's Instructions for Schedule K-1 (Form 1120S).
	5 Net Section 1231 gain (loss) (other than due to casualty or theft)	5		(Enter on applicable line of return.)
	6 Other income (loss) (attach schedule)	6		
Deductions	7 Charitable contributions (attach schedule)	7	310.	Schedule A, line 15 or 16
	8 Section 179 expense deduction	8		See Shareholder's Instructions for Schedule K-1 (Form 1120S).
	9 Deductions related to portfolio income (loss) (attach schedule)	9		
	10 Other deductions (attach schedule)	10		
Investment Interest	11a Interest expense on investment debts	11a		Form 4952, line 1
	b (1) Investment income included on lines 4a, 4b, 4c, and 4f above	b(1)	314.	See Shareholder's Instructions for Schedule K-1 (Form 1120S).
	(2) Investment expenses included on line 9 above	b(2)		
Credits	12a Credit for alcohol used as fuel	12a		Form 6478, line 10
	b Low-income housing credit:			
	(1) From Section 42(j)(5) partnerships for property placed in service before 1990	b(1)		
	(2) Other than on line 12b(1) for property placed in service before 1990	b(2)		Form 8586, line 5
	(3) From Section 42(j)(5) partnerships for property placed in service after 1989	b(3)		
	(4) Other than on line 12b(3) for property placed in service after 1989	b(4)		
	c Qualified rehabilitation expenditures related to rental real estate activities	12c		See Shareholder's Instructions for Schedule K-1 (Form 1120S).
	d Credits (other than credits shown on lines 12b and 12c) related to rental real estate activities	12d		
	e Credits related to other rental activities	12e		
	13 Other credits	13		

BAA For Paperwork Reduction Act Notice, see the instructions for Form 1120S.

Schedule **K-1** (Form 1120S) 1998

SPSA0412 12/01/98

Schedule K-1 (Form 1120S) (1998)   Debbie Black   354-98-7667   Page 2

	(a) Pro rata share items		(b) Amount	(c) Form 1040 filers enter the amount in column (b) on:
Adjustments and Tax Preference Items	14a Depreciation adjustment on property placed in service after 1986	14a	300.	See Shareholder's Instructions for Schedule K-1 (Form 1120S) and Instructions for Form 6251
	b Adjusted gain or loss	14b		
	c Depletion (other than oil and gas)	14c		
	d (1) Gross income from oil, gas, or geothermal properties	d(1)		
	(2) Deductions allocable to oil, gas, or geothermal properties	d(2)		
	e Other adjustments and tax preference items (attach schedule)	14e		
Foreign Taxes	15a Type of income ▶			Form 1116, Check boxes
	b Name of foreign country or U.S. possession ▶			
	c Total gross income from sources outside the United States (attach schedule)	15c		Form 1116, Part I
	d Total applicable deductions and losses (attach schedule)	15d		
	e Total foreign taxes (check one): ▶ ☐ Paid ☐ Accrued	15e		Form 1116, Part II
	f Reduction in taxes available for credit (attach schedule)	15f		Form 1116, Part III
	g Other foreign tax information (attach schedule)	15g		See Instructions for Form 1116
Other	16 Section 59(e)(2) expenditures: a Type ▶			See Shareholder's Instructions for Schedule K-1 (Form 1120S).
	b Amount	16b		
	17 Tax-exempt interest income	17		Form 1040, line 8b
	18 Other tax-exempt income	18		See Shareholder's Instructions for Schedule K-1 (Form 1120S).
	19 Nondeductible expenses	19		
	20 Property distributions (including cash) other than dividend distributions reported to you on Form 1099-DIV	20		
	21 Amount of loan repayments for 'Loans from Shareholders'	21		
	22 Recapture of low-income housing credit:			
	a From Section 42(j)(5) partnerships	22a		Form 8611, line 8
	b Other than on line 22a	22b		

23 Supplemental information required to be reported separately to each shareholder (attach additional schedules if more space is needed):

Supplemental Information

SPSA0412
12/01/98

12-34 2000/CORPORATIONS, PARTNERSHIPS, ESTATES, AND TRUSTS

Form **4562**
Department of the Treasury
Internal Revenue Service (99)

Depreciation and Amortization
(Including Information on Listed Property)
► See instructions.
► Attach this form to your return.

OMB No. 1545-0172
1998
67

Name(s) Shown on Return: Glad's Flower Shop, Inc.
Business or Activity to Which This Form Relates: Form 1120S Line 21
Identifying Number: 37-4536271

Part I — Election to Expense Certain Tangible Property (Section 179)
(Note: If you have any 'listed property,' complete Part V before you complete Part I.)

1	Maximum dollar limitation. If an enterprise zone business, see instructions	$18,500.
2	Total cost of Section 179 property placed in service. See instructions	
3	Threshold cost of Section 179 property before reduction in limitation	$200,000.
4	Reduction in limitation. Subtract line 3 from line 2. If zero or less, enter -0-	
5	Dollar limitation for tax year. Subtract line 4 from line 1. If zero or less, enter -0-. If married filing separately, see instructions	

6	(a) Description of property	(b) Cost (business use only)	(c) Elected cost

7	Listed property. Enter amount from line 27	
8	Total elected cost of Section 179 property. Add amounts in column (c), lines 6 and 7	
9	Tentative deduction. Enter the smaller of line 5 or line 8	
10	Carryover of disallowed deduction from 1997. See instructions	
11	Business income limitation. Enter the smaller of business income (not less than zero) or line 5 (see instrs)	
12	Section 179 expense deduction. Add lines 9 and 10, but do not enter more than line 11	
13	Carryover of disallowed deduction to 1999. Add lines 9 and 10, less line 12	

Note: Do not use Part II or Part III below for listed property (automobiles, certain other vehicles, cellular telephones, certain computers, or property used for entertainment, recreation, or amusement). Instead, use Part V for listed property.

Part II — MACRS Depreciation for Assets Placed in Service Only During Your 1998 Tax Year
(Do Not Include Listed Property)

Section A — General Asset Account Election

14 If you are making the election under Section 168(i)(4) to group any assets placed in service during the tax year into one or more general asset accounts, check this box. See instructions ▶ ☐

Section B — General Depreciation System (GDS) (See instructions)

(a) Classification of property	(b) Month and year placed in service	(c) Basis for depreciation (business/investment use only — see instructions)	(d) Recovery period	(e) Convention	(f) Method	(g) Depreciation deduction
15a 3-year property						
b 5-year property						
c 7-year property		9,750.	7.0 yrs	HY	200DB	929.
d 10-year property						
e 15-year property						
f 20-year property						
g 25-year property			25 yrs		S/L	
h Residential rental property			27.5 yrs	MM	S/L	
			27.5 yrs	MM	S/L	
i Nonresidential real property			39 yrs	MM	S/L	
				MM	S/L	

Section C — Alternative Depreciation System (ADS) (See instructions)

16a Class life					S/L	
b 12-year			12 yrs		S/L	
c 40-year			40 yrs	MM	S/L	

Part III — Other Depreciation (Do Not Include Listed Property) (See instructions)

17	GDS and ADS deductions for assets placed in service in tax years beginning before 1998	
18	Property subject to Section 168(f)(1) election	
19	ACRS and other depreciation	

Part IV — Summary (See instructions)

20	Listed property. Enter amount from line 26	1,500.
21	**Total.** Add deductions on line 12, lines 15 and 16 in column (g), and lines 17 through 20. Enter here and on the appropriate lines of your return. Partnerships and S corporations — see instructions	2,429.
22	For assets shown above and placed in service during the current year, enter the portion of the basis attributable to Section 263A costs	

BAA For Paperwork Reduction Act Notice, see the separate instructions.   FDIZ0812 07/23/98   Form 4562 (1998)

S CORPORATIONS 12-35

Form 4562 (1998) Glad's Flower Shop, Inc. 37-4536271 Page 2

Part V — Listed Property — Automobiles, Certain Other Vehicles, Cellular Telephones, Certain Computers, and Property Used for Entertainment, Recreation, or Amusement

Note: *For any vehicle for which you are using the standard mileage rate or deducting lease expense, complete **only** 23a, 23b, columns (a) through (c) of Section A, all of Section B, and Section C if applicable.*

Section A — Depreciation and Other Information (Caution: See instructions for limits for passenger automobiles.)

23a Do you have evidence to support the business/investment use claimed? ..... [X] Yes [ ] No   23b If 'Yes,' is the evidence written? ..... [X] Yes [ ] No

(a) Type of property (list vehicles first)	(b) Date placed in service	(c) Business/ investment use percentage	(d) Cost or other basis	(e) Basis for depreciation (business/investment use only)	(f) Recovery period	(g) Method/ Convention	(h) Depreciation deduction	(i) Elected Section 179 cost
24 Property used more than 50% in a qualified business use (see instructions):								
truck	05/02/98	100.00	11,250.	11,250.	5.00	200DB/HY	1,500.	
25 Property used 50% or less in a qualified business use (see instructions):								

26 Add amounts in column (h). Enter the total here and on line 20, page 1 ..... 26 1,500.
27 Add amounts in column (i). Enter the total here and on line 7, page 1 27

Section B — Information on Use of Vehicles

Complete this section for vehicles used by a sole proprietor, partner, or other 'more than 5% owner,' or related person.
If you provided vehicles to your employees, first answer the questions in Section C to see if you meet an exception to completing this section for those vehicles.

	(a) Vehicle 1	(b) Vehicle 2	(c) Vehicle 3	(d) Vehicle 4	(e) Vehicle 5	(f) Vehicle 6
28 Total business/investment miles driven during the year (**Do not** include commuting miles)						
29 Total commuting miles driven during the year						
30 Total other personal (noncommuting) miles driven						
31 Total miles driven during the year. Add lines 28 through 30						
	Yes No	Yes No	Yes No	Yes No	Yes No	Yes No
32 Was the vehicle available for personal use during off-duty hours?						
33 Was the vehicle used primarily by a more than 5% owner or related person?						
34 Is another vehicle available for personal use?						

Section C — Questions for Employers Who Provide Vehicles for Use by Their Employees

*Answer these questions to determine if you meet an exception to completing Section B for vehicles used by employees who **are not** more than 5% owners or related persons.*

	Yes	No
35 Do you maintain a written policy statement that prohibits all personal use of vehicles, including commuting, by your employees?		
36 Do you maintain a written policy statement that prohibits personal use of vehicles, except commuting, by your employees? See instructions for vehicles used by corporate officers, directors, or 1% or more owners		
37 Do you treat all use of vehicles by employees as personal use?		
38 Do you provide more than five vehicles to your employees, obtain information from your employees about the use of the vehicles, and retain the information received?		
39 Do you meet the requirements concerning qualified automobile demonstration use? See instructions		

Note: *If your answer to 35, 36, 37, 38, or 39 is 'Yes,' you need not complete Section B for the covered vehicles.*

Part VI — Amortization

(a) Description of costs	(b) Date amortization begins	(c) Amortizable amount	(d) Code Section	(e) Amortization period or percentage	(f) Amortization for this year
40 Amortization of costs that begins during your 1998 tax year:					
organizational costs	05/02/98	700.	248	5.00 yrs	93.
41 Amortization of costs that began before 1998 41					
42 **Total.** Enter here and on 'Other Deductions' or 'Other Expenses' line of your return 42					93.

FDIZ0812 07/23/98

GLAD'S FLOWER SHOP, INC. 37-4536271
Form 1120S 12/31/1998

Page 1, Line 19, Schedule of Other Deductions:

Amortization	$ 93
Insurance	1,445
Office Supplies	480
Telephone	4,324
Bank Service Charge	87
Truck Expenses	838
	$7,267

Amortization of Organization Expenditures
Initial Year May 2, 1998 - December 31, 1998

Glad's Flower Shop elects ("has elected," for later years) to amortize its organizational expenses ratably over a 60-month period, under Code Sec. 248. The following information is submitted as required by Regulation 1.248-1(c):

Description of Expense	Date Incurred	Amount
Legal Fees for incorporation	May 2, 1998	$700.00
Month taxpayer began business	May 1998	
Amortization period:	60 months	

CHAPTER 13

COMPARATIVE FORMS OF DOING BUSINESS

LEARNING OBJECTIVES

After completing Chapter 13, you should be able to:

1. Identify the principal legal and tax forms for conducting a business.

2. Appreciate the relative importance of nontax factors in making business decisions.

3. Distinguish between the forms for conducting a business according to whether they are subject to single taxation or double taxation.

4. Identify techniques for avoiding double taxation and for controlling the entity tax.

5. Understand the applicability and the effect of the conduit and entity concepts on contributions to the entity, operations of the entity, entity distributions, passive activity loss and at-risk rules, and special allocations.

6. Analyze the effect of the disposition of a business on the owners and the entity for each of the forms for conducting a business.

KEY TERMS

Conduit concept
Entity concept
Limited liability company (LLC)
Thin capitalization

OUTLINE

I. **FORMS OF DOING BUSINESS**

   A. The principal legal forms of conducting a business entity are:
   1. Sole proprietorship
   2. Partnership
   3. Corporation

   B. Generally, a taxpayer is bound by the legal form of business he chooses, however, the IRS may, in some cases, employ the 'substance over form' concept to reclassify an entity for tax purposes.

II. **NONTAX FACTORS**

   A. Capital Formation
   1. Sole proprietorships depend upon the funds obtainable by the owner.
   2. Partnerships pool the resources of the partners.
   3. Corporations can issue additional stock to raise capital.

   B. Limited Liability
   1. Corporations generally have limited liability under state law.
      a. Statutes do not provide limited liability for the performance of professional services.
      b. In small corporations, shareholders often guarantee loans to the corporation.
   2. Limited partnerships provide limited liability to limited partners.
   3. LLCs limit the liability of all owners.

   C. Other Factors significant in selecting an organizational form include:
   1. Estimated life of the business.
   2. Number of owners and their role in the management of the business.
   3. Freedom of choice in transferring ownership interests.
   4. Organizational formality and the related cost and extent of government regulation.

III. **SINGLE VERSUS DOUBLE TAXATION**

   A. Overall Impact on Entity and Owners
   1. Sole proprietors and partners are taxed only at the owner level.
   2. Corporations are taxed on earnings at the corporate level and distributions of corporate earnings are taxed at the shareholder level.

3. S corporations generally avoid the corporate level tax and earnings are taxed at the shareholder level.

B. All forms of business are directly or indirectly subject to the alternative minimum tax.
1. Sole proprietors and corporations are taxed directly.
2. Partnerships and S corporations pass through the preferences and adjustments to entity owners.
3. AMT has been repealed for small corporations; corporations
   a. having average annual gross receipts not more than $5 million for the 3 year period beginning after 12/31/93, or
   b. in their first year of existence.

IV. CONTROLLING THE ENTITY TAX

A. Favorable Treatment of Certain Fringe Benefits
1. Some fringe benefits are deductible by the entity and excludable from the recipient's gross income.
2. Of these excludable fringe benefits, some are available only to employees.
   a. For an owner to be an employee the entity must be a corporation.
   b. For an S corporation, a more than 2% shareholder is treated as a partner.
3. Pension and profit sharing plans defer taxation for the recipient.

B. Minimizing Double Taxation, Corporations
1. Double taxation occurs when a corporation distributes earnings.
2. Deductible distributions include reasonable payments for:
   a. salary to shareholder-employees
   b. rent to shareholder-lessors
   c. interest to shareholder-creditors
3. Not making distributions carries the risk that the accumulated earnings tax will eventually apply.
4. Electing S status causes the tax to be levied at the shareholder, rather than, the corporate level; all of the qualification/maintenance requirements need to be considered.

V. CONDUIT VERSUS ENTITY TREATMENT

A. Effect on Recognition at Time of Contribution to the Entity
1. Contributions of personal use assets are valued at the lower of adjusted basis or fair market value.
2. Partnerships have a carryover basis for contributed property and the partner has a substitute basis in his partnership interest.

3. Corporations must satisfy the §351 control requirements to obtain a carryover/substitute basis, otherwise, the transfer will be a taxable event.
4. Special allocation treatment is mandatory for partnerships when the adjusted basis and the fair market value of contributed property is not equal.

B. Effect on Basis of Ownership Interest
1. A partner's basis in a partnership interest recognizes the partnership's profits and losses and includes liability effects.
2. A C corporation shareholder's basis is not affected by corporate profit or loss nor liability increases or decreases.
3. An S corporation shareholder's basis recognizes the corporation's profits and losses but not corporate liability increases or decreases.

C. Effect on Results of Operations
1. Under the entity concept the earnings components of a C corporation lose their identity when passed through to the shareholder as dividends.
2. Under the conduit concept, any item subject to special treatment on the taxpayer-owners' tax return is reported separately to the partner or S corporation shareholder.
3. Only the partnership completely applies the conduit concept; an S corporation is subject to taxation at the entity level in some circumstances.

D. Effect on Passive Activity Losses
1. Passive activity loss rules apply to partnerships, S corporations, personal service corporations and closely held corporations.
2. To be classified as a personal service corporation
   a. the principal activity of the corporation is the performance of personal services.
   b. the services are substantially performed by owner-employees.
   c. owner-employees own more than 10% in value of the stock of the corporation.
3. In a closely held corporation more than 50% of the value of the outstanding stock at any time during the last half of the year is owned by 5 or fewer individuals.
4. For personal service corporations, passive activity losses cannot be offset against either active or portfolio income.
5. For closely-held corporation, passive activity losses can be offset against active income but not against portfolio income.
6. The results of passive activities of a partnership and an S corporation are separately stated and passed through to the partners and shareholders.

VI. DISPOSITION OF A BUSINESS OR OF AN OWNERSHIP INTEREST

A. Sole Proprietorship
   1. The sale of a sole proprietorship is treated as the sale of individual assets.
   2. Classification as ordinary income or capital gain depends upon the nature and holding period of the individual assets.
   3. If the amount realized exceeds the FMV of identifiable assets, the excess is identified as goodwill which produces capital gain for the seller.

B. Partnership
   1. If structured as a sale of assets, the treatment is the same as that of a sole proprietorship.
   2. If structured as a sale of an ownership interest, it is treated as a sale of a capital asset under §741 subject to ordinary income potential under §751. Refer to the description of these Code sections in Chapter 11.

C. Corporation
   1. A corporation is taxed on a sale of assets whether it actually sells the assets or distributes the assets to shareholders.
   2. In a liquidating distribution, the shareholders, in effect, sell their stock back to the corporation and recognize capital gain or loss.
   3. A sale of stock produces capital gain or loss to the selling shareholders. Because the corporation is not involved, there are no tax consequences at the corporate level.

VII. OVERALL COMPARISON OF FORMS OF DOING BUSINESS

A. Overall comparison of forms of doing business. Concept Summary 13-2 of the text provides a detailed comparison of the tax consequences of different forms of business.

B. Considerations should extend beyond the current tax period and include the following:
   1. Asset contributions
   2. Taxation of results of operations
   3. Distributions to owners
   4. Disposition of ownership interests
   5. Business termination

TEST FOR SELF-EVALUATION

True or False

T F 1. The capitalized costs of goodwill or going concern value acquired after August 10, 1993, must be amortized over a 15-year period beginning with the month acquired.
(IRS 95 2A-8)

T F 2. S Corporations are never taxed.

T F 3. The test in determining if the compensation paid to an officer of a corporation is reasonable is based on the total of salaries paid to all of the officers of that corporation.

T F 4. All forms of businesses are subject to AMT.

T F 5. Sole proprietors have the advantage over corporations when the alternative minimum tax applies.

T F 6. Fringe benefits which are not discriminatory are deductible by S Corporations.

T F 7. If a personal use asset is contributed to a corporation, the corporation's basis is the lower of adjusted basis or FMV when contributed.

Fill in the Blanks

1. _____ rules apply to personal service corporations and closely held corporations.

2. _____% or more of the stock value must be held by _____ or fewer individuals during the last half of the tax year for a corporation to meet the definition of a closely held corporation.

3. The At-Risk rules apply to both _____ and _____.

4. Under the _____ the business is an extension of the owners; under the _____ the business is distinct from the owners.

5. The ability to share profits and losses differently from the share in capital is a _____ allowed only to _____.

Multiple Choice

_____ 1.   John bought land with a building on it that he planned to use in his business. His costs in connection with this purchase were as follows:

Cash downpayment	$ 40,000
Mortgage on property	300,000
Survey costs	2,000
Transfer taxes	1,800
Charges for installation of gas lines	3,000
Back taxes owed by seller and paid by John	1,200

What is John's basis in the property?   (IRS 95 1C-57)

a. $348,000
b. $346,800
c. $345,000
d. $343,000

_____ 2.   In 1994, Robert sold a building used in his business. His books and records reflect the following information:

Original cost of building	$150,000
Improvements made to building	50,000
Broker's commissions paid on sale	10,000
Cash received on sale	100,000
Total property taxes for 1993 paid by Robert	3,000
Portion of property taxes imposed on purchaser and reimbursed in a separate payment to Robert by purchaser under IRC 164(d)	500
Mortgage assumed by buyer	80,000
Accumulated depreciation	70,000
Fair market value of other property received	20,000

What is the amount of gain Robert must RECOGNIZE from the sale of the property?   (IRS 95 1C-61)

a. $60,000
b. $61,000
c. $70,000
d. $71,000

___ 3. Matt purchased a high-volume dry cleaning store on January 1, 1994, for $960,000. NO liabilities were assumed. The fair market values of the assets at the time of the purchase were as follows:

Cash in banks	$210,100
U. S. government securities	100,200
Building and land	312,200
Accounts receivable	100,000
Fixtures and equipment	202,000

Matt will NOT change the name of the cleaners. What is Matt's basis for goodwill or going concern value? (IRS 95 2C-46)

a. $0
b. $35,500
c. $91,300
d. $110,560

___ 4. In a sole proprietorship the liabilities of the business:

a. extend to the owner's personal assets
b. extend only to the assets of the business
c. are limited to negligent acts of the owner personally, not employee actions
d. both b and c

___ 5. Alisa purchased a day care center on December 10, 1993. The contract showed the following adjusted basis and fair market value of the assets:

	Adjusted Basis	Fair Market Value
Building	$150,000	$300,000
Land	40,000	50,000
Furniture & Fixtures	60,000	50,000

The contract provided that the agreed sale price wad a lump sum $360,000. What is Alisa's basis in the building? (IRS 94 2C-52)

a. $216,000
b. $250,000
c. $270,000
d. $300,000

SOLUTIONS

True or False

1. T (p. 13-24)
2. F (p. 13-8)
3. F (p. 13-14)
4. F (p. 13-9)
5. F (p. 13-10)
6. T (p. 13-12)
7. T (p. 13-17)

Fill in the Blanks

1. Passive activity loss (p. 13-20)
2. 50; 5 (p. 13-20)
3. partnerships; S Corporations (p. 13-21)
4. conduit concept; entity concept (p. 13-17)
5. special allocation; partnerships (p. 13-22)

Multiple Choice

1. a (40,000 + 300,000 + 2,000 + 1,800 + 3,000 + 1,200)
2. a (Sales Price - Adjusted Basis; (100,000 + 80,000 + 20,000) - (150,000 + 50,000 + 10,000 - 70,000))
3. b (960,000 - (210,100 + 100,200 + 312,200 + 100,000 + 202,000))
4. a (p. 13-7)
5. c (relative fair market value: (300,000/400,000) (360,000))

CHAPTER 14

EXEMPT ENTITIES

LEARNING OBJECTIVES

After completing Chapter 14, you should be able to:

1. Identify the different types of exempt organizations.

2. Enumerate the requirements for exempt status.

3. Know the tax consequences of exempt status, including the different consequences for public charities and private foundations.

4. Determine which exempt organizations are classified as private foundations.

5. Recognize the taxes imposed on private foundations and calculate the related initial tax and additional tax amounts.

6. Determine when an exempt organization is subject to the unrelated business income tax and calculate the amount of the tax.

7. List the reports exempt organizations must file with the IRS and the related due dates.

8. Identify tax planning opportunities for exempt organizations.

KEY TERMS

Debt-financed income
Excess lobbying expenditure
Exempt organization
Feeder organization
Grass roots expenditure
Lobbying expenditure
Private foundation
Unrelated business income
Unrelated business income tax

OUTLINE

I. **EXEMPT ORGANIZATIONS**

    A. To qualify for exempt status an organization must fit one of the categories provided for in the Code. Exhibit 14-1 of the text contains many examples.

    B. Requirements for Exempt Status
        1. Must serve some type of common good,
        2. Must be a not-for-profit entity,
        3. Must not allow net earnings to be used for the benefit of any private shareholder or individual, and
        4. Must not exert political influence.

II. **TAX CONSEQUENCES OF EXEMPT STATUS**

    A. Though generally exempt, Federal taxes may be imposed on an organization classified as exempt if the organization:
        1. Engages in prohibited transactions,
        2. Is a feeder organization,
        3. Is classified as a private foundation, or
        4. Has unrelated business income.

    B. Prohibited transactions include:
        1. Failure to sustain the initial requirements of exempt status,
        2. Certain lobbying activities.

    C. Disqualified organizations, churches, their integrated auxiliaries and private foundations, violate the qualification/maintenance requirements by participating in lobbying activities.

    D. Qualifying §501(c)(3) organizations may elect to participate in lobbying activities on a limited basis. These organizations may not exceed the ceiling amount statutorily imposed on the lobbying expenditures.

    E. Two ceiling amounts apply. The grass roots ceiling limits the amount of expenditures incurred to influence general public opinion. The lobbying expenditures ceiling amount limits expenditures incurred to influence the formulation of legislation.

    F. Though not in excess of the ceiling amount, excess lobbying expenditures are subject to a 25% tax. The ceiling amounts are 150% of the grass roots or lobbying nontaxable amount; the excess lobbying expenditures are more than 100% of the grass roots or lobbying nontaxable amount. See Figure 14-1 of text for calculations of lobbying nontaxable amount.

G. Feeder organizations carry on a trade or business activity for profit and pay all profits to one or more exempt organizations. These types of organizations are subject to Federal income tax with three exceptions. Those engaged in activities:
1. Which generate rental income excluded from the definition of rent for unrelated business income tax purposes,
2. For which substantially all work is performed by volunteers, and
3. Which sell merchandise substantially all of which had been received as contributions or gifts.

III. PRIVATE FOUNDATIONS

A. Private foundations are so classified because these organizations generally do not have broad public support, they are formed to respond to the private interests of a limited number of persons.

B. Though generally exempt from Federal income tax, §§4940-4945 impose excise taxes on private foundations for certain actions or failure to act. These taxes are levied only on private foundations:
1. Tax based on investment income
2. Tax on self-dealing (engaging in transactions with disqualified persons)
3. Tax on failure to distribute income (distributions for exempt purposes)
4. Tax on excess business holdings (controlling unrelated businesses)
5. Tax on investments that jeopardize charitable purposes (speculative investments)
6. Tax on taxable expenditures (expenditures that should not be made by private foundations)

C. See Concept Summary 14-3 of the Text.

IV. UNRELATED BUSINESS INCOME TAX

A. An exempt organization may be subject to income tax on unrelated business income if:
1. The organization conducts a trade or business,
2. The trade or business is not substantially related to the exempt purpose of the organization, and
3. The trade or business is regularly carried on by the organization.

B. Statutory exceptions to classification as unrelated trade or business apply even if all the above factors are present if:
1. All work is performed by volunteers.
2. Substantially all merchandise being sold was received by gift.
3. The business is conducted primarily for the convenience of the organization's members.
4. Gross income from an unrelated trade or business is less than $1,000.

C. When applicable, the tax on unrelated business income is computed at corporate tax rates.
    Gross unrelated business income
- Deductions
= Net unrelated business income
+/- Modifications
= Unrelated business taxable income

V. REPORTING REQUIREMENTS

A. Though only certain types of organizations are required to obtain IRS approval for exempt status, exempt organizations should apply to avoid potential disqualification by the IRS.
1. Application is made on Form 1023 for §501(c)(3) organizations.
2. Form 1024 is used for most other types of exempt organizations.

B. Annual filings of Form 990 are required of exempt organizations other than:
1. Federal agencies,
2. Churches,
3. Organizations having annual gross receipts < $25,000,
4. Private foundations - private foundations are required to file Form 990-PF.

C. Form 990 is due on the 15th day of the 5th month after the end of the organization's tax year.

EXEMPT ENTITIES 14-5

TEST FOR SELF-EVALUATION

True or False

T F 1. Any organization that qualifies for tax-exempt status can receive contributions that are fully deductible by the donor. (IRS 97 4A-6)

T F 2. Exempt status is automatically lost if an exempt organization has any unrelated business income during the year.

T F 3. The ONLY organizations exempt from federal income taxes are those organized and operated exclusively for religious, charitable, scientific or educational purposes. (IRS 96 4A-26)

T F 4. An organization recognized as a tax exempt organization will NOT pay income tax on any income it earns, but is still responsible for withholding, social security taxes and federal unemployment tax for wage payments. (IRS 94 4A-26)

T F 5. A partnership may qualify as an organization exempt from federal income tax if it is organized and operated exclusively for one or more of the purposes found in Section 501(c)(3) of the Internal Revenue Code. (IRS 91 4A-39)

T F 6. An exempt organization with $4,999 gross income from an unrelated business is required to file Form 990-T, Exempt Organization Business Income Tax Return. (IRS 91 4A-40)

T F 7. Organizations recognized as tax exempt are not responsible for withholding, depositing, paying and reporting federal income tax, FICA and FUTA wages paid to their employees. (IRS 91 4A-41)

T F 8. A church, its integrated auxiliaries, or a convention or association of churches is not required to file Form 1023, Application for Recognition of Exemption Under Section 501(c)(3) of the Internal Revenue Code, in order to be tax exempt or to receive tax deductible contributions. (IRS 91 4A-42)

Fill in the Blanks

1. The underlying rationale for all exempt organizations is to _____.

2. Ceiling amounts on lobbying expenditures for exempt organizations are calculated for _____ expenditures and for _____ expenditures.

3. Failure to continue to qualify as a type of exempt organization is a _____.

4. A _____ carries on a trade or business for the benefit of an exempt organization.

5. _____ or _____ includes any activity conducted for the production of income through the sale of merchandise or the performance of services.

Multiple Choice

_____ 1. Which of the following statements is correct in respect to tax-exempt organizations? (IRS 97 4B-44)

   a. A foundation may qualify for exemption from federal income tax if it is organized for the prevention of cruelty to animals.
   b. A partnership may qualify as an organization exempt from federal income tax if it is organized and operated exclusively for one or more of the purposes found in section 501(c)(3).
   c. An individual can qualify as an organization exempt from federal income tax.
   d. In order to qualify as an exempt organization, the organization must be a corporation.

_____ 2. Which of the following organizations, which are exempt from Federal income tax, must generally file an annual information report? (IRS 97 4B-45)

   a. An organization, other than a private foundation, with annual gross receipts that normally are not more than $25,000.
   b. A private foundation.
   c. A church.
   d. A religious order.

_____ 3. If applicable the tax on unrelated business income is:

   a. computed at corporate tax rates
   b. computed at trust tax rates
   c. computed at single individual tax rates
   d. computed at special exempt organization tax rates

_____ 4. Private foundation status of an exempt organization terminates if it:

   a. invests in a functionally related business
   b. becomes a public charity
   c. receives less than 1/3 of its support from a governmental unit
   d. becomes an exempt operating foundation

_____ 5. To qualify as an exempt organization, an entity:

a. can never engage in lobbying activities
b. cannot have a nonresident shareholder
c. must satisfy one of the categories provided for in the Code
d. can be a feeder organization

_____ 6. Income derived from conducting games of chance will be exempt if:

a. allowed by state law only to exempt organizations
b. the games are legal under state and local law
c. both of the above
d. neither of the above

_____ 7. A private foundation may be subject to taxes imposed on:

a. investment income
b. self dealing
c. undistributed income
d. all of the above
e. none of the above

_____ 8. In determining whether or not an exempt organization is broadly supported and not classified as a private foundation, two tests must be satisfied:

a. one-third support test
b. not more than one-third support test
c. $5,000 or 1% support, the greater, test
d. a and c
e. a and b

_____ 9. Low cost items distributed incidental to solicitation for charitable contributions are not considered unrelated trade or business when:

a. the item is requested by the recipient
b. the item is returned in lieu of a donation
c. the items cost less than $6.90 each
d. all of the above
e. none of the above

_____ 10. An exempt organization will be subject to the tax on unrelated business income if:

a. the trade or business is not regularly carried on
b. the trade or business is not substantially related to the exempt purpose of the organization

c. the trade or business is substantially related to the exempt purpose of the organization
d. the trade or business is conducted primarily for the convenience of members

_____ 11. Which of the following might be considered an unrelated trade or business for a hospital:

a. cafeteria
b. pharmacy
c. gift shop
d. all of the above
e. none of the above

_____ 12. A tax-exempt organization that is required to file Form 990, Return of Organization Exempt From Income Tax, must do so by what date (do NOT consider any extensions, weekends, or holidays)? (IRS 96 4B-67)

a. The last day of the month following the end of the organization's accounting period.
b. The 15th day of the 3rd month following the end of the organization's accounting period.
c. The 15th day of the 4th month following the end of the organization's accounting period.
d. The 15th day of the 5th month following the end of the organization's accounting period.

_____ 13. Which of the following organizations, exempt from federal income tax under Section 501(a) of the Internal Revenue Code (IRC), must file an annual information return on Form 990 or Form 990-PF? (IRS 94 4B-68)

a. A private foundation exempt under Sec. 501(c)(3) of the IRC.
b. An organization, other than a private foundation, having gross receipts in each year that normally are NOT more than $5,000.
c. A stock bonus, pension, or profit-sharing trust that qualifies under Sec. 401 of the IRC.
d. A school BELOW college level, affiliated with a church or operated by a religious order, that is NOT an integrated auxiliary of a church.

EXEMPT ENTITIES 14-9

SOLUTIONS

True or False

1. F (p. 14-6; usually exempt; subject to limitations)
2. F (p. 14-15)
3. F (Exhibit 14-1)
4. F (p. 14-6; may pay on unrelated business income)
5. F (Exhibit 14-1)
6. T (p. 14-25)
7. F (p. 4-6; exempt from federal income tax)
8. T (p. 14-24)

Fill in the Blanks

1. serve some type of common good (p. 14-3)
2. lobbying; grass roots (p. 14-7)
3. prohibited transaction (p. 14-6)
4. feeder organization (p. 14-9)
5. trade or business (p. 14-15)

Multiple Choice

1. a
2. b (p. 14-25)
3. a (p. 14-14)
4. b (p. 14-12)
5. c (p. 14-3)
6. c (p. 14-17)
7. d (p. 14-12)
8. e (p. 14-11)
9. c (p. 14-18)
10. b (p. 14-15)
11. c (p. 14-16)
12. d (p. 14-25)
13. a (p. 14-25)

CHAPTER 15

MULTISTATE CORPORATE TAXATION

LEARNING OBJECTIVES

After completing Chapter 15, you should be able to:

1. Illustrate the computation of a multistate corporation's state tax liability.

2. Define nexus and its role in state income taxation.

3. Distinguish between allocation and apportionment of a multistate corporation's taxable income.

4. Describe the nature and treatment of business and nonbusiness income.

5. Discuss the sales, payroll, and property apportionment factors.

6. Apply the unitary method of state income taxation.

7. Discuss the states' income tax treatment of S corporations.

8. Describe other commonly encountered state and local taxes on businesses.

9. Recognize tax planning opportunities available to minimize a corporation's state and local tax liability.

KEY TERMS

Allocate	Passive investment company	Throwback rule
Apportion	Payroll factor	UDITPA
Dock sales	Property factor	Unitary theory
Multistate Tax Commission	Public Law 86-272	Water's edge election
Nexus	Sales factor	

OUTLINE

I. **OVERVIEW OF CORPORATE STATE INCOME TAXATION**

  A. Currently, forty-six states and the District of Columbia impose a tax based on a corporation's income.

  B. Generally, states require use of the same accounting periods and methods as those used on the corporation's Federal return.

  C. In the majority of states, state taxable income is determined by reference to the corporation's Federal return with modification. State modifications:
  1. Reflect differences between state and Federal statutes.
  2. Remove income that a state is constitutionally prohibited from taxing.
  3. Eliminate the recovery of income for which the state did not permit a deduction on an earlier return.

  D. Jurisdiction to Impose Tax
  1. The state in which a business is incorporated has taxing jurisdiction.
  2. For corporations operating in other than their state of incorporation, sufficient nexus must be established.
     a. nexus describes the degree of business activity that must be present before a tax can be imposed.
     b. nexus is measured according to state statute, its definition and sufficiency varies among states.

II. **ALLOCATION AND APPORTIONMENT OF INCOME**

  A. Allocation assigns specific components of corporate net income to a certain state.

  B. Allocable income generally includes:
  1. Income or loss derived from sale of nonbusiness real or tangible property.
  2. Income or loss derived from rentals and royalties from nonbusiness real or tangible property.

  C. Apportionment divides a corporation's business income among the taxing states.

  D. Business and Nonbusiness Income
  1. Business income arises from the taxpayer's regular course of business or constitutes an integral part of the taxpayer's regular business.
  2. Nonbusiness income is "all income other than business income."
  3. Business income is apportioned; nonbusiness income may be apportioned or allocated to the state in which the property is located.

  E. Apportionment Factors

1. Each state chooses the type and number of factors used to establish its apportionment formula.
2. Most states use a three-factor formula which assigns equal weight to sales, payroll and property.
3. Variations in the state's definition of allocable and apportionable income and in apportionment formulas may cause a corporation to be subject to state income tax on more or less than 100% of its Federal taxable income after modifications.

F. Sales Factor
   1. In-state sales/Total sales:
      a. includes sales that generate business income.
      b. excludes income on federal obligations.
      c. sales of capital assets are treated differently by different states.
   2. Most states apply the ultimate destination concept which assumes a sale takes place at the point of delivery to determine in-state sales.
   3. If an origination state has adopted a throwback rule, out-of-state sales not subject to tax in the destination state or sales to the U.S. government are treated as sales in the state of origination.

G. The Payroll Factor
   1. In-state compensation/Total compensation
      a. generally includes compensation includible in the employees' Federal gross income.
      b. in some states, certain fringe benefits excluded from Federal income tax under §401(k) are included.
      c. payments to non-employee, outside contractors, are not included in most states.
   2. Compensation of an employee is not, normally, split between states unless the employee is transferred or changes position during the year.
   3. When services are performed in more than one state, that employee's compensation is allocated to the state in which:
      a. the services are primarily performed.
      b. the employee's base of operations is located and in which services are performed.
      c. the services are directed or controlled and in which services are performed.
      d. the employee resides.
   4. Only compensation related to the production of apportionable income is includes in the payroll factor.

H. The Property Factor
1. In-state property/Total property
   a. is based on the average value of the corporation's real and tangible personal property owned or rented and used during the year.
   b. owned property is usually valued at historic cost plus additions and improvements.
   c. rented property is usually valued at 8 times its annual rent.
2. Only property used to produce apportionable income is included in the property factor.

III. THE UNITARY THEORY

A. The unitary approach, adopted by many states, requires a corporation to file combined or consolidate returns which include the operating results of certain affiliated corporations.

B. The unitary theory
1. Ignores the separate legal existence of the entities and focuses on practical business realities:
   a. unity of ownership
   b. unity of operations
   c. unity of use
2. Treats the separate entities as a single business for state income tax purposes.
3. Applies the apportionment formula to the combined income of the unitary business.

C. Water's Edge Election
1. Permits a multinational corporation to elect to limit a state's taxing jurisdiction over out-of-state affiliates to activities occurring within the U.S.
2. This election usually cannot be revoked for a number of years without permission.
3. Corporation's making this election may be subject to an additional tax for the privilege of excluding out-of-state entities from the combined report.

IV. TAXATION OF S CORPORATIONS

A. Many of the states that recognize S corporations automatically treat them as such if a valid Federal election is in place. Certain states impose additional eligibility requirements.

B. Most states that impose corporate income taxes have special provisions for S corporations.

C. When an S corporation has nonresident shareholders:

1. A corporate-level tax might be imposed.
2. The corporation might be required to withhold tax on the nonresidents' portion of the income.
3. The nonresident shareholder may have to agree to pay state taxes.

V. OTHER STATE AND LOCAL TAXES

   A State and Local Sales and Use Taxes
1. Sales and use taxes are imposed on the final consumer of the taxable item.
2. The seller of taxable property or services acts as an agent of the state in collecting sales tax.
3. The use tax is designed to prevent consumers from evading sales tax by purchasing goods out-of-state for in-state use.
4. States apply a separate set of nexus rules to sales/use tax.

   B. Property Taxes
1. Property taxes are ad valorem taxes because they are based on the value of the property.
2. Property taxes may be assessed on real property and/or personal property.
     a. different tax rates and assessment methods apply to the two classes.
     b. most states limit personal property taxes to tangible property.

IV. TAX PLANNING CONSIDERATIONS include:

   A. Redirection of Corporate Activities within various states

   B. Selecting the Optimal State in Which to Operate
1. Disconnect activities from undesirable states.
2. Create nexus in a desirable state.

TEST FOR SELF-EVALUATION

True or False

T F 1. Total allocable income is included when a state's apportionment percentage is applied.

T F 2. Corporations cannot be subject to tax on more than 100% of their income.

T F 3. States uniformly define business income.

T F 4. Double weighting the sales factor in a state apportionment formula favors corporations domiciled within the state.

T F 5. An employee's salary is always apportioned to his state of residence.

T F 6. A unitary business cannot be an independent division.

T F 7. Generally, if a greater weight is assigned to the sales factor of an apportionment formula, a greater tax burden is imposed on out-of-state taxpayers.

T F 8. States are prohibited from imposing an income tax on U.S. government obligations.

T F 9. States generally accept an organization's classifications of income as active or passive to be business or nonbusiness income respectively.

T F 10. Sales made to a retailer by a manufacturer are exempt from sales tax.

Fill-in-the-Blanks

1. _____ describes the degree of business activity that must be present before a tax can be imposed on the corporation's income.

2. Apportionment formulas are generally based on three factors: _____, _____, and _____.

3. Under the _____, sales are assumed to take place at point of delivery.

4. To simplify the filing of tax returns, approximately 40 states _____ onto the Federal income tax base.

5. _____ divide a corporation's business income among states.

6. _____ directly assigns specific income components to a certain state.

Multiple Choice

Use the following data to answer questions 1-3:

Zack Corporation owns and operates two manufacturing facilities, one in State I and one in State W. Zack had $400,000 of taxable income this year from its manufacturing activities. Zack Corporation had no other income.

	I	W
Sales	$750,000	$500,000
Property	500,000	400,000
Payroll	225,000	150,000

____ 1. Assuming both states use an equally weighted three factor apportionment formula, what is Zack's taxable income in State W?

a. $160,000
b. $165,926
c. $234,075
d. $240,000

____ 2. Assuming State W uses a double weighted sales factor in its three factor apportionment formula, what would Zack's taxable income be in State W?

a. $165,926
b. $160,000
c. $164,444
d. $139,259

____ 3. Assume I uses a single-factor sales only formula and W uses an equally weighted three factor formula, what will Zack's total taxable income be?

a. $400,000
b. $405,926
c. $474,075
d. $440,000

____ 4. Generally, sales are allocated to the state

a. where the shipment originates
b. at point of delivery
c. of ultimate destination

_____ 5. Under UDITPA, compensation is treated as paid in the state if:

   a. service is performed entirely within the state
   b. the base of operations is within the state
   c. neither of the above
   d. both of the above

_____ 6. A furniture store purchased 20 desks for $500 each. One desk was taken from the inventory and used by the storekeeper. Assuming a 5% use tax rate, how much tax does the store owe?

   a. $0
   b. $4
   c. $25
   d. $50

Zinc, a multistate S corporation, apportioned its $500,000 of ordinary income 40% to state A and 60% to state B. Zinc is owned equally by Larry and Mike. Larry resides in State A; Mike resides in state B.

_____ 7. On their resident income tax returns, Larry and Mike will each report income of:

   a. $500,000
   b. $300,000
   c. $250,000
   d. $200,000

_____ 8. On his state B return, Larry will report income of:

   a. $250,000
   b. $150,000
   c. $125,000
   d. $100,000

_____ 9. On Mike's state A return, he will report income of:

   a. $250,000
   b. $150,000
   c. $125,000
   d. $100,000

Wren Corporation owns property in States A and B. A values property at its historical cost, B values property at its net book value, both use the average value of assets.

	January 1, 1990		December 31, 1990	
	State A	State B	State A	State B
Inventories	$125,000	$100,000	$150,000	$175,000
Buildings & Machinery	225,000	400,000	225,000	400,000
Accumulated Depreciation	(75,000)	(50,000)	(100,000)	(100,000)
Land	25,000	50,000	25,000	50,000
Totals	$300,000	$500,000	$300,000	$525,000

_____ 10. Compute the property factor for State A.

_____ 11. Compute the property factor for State B.

_____ 12. What is the aggregate of Wren's property factors?

    a. 100%
    b. 98%
    c. 102%

SOLUTIONS

True or False

1. F (p. 15-11)
2. F (p. 15-12)
3. F (p. 15-13)
4. T (p. 15-15)
5. F (p. 15-22)
6. T (p. 15-28)
7. T (p. 15-16)
8. T (p. 15-6)
9. F (p. 15-14)
10. T (p. 15-33)

Fill-in-the-Blanks

1. Nexus (p. 15-9)
2. property, payroll, sales (p. 15-15)
3. ultimate destination concept (p. 15-19)
4. piggyback (p. 15-6)
5. apportionment formulas (p. 15-11)
6. allocation (p. 15-11)

Multiple Choice

1. b ((500,000/1,250,000) + (400,000/900,000) + (150,000/375,000) /3) times 400,000
2. c ((500,000/1,250,000)2 + (400,000/900,000) + (150,000/375,000) /4) times 400,000
3. b (750,000/1,250,000(400,000) + 165,926)
4. c (p. 15-19)
5. a (p. 15-22)
6. c ($500 x 5%)
7. c ($500,000 x 50%)
8. b ($500,000 x 60% x 50%)
9. d ($500,000 x 40% x 50%)
10.   39.7436% (Example 19)
11.   63.0769% (Example 19)
12. c (p. 15-24, 25; Example 19)

CHAPTER 16

TAX ADMINISTRATION AND PRACTICE

LEARNING OBJECTIVES

After completing Chapter 16, you should be able to:

1. Describe the organization and structure of the IRS.

2. Identify the various administrative pronouncements issued by the IRS and explain how they can be used in tax practice.

3. Describe the audit process, including how returns are selected for audit and the various types of audits.

4. Explain the taxpayer appeal process, including various settlement options available.

5. Determine the amount of interest on a deficiency or a refund and when it is due.

6. Discuss the various penalties that can be imposed on acts of noncompliance by taxpayers and return preparers.

7. Understand the rules governing the statute of limitations on assessments and on refunds.

8. Summarize the legal and ethical guidelines that apply to those engaged in tax practice.

KEY TERMS

Accuracy-related penalty	Negligence	Statute of limitations
Closing agreement	Ninety-day letter	Substantial authority
Determination letter	Offer in compromise	Technical advice
Enrolled agent (EA)	Reasonable cause	memorandum
Fraud	Revenue Agent's	Thirty-day letter
Letter ruling	Report (RAR)	

OUTLINE

I. TAX ADMINISTRATION

   A. IRS responsibilities include:
      1. providing adequate information,
      2. identifying delinquent tax payments,
      3. carrying out assessment and collection procedures.

   B. IRS Procedures - Letter Rulings
      1. Letter Rulings, issued by the National Office, are written statements of the IRS' current position on the tax consequences of a course of action contemplated by a taxpayer.
      2. Rulings are issued only on uncompleted, actual transactions or transactions which have been completed prior to filing the tax return for the year in question.
      3. Rulings are not issued:
         a. in hypothetical situations
         b. in cases involving a question of fact
      4. Rulings may be revoked if substantial discrepancies are found between the facts in the ruling request and the actual situation.
      5. A Ruling may be relied on only by the taxpayer who requested and received it.
      6. Rulings must be attached to the tax return for the year in question.

   C. IRS Procedures - Other Issuances
      1. Determination Letters are issued by the District Director and cover completed transactions when the issue involved is covered by judicial or statutory authority, Regulations or rulings.
      2. A Technical Advice Memorandum is issued by the National Office to the District Director and/or Regional Commissioner in response to a specific request from either an agent, an Appellate Conferee or a District Director. Technical advice requests arise from the audit process.

   D. Administrative Powers of the IRS
      1. The Code empowers the IRS to:
         a. Examine the books and records of the taxpayer.
         b. Assess a deficiency and demand a payment for the tax.
      2. The files, work papers and other material of a tax practitioner are subject to subpoena.

E. The Audit Process
1. Selection of returns for audit
   a. A computer-assisted procedure, through the use of mathematical formulas, attempts to select returns likely to contain errors.
   b. Certain groups, self-employed individuals and cash businesses, are subject to audit more frequently than other taxpayers.
   c. If corresponding informational returns are not in substantial agreement with the taxpayer's return, the return may be audited.
   d. Itemized deductions in excess of norms may trigger an audit.
   e. Certain returns are selected on a random sampling basis.
2. An initial review corrects math errors or failures to comply with deduction limitations. These matters are usually settled through correspondence without a formal audit.
3. Office audits usually require substantiation of a particular item on an individual's return having few or no items of business income.
4. Field audits generally entail a more complete examination of a taxpayer's transactions. Field audits usually deal with corporate returns and individuals engaged in business or professional activities.
5. Taxpayer Rights
   a. Prior to or at the initial interview, the IRS must provide an explanation of the audit process and describe the taxpayer's rights under that process.
   b. Upon advance request, the IRS must allow an audio recording of any in-person interview.
6. Settlement with the revenue agent
   a. The IRS agent may accept the return as filed or recommend certain adjustments following an audit.
   b. Usually, questions of fact can be resolved at the agent level. Agents must adhere strictly to published IRS policy.
   c. If agreement is reached, Form 870, Waiver of Restrictions on Assessment and Collection of Deficiency in Tax, is signed by the taxpayer. Form 870 generally closes the case; however, the IRS may assess additional deficiencies if deemed necessary.

F. The Taxpayer Appeal Process
1. If agreement cannot be reached at the agent level, the taxpayer receives a copy of the Revenue Agent's Report and a letter which grants the taxpayer 30 days to request an administrative appeal.
2. If an appeal is not requested, a statutory notice of deficiency, 90 day letter, will be issued.
3. A request for appeal must be made to the Appeals Division and must be accompanied by a written protest unless:
   a. the proposed tax deficiency does not exceed $10,000 or
   b. the deficiency resulted from a correspondence or office audit.

4. The Appeals Division of the IRS has authority to settle all tax disputes based on the hazards of litigation: the probability of winning a court case.
5. If agreement is reached, Form 870AD is signed by the taxpayer. This agreement is usually binding upon both parties.
6. If agreement is not reached, the IRS issues a statutory notice of deficiency which gives the taxpayer 90 days to file a petition with the Tax Court or to pay the tax and file a claim for refund.

G. Offers in Compromise and Closing Agreements
1. Offers in Compromise are generally used only in extreme cases where the taxpayer's ability to pay the total amount of tax is doubtful.
2. Closing Agreements are used in situations when disputed issues involve future years. A closing agreement is generally binding on both parties.

H. Interest
1. Interest accrues on tax underpayments and overpayments.
2. Interest usually accrues from the unextended due date of the return until 30 days after the taxpayer agrees to the deficiency by signing Form 870.
3. Quarterly adjustments to the interest rates are based on the average market yield of outstanding U.S. marketable obligations maturing in 3 years or less.
   a. underpayments are subject to this short term rate plus 3%,
   b. overpayments earn 1% less,
      1. if an overpayment is refunded within 45 days no interest is allowed
      2. when a return is filed after the due date, interest accrues from the date of filing.
   c. both are compounded daily.

I. Taxpayer Penalties
1. Penalties are additions to tax liability and are not tax-deductible.
2. "Ad valorem" penalties are
   a. based on a percentage of the tax owed,
   b. subject to the same deficiency procedures that apply to the underlying tax.
3. "Assessable" penalties are typically a flat dollar amount.
4. Failure to file penalty is 5% per month up to 25% of the tax liability, a minimum penalty of $100 may be imposed.
5. Failure to pay penalty is 0.5% per month up to 25% of the tax liability.
6. If both the failure to file and the failure to pay penalties apply in any month, the failure to file penalty is reduced by the failure to pay penalty amount.

7. "Accuracy-related" penalties are applied when the taxpayer fails to show reasonable cause for the underpayment or a good faith effort to comply with the tax law. The penalty is 20% of the underpayment for:
   a. negligence or disregard of rules or regulations
   b. substantial understatement of tax liability
8. Negligence includes any failure to make a reasonable attempt to comply with tax law.
   a. substantial valuation overstatement
   b. substantial valuation understatement
9. Fraud is when the taxpayer had a specific intent to evade a tax
   a. civil fraud must be proved by a preponderance of evidence,
   b. criminal fraud must be proved beyond the shadow of a reasonable doubt,
   c. any underpayment resulting from fraud, 75% of the tax liability.

J. Statute of Limitations
1. Generally, any tax imposed must be assessed within three years of the filing of the return. Exceptions to the above rule are:
   a. If no return was filed, or if a fraudulent return was filed, an assessment may be made at any time.
   b. The statute is increased to six years if the taxpayer omits from gross income an amount in excess of 25% of the gross income as stated on the return.
   c. The statute may be extended by mutual consent of the District Director and the taxpayer.
2. If after the IRS issues a statutory notice of deficiency, the taxpayer, within the allotted time, files a Tax Court petition, the statute of limitations is suspended on both the assessment and period of collection until 60 days after the court's final decision.
3. A taxpayer who wishes to file a tax refund claim must file the appropriate form within three years of the filing of the original tax return, or within two years following the payment of the tax, whichever is later. Individuals use Form 1040X, and corporations use Form 1120X.

II. TAX PRACTICE

A. While anyone can prepare a tax return or give tax advice, practice before the IRS is usually limited to CPA's, attorneys, and IRS enrollees who have passed an IRS-administered examination.

B. Rules governing tax practice require the tax preparer:
1. To make known to a client any error or omission on any return or document submitted to the IRS.
2. To submit records or information lawfully requested by the IRS.
3. To exercise due diligence as to accurately preparing and filing returns.

C. Tax preparers are also subject to restrictions:
1. Against unreasonably delaying prompt disposition of any matter before the IRS.
2. Against charging clients "an unconscionable fee".
3. Against representing clients with conflicting interests.

D. Preparer penalties include:
1. A $250 penalty for the understatement of tax liability due to unrealistic positions.
2. A $1,000 penalty for willful and reckless conduct.
3. A $1,000 ($10,000 for corporations) penalty per return or document is imposed against those who aid in the preparation of returns or other documents which they know will result in understatement of tax liability.
4. A $50 fine is assessed for each of the following:
   a. failure to sign the return
   b. failure to furnish preparer's identifying number
   c. failure to furnish the taxpayer with a copy of the return
5. A $500 penalty may be assessed if a preparer endorses a check for a tax refund which is issued to the taxpayer.

E. The AICPA Tax Committee has issued statements to guide CPAs in resolving ethical questions related to tax practice. Some of these statements are summarized below.
1. Positions Contrary to IRS Interpretations: The CPA must believe the position has a realistic possibility of being accepted if challenged and must advise the client of the risks and penalties if the position is not accepted.
2. Questions on Returns: Reasonable efforts should be made to provide answers to all questions on a tax return.
3. Procedural Aspects of Preparing Returns: The CPA must inform the client of any applicable expenditure verification rules and must make reasonable inquiries if client representations appear to be incorrect, incomplete or inconsistent.
4. Estimates: Estimates may be used in preparing a tax return if reasonable and indicated as such if it is impracticable to obtain exact data.
5. Recognition of Administrative Proceeding: A CPA is not bound by proceedings involving a prior year but is to use his/her own judgment depending on the facts and circumstances of the particular situation.

6. Knowledge of Error: The CPA should promptly advise the client and recommend corrective measures of any errors or omissions on returns.
7. Advice to Clients: The CPA must use judgment in advising clients. His advice should be professionally competent and appropriate for the particular client.

F. These statements are representative of standards followed by members of the profession. Deviations from these statements could indicate that a lack of due care was exercised.

TEST FOR SELF-EVALUATION

True or False

T F 1. Trusts, receiverships guardianships or estates may be represe4nted before any office of the Internal Revenue Service by their trustees, receivers, guardians administrators or executors. (IRS 97 4A-5)

T F 2. A check drawn on the United States Treasury for a refund of Internal Revenue Service taxes, penalties or interest CANNOT be mailed to the recognized representative of the taxpayer even if there is a valid power of attorney containing specific authorization. (IRS 97 4A-10)

T F 3. Doyle, an enrolled agent, knows that his client has not complied with the revenue laws of the United States. Doyle has the responsibility to advise his client promptly of such noncompliance. (IRS 97 4A-18)

T F 4. A taxpayer, during an interview conducted by the preparer, stated that he paid $6,500 in doctor bills and $5,000 in deductible travel and entertainment expenses during the tax year, when in fact he had paid smaller amounts. On the basis of this information, the preparer properly calculated the deductions for medical expenses and for travel and entertainment expenses which resulted in an understatement of tax liability. The preparer had NO reason to believe that the medical expenses and the travel and entertainment expense information was incorrect or incomplete. The preparer did NOT ask for underlying documentation of the medical expenses but inquired about the existence of travel and entertainment expense records. The preparer was reasonable satisfied by the taxpayer's representations that the taxpayer had adequate records (or other corroborative evidence) for the deduction of $5,000 for travel and entertainment expenses. The preparer is NOT subject to a penalty under section 6694. (IRS 97 4A-25)

T F 5. A revenue ruling holds that certain expenses incurred in the purchase of a business must be capitalized. The Code is silent as to whether these expenses must be capitalized or may be deducted currently, but several cases from different courts hold that these particular expenses may be deducted currently. There is NO other authority. Under these circumstances, a return preparer taking a position contrary to the revenue ruling would NOT be subject to the penalty for understatement due to willful or reckless conduct(IRC 6694(b)) (IRS 97 4A-26)

T F 6. If the proposed increase or decrease in tax resulting from an IRS examination, conducted at the taxpayer's place of business, exceeds $2,500, but not more than $10,000, the taxpayer or the taxpayer's representative who wishes to appeal, must provide a brief written statement explaining the disputed issues. (IRS 97 4A-31)

T F 7. The trust fund recovery penalty may be imposed against any person who is responsible for collecting or paying withheld income and employment taxes AND who willfully fails to collect OR pay them. (IRS 96 4A-32)

T F 8. A taxpayer can only submit an Offer in Compromise if it is submitted based on doubt as to the liability owed and doubt as to the ability of the taxpayer to fully pay the amount owed. (IRS 96 4A-33)

T F 9. Audrey's 1993 income tax return is under examination by the Internal Revenue Service. She agrees with several proposed changes by the examiner. Audrey thinks that she will owe additional tax of $3,000 and deposits a cash bond in that amount with the IRS. This deposit will stop the further accrual of interest on BOTH the tax and on the interest accrued to that point. (IRS 96 4A-12)

T F 10. If you are filing a claim for credit or refund based on contested income tax issues considered in previously examined returns and do NOT want to appeal within the IRS, you should request in writing that the claim be immediately rejected.
(IRS 96 4A-10)

Fill in the Blanks

1. When agreement cannot be reached between the taxpayer and the Appeals Division, the IRS issues a _____.

2. The _____ defines the period of time during which one party may pursue legal action against another party.

3. The position of Commissioner of the Internal Revenue Service is an _____ position.

4. In addition to issuing Letter Rulings and Revenue Rulings, the IRS also issues _____, and _____.

5. The Tax Committee of the AICPA has issued "_____," the purpose of which is to guide the conduct of CPA's in tax practice.

6. "_____ of _____" is a term used to describe the possibility of winning or losing a tax issue if the case goes to court.

7. An _____ in _____ gives the IRS the authority to negotiate a compromise settlement if there is doubt as to the amount or ability to collect a tax liability.

8. _____ are additions to the tax liability and are not deductible as itemized or business expense items.

9. The statement which is filed with the IRS District Office following an audit which recommends acceptance of adjustment of the tax return is known as the _____.

Multiple Choice

_____ 1. Which of the following is NOT practice before the Internal Revenue Service?
(IRS 97 4B-41)

    a. Preparing the tax return, furnishing information at the request of the IRS, or appearing as a witness for a taxpayer.
    b. Communicating with the IRS for a taxpayer regarding the taxpayer's rights, privileges, or liabilities under laws and regulations administered by the IRS.
    c. Preparing and filing necessary documents with the IRS for the taxpayer whose tax returns were prepared by a different practitioner.
    d. Representing a taxpayer at conferences, hearings, or meetings with the IRS.

_____ 2. All of the following can practice before the Internal Revenue Service except:
(IRS 97 4B-43)

    a. An individual family member representing members of his or her immediate family.
    b. An individual convicted of any offense involving dishonesty or lack of trust.
    c. A regular full-time employee representing his or her employer.
    d. A bona fide officer of a corporation, association or organized group representing the corporation, association or group.

_____ 3. Late payments by a taxpayer on an installment agreement to pay a tax liability will:
(IRS 97 4B-48)

    a. Necessitate payment by certified check.
    b. Extend the statute of limitations.
    c. Generate a Notice of Intent to Levy.
    d. Generate a 30-day notice as to the cessation of the agreement.

_____ 4. Which of the following statements with respect to taxpayers' offers in compromise on unpaid tax liabilities is correct? (IRS 97 4B-55)

    a. A taxpayer does NOT have the right to submit an offer in compromise on his/her tax bill but is given the opportunity in order to increase voluntary compliance with the tax law.
    b. Doubt as to the liability for the amount owed must be supported by evidence and the amount acceptable under the offer in compromise will depend on the degree of doubt found in the particular case.

c. Submission of an offer in compromise automatically suspends the collection of an account.
d. If the offer in compromise is made on the grounds that there is doubt as to the taxpayer's ability to make full payment on the amount owed, the amount offered must give sufficient consideration ONLY to the taxpayer's present earning capacity.

_____ 5. With regard to an installment agreement with the IRS to pay a federal tax debt, all of the following statements are correct except: (IRS 97 4B-56)

a. Once an installment payment plan has been approved, the IRS will NOT continue to charge the taxpayer's account with interest on the taxpayer's unpaid balance of penalties and interest.
b. Installment payments may be paid by electronic transfers from the taxpayers' bank account.
c. While the taxpayer is making installment payments, the IRS may require the taxpayer to provide financial information on his/her financial condition to determine any change in his/her ability to pay.
d. The IRS may file a Notice of Federal Tax Lien to secure the government's interest until the taxpayer makes the final payment.

_____ 6. Which of the following situations describes a disclosure of tax return information by a tax return preparer which would subject the preparer to a penalty? (IRS 97 4B-63)

a. Grandfather's tax information is made available to his grand-daughter to inform her she will be claimed as a dependent on the grandfather's return.
b. Employee of the tax return preparer makes corporate return information available to shareholders.
c. After a client files for bankruptcy, the tax return preparer provides a copy of the last return filed to the court-appointed fiduciary without written permission.
d. None of the above.

_____ 7. In which of the following situations may the tax return preparer disclose the tax return information requested WITHOUT first obtaining consent of the taxpayer/client? (IRS 97 4B-64)

a. The preparer receives a state grand jury subpoena requesting copies of federal and state income tax returns.
b. An IRS agent, in his or her official capacity, makes a visit to the preparer and requests copies of state and federal income tax returns, related returns, schedules and records of the taxpayer used in the preparation of the tax returns.

c. A partner in a partnership, who was not involved with the return preparation or partnership records, requests a copy of the partnership return including the schedule K-1S for ALL partners.
d. All of the above.

_____ 8. Mr. Congenial's 1994 income tax return was examined by the IRS and he agreed with the proposed changes. He has several ways by which he may setttle his account and pay any additional tax that is due. All of the following statements with respect to this situation are correct except: (IRS 97 4B-65)

a. If he pays when he signs the agreement, the interest is generally figured from the due date of the return to the date of his payment.
b. If he does NOT pay the additional tax when he signs the agreement, he will receive a bill. The interest on the additional tax is generally figured from the due date of the return to the billing date.
c. If the bill is delayed, he will NOT be billed for additional interest for more than 60 days from the date he signed the agreement.
d. If he pays the amount due within 10 days of the billing date, he will NOT have to pay more interest or penalties.

_____ 9. Which of the following persons would be subject to the penalty for improperly negotiating a taxpayer's refund check? (IRS 97 4B-73)

a. An income tax return preparer who operates a check-cashing agency that cashes, endorses, or negotiates income tax refund checks for returns he prepared.
b. An income tax return preparer who operates a check-cashing business and cashes checks for his clients as part of a second business.
c. The firm which prepared the tax return and is authorized by the taxpayer to receive an income tax refund, but NOT to endorse or negotiate the check.
d. A business manager who prepares income tax returns for clients who maintain special checking accounts against which the business manager is authorized to sign certain checks on their behalf. The clients' federal income tax refunds are mailed to the business manager, who has the clients endorse the checks and deposits them in the special accounts.

SOLUTIONS

True or False

1. T (p. 16-24)
2. F
3. T (p. 16-25)
4. T (p. 16-25, 28)
5. T (p. 16-26)
6. T (p. 16-11; field audit)
7. T (p. 16-21)
8. F (p. 16-13)
9. F (p. 16-14; interest stops only on amount remitted)
10. T (p. 16-12; Figure 16-3)

Fill in the Blanks

1. 90 day letter: statutory notice of deficiency (p. 16-11)
2. statute of limitations (p. 16-22)
3. appointed (p. 16-5)
4. Determination Letters, and technical advices (p. 16-6)
5. "Statements on Responsibilities in Tax Practice" (p. 16-26)
6. "Hazards; litigation" (p. 16-11)
7. offer; compromise (p. 16-13)
8. Penalties (p. 16-15)
9. Revenue Agent's report (p. 16-10)

Multiple Choice

1. a (p. 16-24)
2. b (p. 16-24)
3. d
4. b (p. 16-13)
5. a
6. d (p. 16-25; not third parties)
7. d (p. 16-25)
8. c
9. a (p. 16-26)

CHAPTER 17

THE FEDERAL GIFT AND ESTATE TAXES

LEARNING OBJECTIVES

After completing Chapter 17, you should be able to:

1. Understand the nature of the Federal gift and estate taxes.

2. Work with the Federal gift tax formula.

3. Work with the Federal estate tax formula.

4. Explain the operation of the Federal gift tax.

5. Illustrate the computation of the Federal gift tax.

6. Review the components of the gross estate.

7. Describe the components of the taxable estate.

8. Determine the Federal estate tax liability.

9. Appreciate the role of the generation skipping transfer tax.

KEY TERMS

Alternate valuation date
Annual exclusion
Disclaimers
Exemption equivalent
Future interest
Gross estate
Inheritance tax
Joint tenants
Marital deduction
Power of appointment
Probate estate
Qualified family-owned business interest
Qualified terminable interest property
Taxable estate
Taxable gift
Tenants by the entirety
Tenants in common
Terminable interests
Unified tax credit
Unified transfer tax

OUTLINE

I. TRANSFER TAXES

    A. Nature of the Taxes
        1. Transfer taxes are based on the value of the property transferred, not the income derived from the property.
        2. The Unified Transfer Tax covers all gratuitous transfers.
            a. the gift tax is a tax on transfers during the donor's lifetime.
            b. the estate tax is a tax on transfers at or after death.
        3. Persons subject to the tax
            a. Federal gift tax
                1. applies to all transfers of property by individuals who, at the time of the gift, were citizens or residents of the U.S.
                2. applies to gifts of property located in the U.S. for individuals who were neither citizens or residents.
            b. Federal estate tax
                1. applies to the entire estate of decedents who, at the time of death, were U.S. citizens or residents.
                2. applies to property located in the U.S. for decedents who were neither citizens or residents.
            c. for nonresidents and/or non-citizens, application of these taxes may be different under treaties between the U.S. and various foreign countries.
        4. Formulas
            a. the gift tax
                  current year taxable gifts
              + prior years taxable gifts
              = total taxable gifts
                  tax on total taxable gifts
              - tax paid or deemed paid on prior taxable gifts
              - the unified tax credit
              = tax on current year gifts
            b. the estate tax
                  gross estate
              - deductions allowed
              = taxable estate
              + post-1976 taxable gifts
              = tax base
                  tentative tax on total transfers
              - tax paid or deemed paid on prior taxable gifts
              - tax credits
              = estate tax

B. Valuation for Estate and Gift Tax Purposes
1. The fair market value of property on the date of transfer is generally the amount subject to the gift or estate tax.
2. An estate may elect the alternate valuation date if:
   a. the estate is required to file an Estate Tax Return, and
   b. the election would decrease both the value of the gross estate and the estate tax liability.
3. The alternate valuation date values all property six months after the date of death or on their date of disposition, the earlier.

C. Key Property Concepts
1. Undivided ownership
   a. joint tenants and tenants by the entirety have rights of survivorship.
   b. tenants in common or community property interests pass to the estate or heirs.
2. Partial interests are interests in assets divided as to rights to the income or principal.

II. THE FEDERAL GIFT TAX

A. General Considerations
1. Under state law, for a gift to be complete, the following conditions must be present:
   a. A donor competent to make the gift,
   b. A donee capable of receiving and possessing the gifted property,
   c. Donative intent on behalf of the donor,
   d. Actual or constructive delivery of the property to the donee or donee's representative,
   e. Acceptance of the gift by the donee.
2. Certain excluded transfers
   a. transfers to political organizations
   b. payments made on another's behalf for
      1. tuition payments made to an educational organization
      2. medical care

B. Transfers Subject to the Gift Tax
1. Gift loans
   a. A gift loan is any below-market loan where the foregoing of interest is in the nature of a gift.
   b. The gift is determined as the difference between interest charged and the market rate.
   c. Special limitations apply if the gift loan does not exceed $100,000, unless tax avoidance is a principal purpose of the loan. In such a case,

1. the interest element may not exceed the borrower's net investment income,
2. when net investment income is under $1,000, the interest element is disregarded.
2. Generally, the settlement of certain marital rights are subject to the Federal gift tax. An exception to the general rule is if, in settlement of their marital or property rights,
   a. a written agreement between spouses is executed.
   b. a final divorce is obtained within the three-year period beginning on the date one year before such agreement is entered into.

C. Disclaimers
1. A disclaimer is a refusal by a person to accept property that is designated to pass to him or her.
2. The effect of the disclaimer would be to pass the property to someone else, thereby avoiding the payment of a transfer tax.
3. Care should be taken to satisfy the requirements of Section 2518 to avoid the application of a gift tax.

D. Annual Exclusion
1. A donor may deduct the first $10,000 of gifts to each donee.
2. The gifts must be of a present interest, and may be doubled through gift splitting with one's spouse.
3. For gifts in trust the annual exclusion applies to each beneficiary of the trust as a separate individual.

E. An exception to the future interest rule concerns gifts to minors. Provided the following conditions are met, the gift will be considered a gift of a present interest:
1. both the property and the income from the property may be expended by or for the benefit of the minor donee before he or she attains the age of 21;
2. if the property is not expended, it will pass to the minor at his or her attainment of age 21;
3. if the donee dies before reaching the age of 21, the property will pass to his or her estate, or as he or she may appoint under a general power of appointment.

F. Procedural Matters.
1. Form 709 must be filed whenever the gifts for one calendar year exceed the annual exclusion, $10,000, or involve a gift of a future interest.
2. The due date is April 15 of the following year.
3. To elect gift splitting between spouses, Forms 709 must be filed.

III. THE FEDERAL ESTATE TAX

  A. The Gross Estate
     1. The gross estate is composed of the value of all property in which the decedent has an interest at his death.
     2. Adjustments for gifts made within three years of death, include
        a. any gift tax paid on gifts made within 3 years of death
        b. any incomplete transfers, property interests transferred by gift within the 3 years, and, in which the donor retained some rights:
           1. retained life estate
           2. revocable transfers
           3. proceeds of life insurance
     3. Survivorship annuities are included in the gross estate if any portion of the annuity is receivable after the decedent's death.
     4. Certain property held in joint tenancy will be included in the decedent's estate unless it can be proved that the surviving co-owners contributed to the cost of the property.
        a. funds received as a gift from the deceased co-owner and applied to the cost cannot be counted as funds provided by a surviving co-owner.
        b. for married persons, one-half of the value of the property is included in the estate of the spouse who dies first.
     5. In joint ownership cases having equal ownership and disproportionate consideration, generally, gift treatment results.
        a. for a joint bank account, a gift occurs when the noncontributing party withdraws funds provided by the other joint tenant.
        b. for U.S. savings bonds, a gift occurs when the noncontributing party uses some or all of the proceeds for himself.
     6. Property over which the decedent possessed a general power of appointment is included in the gross estate.
     7. Life insurance proceeds on the decedent's life are included if:
        a. receivable by the estate
        b. receivable for the benefit of the estate
        c. the decedent possessed an incident of ownership

  B. Taxable Estate
     1. Deductions are allowed for certain expenses, indebtedness, and taxes.
        a. funeral expenses
        b. administrative expense
           1. commissions
           2. attorney fees
           3. accountant fees
           4. court costs
           5. selling expenses for asset dispositions
        c. unpaid mortgages

d. claims against the estate, enforceable personal obligations of the decedent at the time of death
e. casualty or theft losses incurred while administering the estate
2. Deductions are allowed for charitable bequests to:
a. the United States or any of its political subdivisions
b. any corporation or association orgainzed and operated exclusively for religious, charitable, scientific, literary, or educational purposes.
c. various veterans' organizations.
3. Deductions for transfers to the surviving spouse include any interest received as:
a. the decedent's heir or donee
b. the decedent's surviving tenant by the entirety or joint tenant
c. the appointee under the decedent's exercise, lapse or release of a general power of appointment
d. the beneficiary of insurance on the life of the decedent.
4. Deductions for qualified family-owned business interests are available after 1997.
a. this deduction is intended to keep the business intact to benefit the deceased owner's family.
b. this deduction applies when
1. at date of death, the decedent was a citizen or resident of the U.S.
2. the value of the business interest exceeds 50% of the adjusted gross estate.
3. the decedent or a family member owned and materially participated in the business for at least 5 of the 8 years prior to death.
4. a qualified heir must materially participate in the business for at least 5 years in an 8 year period during the 10 years following the decedent's death.
c. tax savings are recaptured when,
1. the qualified heir ceases to materially participate.
2. the business is disposed of to outsiders.
3. the business is moved outside of the U.S. or the qualified heir losses his/her citizenship.
d. the deduction is elective and is made by the executor. The election must include an agreement that the qualified heirs will accept liability for recapture tax consequences should they arise.

C. Computing the Federal Estate Tax
1. Determine the taxable estate
2. Add back post-1976 taxable gifts
3. Compute the tentative tax
4. Subtract available estate tax credits

D. Estate Tax Credits
1. Unified tax credit
2. Credit for state death taxes
3. Credit for tax on prior transfers
4. Credit for foreign death taxes

E. Procedural Matters
1. Filing requirements parallel the exemption equivalent amounts.
2. Form 706, if required, is due nine months after the date of death.
3. An extension of time for filing may be requested.

IV. THE GENERATION SKIPPING TRANSFER TAX

A. The GSTT is imposed when a younger generation is bypassed in favor of a later generation.

B. Generation skipping transfers are taxed at 55% however, a $1 million exemption is allowed.

TEST FOR SELF-EVALUATION

True or False

T F 1. Mr. Goulart, a U.S. resident alien, died on July 1, 1996. As the executor of the estate, you must file an estate tax return if the value of the estate at the date of death was $150,000 or more. (IRS 97 3A-2)

T F 2. During 1996, Bethany gave $5,000 to her mother; $6,000 to her father; and $3,000 to her aunt. Bethany must file Form 709, United States Gift and Generation Skipping Transfer Tax Return. (IRS 97 3A-7)

T F 3. In January 1996, Jon gave an interest free loan of $10,500 to his son so that he could buy a boat. His son repaid the entire $10,500 in December 1996. In addition, Jon gave other gifts to his son during 1996 totaling $85,000. Jon must include an amount for the forgone interest on the boat loan on his gift tax return for 1996. (IRS 97 3A-8)

T F 4. Mr. Hodges, a U. S. citizen, died on August 1, 1995. As the personal representative of the estate, you must file Form 706, United States Estate (and Generation-Skipping Transfer) Tax Return if the value of the GROSS estate at the date of death was $700,000. (IRS 96 3A-13)

T F 5. The gross estate includes property that was owned by a decedent at the time of death and was transferred at death by a will or intestacy laws. (IRS 96 3A-15)

T F 6. Your taxable gifts are your total gifts reduced by the annual exclusion, the charitable deduction AND the marital deduction. (IRS 96 3A-19)

T F 7. An extension of time to file an INCOME TAX RETURN for any tax year that is a calendar year automatically extends the time for filing the ANNUAL GIFT TAX RETURN for that calendar year UNTIL the due date of the income tax return. (IRS 95 3A-18)

T F 8. Herman, as executor of the estate of his deceased father, must sell his father's house to make distributions to all beneficiaries. Herman pays $9,000 to paint and carpet the house to enhance its marketability. The $9,000 Herman pays is deductible from the gross estate to compute the taxable estate. (IRS 94 3A-13)

T F 9. If the alternate valuation method is elected in valuing the decedent's property, any property NOT disposed of within 6 months after the decedent's death is valued as of 6 months after the date of the decedent's death. (IRS 93 3A-14)

Fill in the Blanks

1. A gift is the transfer of property from one person to another for less than _____ and _____ consideration.

2. The Federal gift tax is _____ in effect.

3. The deductions and exclusions which are allowed in arriving at the taxable gifts are _____, _____, and _____.

4. Gift splitting must be between _____.

5. The _____ comprises all property which is subject to the Federal estate tax.

6. _____ is a right that a husband has in his deceased wife's property.

7. An _____ is "one or more payments extending over a period of time."

8. The three things that can happen to a power of appointment are _____, _____ and _____.

9. Powers of appointment fall into two categories: _____ power of appointment and _____ power of appointment.

10. A _____ power of appointment is one in which the decedent could have appointment himself, his creditors, his estate, or the creditors of his estate.

11. The Federal estate tax is imposed on the decedent's right to _____ at death.

Multiple Choice

_____ 1. Eileen, a U.S. citizen, died on June 28, 1996. The value of her gross estate as of the date of death was determined to be in excess of $1,000,000. Without regard to extensions, what is the due date of Form 706, United States Estate and Generation Skipping Transfer Tax Return? (IRS 97 3B-26)

    a. September 15, 1996
    b. December 31, 1996
    c. March 28, 1997
    d. June 30, 1997

_____ 2. Form 706, United States Estate (and Generation Skipping Transfer) Tax Return, was filed for the estate of Erik Cage in 1996. The gross estate tax was $250,000. All of the following items are credited against the gross estate tax to determine the net estate tax payable, except: (IRS 97 3B-27)

a. Marital deduction.
b. Credit for state and foreign death taxes.
c. Unified Credit.
d. Credit for gift taxes.

_____ 3. Nancy's books and records reflect the following for 1996. Which transaction would require filing Form 709, United States Gift (and Generation Skipping Transfer) Tax Return? (IRS 97 3B-27)

a. Gratuitously transferred a vehicle with a fair market value of $20,000 to her fiancé a month before they were married.
b. Donated $12,000 to a qualified political organization.
c. Paid $20,000 to St. Francis Hospital for her aunt's unreimbursed medical expenses.
d. Paid $11,000 to State University for her brother's tuition and books.

_____ 4. All of the following statements concerning gift-splitting are true except:
(IRS 97 3B-29)

a. To qualify for gift-splitting, a couple must be married at the time the gift is made to a third party.
b. Both spouses must consent to the use of gift-splitting.
c. For gift tax purposes, a husband and wife must file a joint income tax return to qualify for the gift-splitting benefits.
d. The annual gift tax exclusion allows spouses who consent to split their gifts to transfer up to $20,000 to any one person during any calendar year without gift tax liability, if the gift qualifies as a present interest.

_____ 5. Listed below are gifts Joan made during 1996.
Gift to a nonprofit home for the underprivileged	$ 25,000
Gift to her daughter	$ 10,000
Contributions to an historical museum	$ 10,000
Gift to her spouse	$ 40,000

What is the amount of taxable gifts to be reported on Form 709 for 1996?
(IRS 97 3C-50)

a. $0
b. $35,000
c. $45,000
d. $75,000

THE FEDERAL GIFT AND ESTATE TAXES   17-11

_____ 6.   What amount of a decedent's taxable estate is effectively tax-free if the maximum unified estate and gift tax credit is taken, in 1997?   (IRS 96 3B-34)

a. $0
b. $10,000
c. $192,000
d. $600,000

_____ 7.   On June 15, 1995, Marlo made a transfer by gift in an amount sufficient to require the filing of a gift tax return. If Marlo did not request an extension of time for filing the 1995 gift tax return, the due date for filing was   (IRS 96 3B-37)

a. December 31, 1995
b. March 15, 1996
c. April 15, 1996
d. June 15, 1996

_____ 8.   For transfers by gift during 1995, one must file a gift tax return for which of the following?   (IRS 96 3B-38)

a. a transfer of $18,000 to a son for which one's spouse has agreed to gift-splitting.
b. A qualified transfer for educational or medical expenses.
c. A transfer of a present interest in property that is not more than the annual exclusion.
d. A transfer to one's spouse that qualified for the unlimited marital deduction.

_____ 9.   Valerie and Dino, who were married in 1992, made a gift to their son Michael on January 2, 1995. In July 1995, Valerie and Dino were legally divorced. Valerie married Scott on December 20, 1995. Which answer below best describes this situation?   (IRS 96 3B-39)

a. The gift-splitting benefits are available to Valerie and Dino if Valerie consents.
b. The gift-splitting benefits are NOT available to Valerie and Dino because they were divorced in 1995.
c. The gift-splitting benefits are NOT available to Valerie and Dino because Valerie remarried in 1995.
d. The gift-splitting benefits ARE available to Valerie and Dino because they were married at the time the gift was made.

_____ 10. Jason died on October 1, 1995. The alternate valuation method was NOT elected. The assets in his estate were valued as of the date of death as follows:

Home	$300,000
Car	20,000
Stocks, bonds & savings	250,000
Jewelry	50,000
Dividends declared July 1, 1995, not paid as of October 1, 1995	1,000
Accrued interest on savings as of October 1, 1995	6,500

What is the amount of Jason's gross estate? (IRS 96 3C-73)

a. $570,000
b. $620,000
c. $621,000
d. $627,500

_____ 11. Ellie died on June 15, 1995. The assets in her estate were valued on her date of death and alternate valuation date respectively as follows:

Asset	Date of Death Valuation	Alternate Valuation
Home	$250,000	$300,000
Stock	$425,000	$450,000
Bonds	$200,000	$125,000
Patent	$100,000	$ 95,000

The patent had 10 years of its life remaining at the time of Ellie's death. The executor sold the home on August 1, 1995, for $275,000. If Ellie's executor elects the alternate valuation date method, what is the value of Ellie's estate?
(IRS 96 3C-74)

a. $895,000
b. $945,000
c. $950,000
d. $970,000

_____ 12. Chris, who is single and a U.S. citizen, made the following gifts in 1995:

Cash to nephew	$100,000
Cash to sister	$100,000
Property to brother	$200,000
Cash to local university building fund	$100,000

Chris had not made any gifts in prior years. What is the amount of taxable gifts?
(IRS 96 3C-75)

a. $370,000
b. $470,000
c. $480,000
d. $500,000

13. In 1995, Linda gave her daughter a gift of land that had a fair market value of $1,000,000. She made no gifts in years 1987 through 1994. In 1986, she used $121,800 of her unified credit to offset gift tax otherwise due. What amount of unified credit can Linda use to offset gift tax due on the 1995 gift?
(IRS 96 3C-76)

   a. $192,800
   b. $71,000
   c. $10,000
   d. $0

14. During 1995, Wellington made the following gifts:

Cash to son Willis	$40,000
Land to wife Paula	100,000
Painting to niece Marlene	16,000

   Wellington and Paula elect gift-splitting. Paula's only gift in 1995 was a $50,000 cash gift to her mother. What is the amount of the taxable gifts to be reported by Wellington in 1995? (IRS 96 3C-77)

   a. $25,000
   b. $38,000
   c. $156,000
   d. $206,000

15. All of the following provisions with respect to the election of the alternate valuation method for property included in the decedent's gross estate are correct except: (IRS 96 3B-33)

   a. The election must be made on a return filed within one year of the due date, including extensions, for filing the return.
   b. The election may be changed after filing the return by filing an amended return.
   c. The election may be made only if it will DECREASE the value of the gross estate and the sum of the estate tax and the generation skipping transfer tax (reduced by any allowable credits).
   d. The election applies to all of the property in the estate and does NOT preclude you from electing the special-use valuation for qualified real property.

SOLUTIONS

True of False
1. F (p. 17-7; in excess of exemption amount)
2. F (p. 17-13; annual exclusion is $10,000 per donee)
3. T (p. 17-12)
4. T (p. 17-7; value of gross estate exceeds exemption amount)
5. T (p. 17-18)
6. T (p. 17-5)
7. T (p. 17-18; footnote)
8. F (p. 17-28; administrative expense)
9. T (p. 17-8)

Fill in the Blanks
1. full and adequate (p. 17-4)
2. cumulative (p. 17-6)
3. charitable, marital, and annual exclusion (p. 17-5)
4. spouses (p. 17-16)
5. gross estate (p. 17-18)
6. curtesy (p. 17-19)
7. annuity (p. 17-22)
8. exercise, lapse and release (p. 17-26)
9. general; special (p. 17-26)
10. general (p. 17-26)
11. pass property (p. 17-3)

Multiple Choice
1. c (p. 17-40)
2. a (p. 17-37; marital deduction reduces gross estate not estate tax)
3. a (p. 17-11)
4. c (p. 17-16)
5. a (p. 17-5)
6. d (p. 17-7; unified credit exemption equivalent amount)
7. c (p. 17-18; April 15 of the following year)
8. a (p. 17-16; must file to elect gift-splitting)
9. d (p. 17-16; Valerie remarried)
10. d (p. 17-19)
11. c (p. 17-8; the patent is valued at $100,000; 10 years = $10,000 per year, 6 mo. = 5,000)
12. a (p. 17-14; nephew 100,000-10,000; sister 100,000 -10,000; brother 200,000-10,000)
13. b (p. 17-7; 1995 unified credit 192,800 - 121,800)
14. a (p. 17-14; son 20,000-10,000; mother-in-law 25,000-10,000)
15. b (p. 17-9; irrevocable election)

CHAPTER 18

FAMILY TAX PLANNING

LEARNING OBJECTIVES

After completing Chapter 18, you should be able to:

1. Use various established concepts in carrying out the valuation process.

2. Apply the special use valuation method in appropriate situations.

3. Identify problems involved in valuing an interest in a closely held business.

4. Compare the income tax basis rules applying to property received by gift and by death.

5. Plan gifts so as to minimize gift taxes and avoid estate taxes.

6. Make gifts so as to avoid income taxes for the donor.

7. Reduce probate costs in the administration of an estate.

8. Apply procedures that reduce estate tax consequences.

9. Obtain liquidity for an estate.

KEY TERMS

Blockage rule
Buy-sell agreement
Cross-purchase buy-sell agreement
Entity buy-sell agreement
Estate freeze
Living Trust
Probate costs
Special use value
Step-down in basis
Step-up in basis

OUTLINE

I. VALUATION CONCEPTS

    A. Valuation in General
       1. Fair Market Value is "the price at which property would change hands between a willing buyer and a willing seller, neither being under any compulsion to buy or sell and both having reasonable knowledge of relevant facts."
       2. FMV is not determined by a forced sale price.
       3. FMV is not determined by the sale price of the item in a market other than that in which the item is most commonly sold to the public.
       4. FMV is based on what the general public would pay, sentiment should not play a part in the determination.

    B. Valuation of Specific Assets
       1. Stocks and bonds
          a. **traded** on valuation date: mean between highest and lowest quoted **prices** on that date.
          b. recently traded: the inverse weighted-average of the mean between the **highest** and lowest prices quoted on the nearest dates before and after the valuation date.
       2. Notes receivable
          a. unpaid principal plus accrued interest.
          b. a lower value might be established due to:
              1. a low interest rate
              2. distant maturity date
              3. proof of entire or partial worthlessness.
       3. Insurance policies and annuity contracts
          a. for a life insurance policy on the life of a person other than the decedent or an annuity contract issued by a company regularly engaged in selling annuities, the value is the cost of a comparable contract.
          b. for noncommercial annuity contracts, special tables are issued by the IRS.
       4. Life estates, terms for years, reversions and remainders involve using IRS tables.

    C. Real Estate and the Special Use Valuation Method
       1. §2032A permits an executor to elect to value certain classes of real estate at "current" use value.
       2. All of the following conditions must be satisfied.
          a. At least 50% of the adjusted value of the gross estate must consist of real or personal property devoted to the qualifying use.

- b. At least 25% of the adjusted gross estate must consist of the real property devoted to qualifying use (qualifying property is considered at its "most suitable use" value for purposes of these tests).
- c. A qualifying heir of the decedent is the recipient of the qualifying property.
- d. The real property has been owned by the decedent or the decedent's family for five out of the last eight years, and the property was being used for its qualifying purpose during that time.
- e. The decedent or a member of his family has participated materially in the operation of the qualifying purpose during that period of time.
3. The special use valuation method permits a reduction of no more than $750,000.
4. Estate tax savings are recaptured from the heir if the property is sold or withdrawn from its qualifying use within 10 years.

D. Valuation Problems with a Closely Held Business
1. Goodwill may be present if the corporation's past earnings are higher than usual for the industry.
2. A discounted valuation may be justified if a minority interest is involved and the corporation has a poor dividend paying record.
3. The "blockage rule" permits a discount from the amount at which smaller lots are selling for when a controlling interest is held and the per unit value might fall if a large block of shares were marketed at one time.
4. A discount may be in order for lack of marketability of shares not traded in a recognized market.
5. Buy Sell Agreements and Valuation
- a. In an entity agreement, the business buys the interest of the withdrawing owner.
- b. In a cross-purchase agreement, the surviving owners buy out the withdrawing owner.
- c. The purchase price will be included in the deceased owner's estate and will control for valuation purposes if:
  1. the price is the result of a bona fide business agreement.
  2. the agreement is not a device to transfer property to family members.
  3. the agreement is comparable to other arrangements entered into by persons dealing at arm's length.

II. INCOME TAX CONCEPTS

A. Basis of Property Acquired by Gift

1. Depends upon when the gift was made and whether it was sold for a gain or loss:
   a. after 1920 and before 1977
      1. basis for gain is the donor's adjusted basis plus any gift tax paid.
      2. basis for gain cannot be higher than FMV on the date of the gift.
      3. basis for loss is the lower of the basis for gain or the FMV at the date of the gift.
   b. after 1976
      1. basis for gain is the donor's adjusted basis plus the gift tax attributable to any appreciation up to the date of the gift.
      2. basis for loss is the lower of the gain basis or the FMV at the date of the gift.
2. The donee's holding period includes the holding period of the donor.

B. Basis of Property Acquired by Death
   1. Generally property acquired from a decedent is valued at its FMV on the date of death or alternate valuation date and the holding period is automatically long-term.
   2. The surviving spouse's half of community property takes the same basis as the half included in the deceased spouse's gross estate.
   3. Under the §1014(e) exception, the original donor assumes the property with the same basis as existed in the hands of the deceased prior to his or her death. For section 1014(e), the following conditions must be satisfied:
      a. The decedent must have received appreciated property as a gift during the one-year period ending with his or her death.
      b. The property is acquired from the decedent by the donor or the donor's spouse.
   4. Income in respect of a decedent is income which was earned by a decedent prior to his death but not reported on his final tax return due to his method of accounting.
      a. For estate tax purposes income in respect of a decedent is valued at fair market value on the valuation date.
      b. For income tax purposes, the decedent's basis and classification is transferred to the estate or heirs.

III. PLANNING

A. A plan of lifetime giving can minimize transfer taxes and income taxes through use of the annual exclusion by
   1. spacing gifts over several years.
   2. making successive gifts of partial interests to transfer real property.

B. Gifts of property expected to appreciate in value removes the appreciation from the donor's gross estate.

C. Estate planning should consider reducing the probate estate through:
1. holding property in joint ownership with rights of survivorship.
2. naming a life insurance beneficiary other than the estate.
3. using a revocable, living, trust which at death becomes irrevocable.

D. The liquidity of an estate is often strained between the date of death and the final disposition of the estate assets. The following should be considered.

1. life insurance payable to the estate,
2. a carefully drawn will,
3. the judicious use of trust arrangements,
4. qualifying for the extension of time for the payment of death taxes.

TEST FOR SELF-EVALUATION

True or False

T F 1. If a federal estate tax return does NOT have to be filed, an individual's basis in inherited property is the property's adjusted basis to the decedent at the date of death. (IRS 97 1A-7)

T F 2. When a taxpayer dies, no gain is reported on depreciable personal property or real property that is transferred to his or her estate or beneficiary. (IRS 97 3A-3)

T F 3. On February 1, 1995, John Smith, a cash basis taxpayer, sold his machine for $5,000, payable March 1 of the same year. His adjusted basis in the machine was $4,000. Mr. Smith died on February 15, 1995, before receiving payment. The gain to be reported as income in respect of the decedent is the $1,000 difference between the decedent's basis in the property and sales proceeds.
(IRS 96 3A-12)

T F 4. There are provisions that allow additional time for paying the estate tax. The usual extension of time to pay is up to 12 months from the date the payment is due. However, if you can show reasonable cause why it is impractical for you to pay the full amount of the tax due on the due date, the IRS may extend the time for payment up to 10 years. (IRS 96 3A-14)

T F 5. Generally, any income generated by the property after the owner's death must be accounted for separately.

T F 6. Generally, the income tax basis of property acquired from a person who died will be its fair market value on the date of death, or, if elected, on the alternate valuation date.

T F 7. As it is possible to have a "step-up" in basis, it is also possible to have a "step-down" in basis for property received as the result of a death transfer.

T F 8. When income must be included in the income tax computation and gross estate of a decedent, the individual is allowed a credit on his final tax return in order to avoid double taxation.

T F 9. To determine your basis in the property you receive as a gift, it is sometimes necessary to add all or part of the gift tax paid on the property.
(IRS 94 1A-11)

T F 10. The only importance in properly determining the value of property is to correctly compute the possible gift or estate tax.

FAMILY TAX PLANNING 18-7

T F 11. Due to the conservative nature of the IRS, taxpayers are required to use wholesale prices when determining the fair market value of property.

T F 12. Shares in a mutual fund should be valued at the redemption or bid price of the security.

T F 13. The value of property reflected on the estate tax return and subsequently accepted by the IRS is presumed to be correct in any case of future changes to that valuation and must be rebutted by the heir.

T F 14. The special valuation method allows certain classes of real estate to be valued at their "most suitable" use.

T F 15. Buy-sell agreements are useful tools in planning estate liquidity.

Fill in the Blanks

1. The special use valuation procedure permits a reduction in estate tax valuation of no more than $_____.

2. To qualify for the special use valuation method, at least _____% of the adjusted value of the gross estate must consist of real or personal property devoted to the qualifying use.

3. The concept that recognizes that the per unit value of shares may fall when a large number of shares are sold at one time is called the "_____."

4. To meet the requirements of section 6166, a decedent's interest in a farm or closely-held business must be more than _____ of his or her adjusted gross estate.

Multiple Choice

_____ 1. Darryl received several acres of land from his father as a gift. At the time of the gift, the land had a fair market value of $85,000. The father's adjusted basis in the land was $105,000. Two years later, Darryl sold the land for $90,000. No events occurred that increased or decreased Darryl's basis in the land. What was Darryl's gain or (loss) on the sale of the land? (IRS 97 1C-49)

    a. ($15,000)
    b. $5,000
    c. $20,000
    d. $0

_____ 2. Jack received 50 shares of stock as an inheritance on July 15, 1996 from his father who died April 25, 1996. His father's adjusted basis in the stock was $65,000. The stock's fair market value on April 25, 1996, was $75,000. On October 25, 1996, its value was $85,000 and on the date Jack received the stock, it was $70,000. The alternative valuation date was NOT selected for filing a federal estate tax return. Jack's basis in the inherited stock is: (IRS 97 1C-50)
   a. $65,000
   b. $70,000
   c. $75,000
   d. $85,000

_____ 3. Mr. Fitch died on December 1, 1996. The alternate valuation method was NOT elected. The assets in his estate were valued as of the date of death as follows:

Home	$400,000
Car	30,000
Stocks, bonds & savings	350,000
Jewelry	25,000
Dividends, declared November 15, 1996, not paid as of December 1, 1996	5,000
Accrued interest on savings as of December 1, 1996	2,500
Life insurance (proceeds receivable by the estate)	300,000

What is the amount of Mr. Fitch's gross estate? (IRS 97 3C-48)

   a. $1,112,500
   b. $1,110,000
   c. $1,105,000
   d. $812,500

_____ 4. Loretta died on January 20, 1996. The assets included in her estate were valued as follows:

	1-20-96	7-20-96	10-20-96
House	$900,000	$800,000	$ 700,000
Stocks	850,000	600,000	1,000,000

The executor sold the house on October 20, 1996 for $700,000. The alternative valuation date was properly elected. What is the value of Loretta's estate?
(IRS 97 3C-49)

   a. $1,750,000
   b. $1,700,000
   c. $1,400,000
   d. $1,300,000

_____ 5.   Donna received land as a gift from her grandfather. At the time of the gift, the land had a fair market value of $80,000 and an adjusted basis of $100,000 to Donna's grandfather. One year later, Donna sold the land for $105,000. What was her gain or (loss) on this transaction?   (IRS 96 1C-55)

   a. $5,000
   b. $15,000
   c. $20,000
   d.   No gain or loss

_____ 6.   During 1995, Juan received a gift of property from his uncle. At the time of the gift, the property had a fair market value of $100,000 and an adjusted basis to his uncle of $40,000. Juan's uncle paid a gift tax on the transfer of $18,000. What is Juan's basis in the property?   (IRS 96 1C-56)

   a. $40,000
   b. $50,800
   c. $60,000
   d. $128,000

_____ 7.   Mr. Hill inherited 1,000 shares of Pro Corporation stock from his father who died on March 8, 1995. His father paid $10 per share for the stock on September 1, 1975. The fair market value of the stock on the date of death was $50 per share. On September 8, 1995, the fair market value of the stock was $60 per share. Mr. Hill sold the stock for $75 a share on December 5, 1995. The estate qualified for, and the executor elected, the alternate valuation method. A federal estate tax return was filed. What was Mr. Hill's basis in the stock on the date of sale?
        (IRS 96 1C-57)

   a. $50,000
   b. $60,000
   c. $75,000
   d. $150,000

_____ 8.   On June 1, 1995, Kirk received a gift of income-producing real estate having a donor's adjusted basis of $50,000 at the date of the gift. The fair market value of the property at the date of the gift was $40,000. Kirk sold the property for $46,000 on August 1, 1995. How much gain or loss should Kirk report for 1995?
        (IRS 96 1C-67)

   a.   No gain or loss
   b. $4,000 short-term capital loss
   c. $4,000 ordinary loss
   d. $6,000 short-term capital gain

_____ 9. In 1995, Daniel inherited 100% of Candy Corporation's outstanding stock from his mother. The stock had a fair market value of $250,000 at the date of death and was reflected on Candy's balance sheet as:

Cash	$250,000
Capital stock	$150,000
Accumulated earnings & profits	$100,000

Daniel immediately withdrew $50,000 out of Candy Corporation as a dividend distribution. Later in 1995, pursuant to a plan of liquidation, Daniel withdrew the remaining $200,000 out of Candy. For 1995, how much will Daniel be required to report as ordinary dividend income and capital gain or (loss)? (IRS 96 3C-63)

	Ordinary Dividend	*Capital Gain or (Loss)*
a.	$0	$0
b.	$50,000	($50,000)
c.	$100,000	($100,000)
d.	$50,000	($250,000)

_____ 10. Mrs. Butler, a cash method taxpayer, died on July 31, 1995. A review of her records reflected that, as of July 31, 1995, she had received interest of $500 and wages of $80,000. Also, on stock that she owned, an $800 dividend was declared on June 20, 1995, and was payable on July 31, 1995. The dividend check was not received until August 3, 1995. What is the amount of income to be reported on Mrs. Butler's final income tax return? (IRS 96 3C-71)

a. $80,000
b. $80,500
c. $80,800
d. $81,300

SOLUTIONS

True or False

1. F (FMV on date of death)
2. T
3. T
4. T
5. T
6. T
7. T
8. F (transfer tax and income tax)
9. T
10. F (basis for depreciation, later disposition)
11. F (fair market value)
12. T
13. T
14. F (current use)
15. T

Fill in the Blanks

1. $750,000
2. 50%
3. "blockage rule"
4. 25%

Multiple Choice

1. d (gain basis is adjusted basis + gift tax on appreciation; loss basis is lesser of gain basis or FMV)
2. c (FMV on date of death)
3. a (all listed assets are included)
4. c (6 months after death, prior to house sale)
5. a (105,000 -100,000 = 5,000)
6. b (60% of gift tax (appreciation) +donor's adjusted basis)
7. b (1,000 shares @ $60 per share, alternate valuation date, Sept. 8)
8. a (donor's basis = gain basis, loss basis is lesser of FMV, 40,000 or gain basis, 50,000)
9. b ($50,000 dividend is ordinary, basis $250,000 - proceeds 200,000 capital)
10. b (dividend and wages are IRD)

CHAPTER 19

INCOME TAXATION OF TRUSTS AND ESTATES

LEARNING OBJECTIVES

After completing Chapter 19, you should be able to:

1. Use working definitions with respect to trusts, estates, beneficiaries, and other parties.

2. Identify the steps in determining the accounting and taxable income of a trust or estate and the related taxable income of the beneficiaries.

3. Illustrate the uses and implications of distributable net income.

4. Use the special rules that apply to trusts where the creator (grantor) of the trust retains certain rights.

KEY TERMS

Complex trust	Grantor	Reversionary interest
Corpus	Grantor trust	Simple trust
Distributable net income (DNI)	Income in respect of	Sprinkling trust
Expenses in respect of a decedent	a decedent (IRD)	

OUTLINE

I. **DEFINITIONS**

   A. A 'trust' usually refers to: an arrangement created by a will or by an inter vivos declaration through which the trustee takes title to property for the purpose of protecting or conserving it for the beneficiaries.

   B. Typically, three parties are involved in creating a trust:
   1. The grantor - transfers property which becomes the principal or corpus of the trust.
   2. The trustee - manages the trust according to the terms of the trust document and applicable law.
   3. The beneficiary - receives the benefits from the trust,
      a. income interest - receives the accounting income,
      b. remainder interest - receives the trust corpus at termination of the trust entity.
   4. When the same individual is grantor, trustee and sole beneficiary, the trust is not recognized for tax purposes.

   C. Each year trusts must be classified as either simple or complex.
   1. A simple trust:
      a. is required to distribute its entire accounting income each year,
      b. has no qualified charitable organizations as beneficiaries, and
      c. makes no distribution of corpus during the year.
   2. A complex trust is any trust that is not a simple trust.

   D. An estate is created upon the death of every individual to:
   1. collect and conserve the individual's assets,
   2. satisfy his liabilities, and
   3. distribute the remaining assets to his heirs.

II. **NATURE OF TRUST AND ESTATE TAXATION**

   A. Taxable income of an estate or trust is taxed to the entity or its beneficiaries to the extent that each received the accounting income.

   B. Filing Requirements
   1. Form 1041, U.S. Fiduciary Income Tax Return is used by trusts and estates.
   2. An estate must file if it has $600 or more gross income for the year.
   3. A trust must file if it has $600 or more gross income and/or any taxable income.
   4. The return is due on the 15th day of the fourth month after the close of the entity's tax year.

C. Tax Accounting Periods and Payments
1. An estate may select any fiscal year or a calendar year.
2. A trust, other than tax-exempt trusts, must use a calendar year.
3. Trusts and estates having tax years ending 2 or more tax years after the death of the decedent, are required to make quarterly estimated tax payments.

D. Tax Rates and Personal Exemptions
1. Trusts and estates use a compressed tax rate schedule.
2. Tax on net long-term capital gains are taxed at no more than 20%.
3. The alternative minimum tax may apply.
4. Trusts and estates are allowed a personal exemption.
   a. simple trusts, $300
   b. complex trusts, $100
   c. estates, $600

III. TAXABLE INCOME OF TRUSTS AND ESTATES

A. Trust and estate taxable income computation involves 5 steps:
1. Determine the accounting income of the entity.
2. Compute entity taxable income before the distribution deduction.
3. Determine distributable net income, (DNI), and the distribution deduction.
4. Compute entity taxable income.
5. Allocate DNI and its character to the beneficiaries.

B. Entity Accounting Income
1. Is the amount that the beneficiary of a simple trust or estate is eligible to receive.
2. May be defined in the will or trust agreement, if not, state law prevails.
3. Allocates specific items of income and expenditures to the income beneficiaries or to corpus.

C. Gross Income
1. Is determined similar to that of individuals:
2. The basis of assets
   a. acquired from a decedent = FMV on date of death or alternate valuation date.
   b. acquired by gift = donor's basis
   c. acquired by purchase = cost
3. Income in respect of decedent is included in the gross income of an estate or trust.

D. Ordinary Deductions

1. Are determined similar to those of individuals, many are subject to the 2% of AGI floor.
2. Are allowed for reasonable administration expenses.
3. Are allowed for expenses in respect of a decedent.

E. Deductions for Losses
1. Casualty or theft losses not covered by insurance.
2. NOLs, where trade or business income is generated.
3. Net capital losses are used only on the fiduciary income tax return.

F. Charitable Contributions
1. Must be made pursuant to the will or trust agreement, and its amount must be determinable in the document.
2. Must be made to a qualified organization.
3. Generally, must be paid in the year claimed.

G. Deductions for Distributions to Beneficiaries
1. DNI approximates current economic income and
   a. is the maximum amount of the distribution on which the beneficiaries may be taxed.
   b. is the maximum amount that can be used by the entity as a distribution deduction for the year.
   c. its composition carries over to the beneficiaries.
2. DNI computation begins with the entity's taxable income before the distribution deduction, then:
   a. adds back the personal exemption,
   b. adds back net tax exempt interest,
   c. adds back net capital losses,
   d. subtracts any net capital gains allocable to corpus.

IV. TAXATION OF BENEFICIARIES

A. Distributions by Simple Trusts
1. DNI limits the amount taxable to the beneficiaries.
2. When there is more than one income beneficiary, the elements of DNI are apportioned ratably according to the amount required to be distributed.

B. Distributions by Estates and Complex Trusts
1. Two-tier system
   a. first tier distributions = income required to be distributed currently.
   b. second tier distributions = all other amounts properly paid, credited, or required to be distributed.
2. If first tier distributions exceed DNI, second tier distributions are not taxed.
3. If first tier distributions do not exceed DNI, second tier distributions are taxed to the extent of remaining DNI.

C. Character of Income
1. Distributions are treated as consisting of the same proportionate classes of income as the items that enter into the computation of DNI.
2. Special allocations are permitted to the extent required in the trust agreement and to the extent that the allocation has an economic effect independent of cash-flow and income tax consequences.

D. Losses in the Termination Year
1. An NOL incurred in the last year of the entity's existence is a deduction from AGI. It is passed through to the beneficiaries and deductible as a miscellaneous deduction, subject to the 2% of AGI floor.
2. Carryovers of other losses, NOLs and net capital losses flow through to the beneficiaries in the termination year and may be used as deductions for AGI.

V. GRANTOR TRUSTS

A. The creation of a reversionary trust is subject to the Federal gift tax. Also, if the grantor dies before the income interest expires, the present value of the reversionary interest will be included in his gross estate, and may be subject to the Federal estate tax.

B. Section 674 provides that the grantor will be treated as the owner of any portion of a trust and taxed on the income therefrom, if he or she retains
1. the beneficial enjoyment of the corpus and/or
2. power to dispose of the trust income without the approval or consent of any adverse party.

C. There are exceptions to the above rule which will not result in the income being taxed to the grantor. These include the power to:
1. Apply the income toward the support of the grantor's dependents.
2. Allocate trust income or corpus among charitable beneficiaries.
3. Invade corpus on behalf of a designated beneficiary.
4. Withhold income from a beneficiary during his or her minority or disability.
5. Allocate receipts and disbursements between income and corpus.

D. If certain administrative power are retained by the grantor or a non-adverse party, the income from the trust will be taxed to the grantor. These powers include:
1. the power to deal with the trust income or property for less than full and adequate consideration.
2. the power to borrow from the trust without adequate interest or security.
3. the power to revoke the trust.

E. A grantor is taxed on all or part of the income of a trust when, at the discretion of the grantor or a non-adverse party, without consent of any adverse party the income is or may be:
1. distributed to the grantor or the grantor's spouse.
2. accumulated for future distribution to the grantor or the grantor's spouse.
3. applied to premium payments on life insurance policies on the life of the grantor or the grantor's spouse.

INCOME TAXATION OF TRUSTS AND ESTATES 19-7

TEST FOR SELF-EVALUATION

True or False

T F 1. Les, as executor of the estate of his deceased father, must sell his father's house to make distributions to all beneficiaries. Les paid $9,000 to paint and carpet the house to enhance its marketability. The $9,000 Les paid is deductible from the gross estate to compute the taxable estate. (IRS 97 3A-4)

T F 2. The beneficiaries succeeding to the estate's property are NOT permitted to claim unused net operating loss carryovers from the estate's last tax year. (IRS 97 3C-6)

T F 3. A beneficiary of a complex trust must include in his taxable income the income that is required to be distributed only if the income is actually distributed during the tax year. (IRS 97 3C-11)

T F 4. If the estate has unused loss carryovers or excess deductions for its last tax year, they are allowed to those beneficiaries who succeed to the estate's property. (IRS 96 3A-18)

T F 5. A trust may be a simple trust for one year and a complex trust for another year. (IRS 96 3A-20)

Fill in the Blanks

1. A trust involves three parties: a _____, a _____, and a _____.

2. A _____ is the transferor of the property who is the creator of the trust.

3. Beneficiaries fall into two categories: those entitled to _____ from the trust and those entitled to the _____ upon the expiration of the _____ interest.

4. The fiduciary return is due not later than the fifteenth day of the _____ month following the close of the entity's taxable year.

5. _____ is the maximum amount that can be used by the entity as a distribution deduction for the year.

6. Income required to be distributed currently, whether distributed or not, is classified as a _____ distribution.

7. Undistributed net income is the _____ net income of the trust, reduced by _____ and _____ distributions, plus any _____ paid by the trust on the remaining undistributable net income.

8. The creation of a reversionary trust is subject to the Federal _____ tax.

9. When an income interest in a trust is based on a beneficiary's life, he is known as a _____.

Multiple Choice

_____ 1. Joan died on August 18, 1996. All of the following statements are correct except:
(IRS 97 3B-23)
   a. Joan's death does NOT close the tax year of the partnership in which she was a partner before it normally ends.
   b. Medical expenses paid by Joan before her death are deductible on her final income tax return if deductions are itemized.
   c. On Joan's final return, all income is reported on the accrual method of accounting regardless of the accounting method that Joan had employed.
   d. Any tax credits that applied to Joan before her death may be claimed on her final income tax return.

_____ 2. In which circumstance must an estate of a decedent make estimated tax payments?
(IRS 97 3B-24)
   a. The estate has a tax year ending 2 or more years after the date of the decedent's death.
   b. The estate has income in excess of $400.
   c. The estate has a first tax year that covers 12 months.
   d. None, since an estate is NOT required to make estimated tax payments.

_____ 3. Stuart died on May 15, 1996. After his death, his estate received interest of $500, dividends of $700, salary of $4,000 and life insurance proceeds of $35,000. How much should Stuart's estate include in income on its 1996 income tax return?
(IRS 97 3B-25)
   a. $40,200
   b. $36,200
   c. $5,200
   d. $1,200

_____ 4. With regard to a trust, all of the following statements are correct except:
(IRS 97 3B-30)
   a. A trust is a separate taxable entity.
   b. The income allocated to a beneficiary retains the same character in his hands as it had in the hands of the trust.
   c. If income is required to be distributed currently or is properly distributed to a beneficiary, the trust is regarded as a conduit with respect to that income.
   d. Generally, the trust is taxed on the income currently distributed and on the portion it has accumulated.

_____ 5. A trust which is required to distribute all of its income currently, does NOT make a distribution other than of current income and does NOT make charitable contributions is called a   (IRS 97 3B-31)

   a. Complex trust
   b. Simple trust
   c. Estate
   d. Totten trust

_____ 6. Which of the following is a characteristic of a "simple" trust?   (IRS 97 3B-32)

   a. A trust in the final year of administration.
   b. A trust which is partially liquidated during the taxable year.
   c. A trust which is allowed a personal exemption deduction of $300.
   d. A trust which distributes an amount out of corpus.

_____ 7. Dave, the grantor, set up two irrevocable trusts; Trust D and Trust G. The income of Trust D is to be accumulated for distribution to Dave's spouse after Dave's death. The income of Trust G is to be accumulated for Dave's children, whom Dave is legally obligated to support. The trustee has the discretion to use any part of the income for the children's support. Half of the income was so used in 1996. Based on this information, which of the following statements is correct?
                                                                 (IRS 97 3B-33)
   a. None of the income from either trust is taxed to Dave.
   b. No income from Trust D is taxed to Dave and half of the income from Trust G is taxed to Dave.
   c. All the income from Trust D and half the income from Trust G is taxed to Dave.
   d. All the income from both trusts is taxed to Dave.

_____ 8. Under terms of the will of Rick Waters, $6,000 a year is to be paid to his widow and $3,000 a year to his daughter out of the estate's income during the period of administration. There are no charitable contributions. For the year, the estate's distributable net income is only $6,000. How much must the widow and the daughter include in their gross income?   (IRS 97 3C-47)

	Widow	Daughter
a.	$6,000	$3,000
b.	$4,000	$2,000
c.	$3,000	$3,000
d.	$2,000	$1,000

____ 9. Trust C, a simple trust, has taxable interest of $8,000, tax-exempt interest of $12,000 and a short-term capital gain of $16,000. The trust instrument provides that capital gains are allocable to corpus. There are two equal beneficiaries. How much gross income does each beneficiary have from Trust C? (IRS 97 3C-51)

   a. $4,000
   b. $6,000
   c. $10,000
   d. $12,000

____ 10. Under the terms of the trust agreement, the income of Murphy Trust is required to be currently distributed to Kathy during her life. Capital gains are allocable to corpus, and all expenses are charged against corpus. During the taxable year, the trust had the following items of income and expense:

Dividends	$35,000
Taxable interest	25,000
Nontaxable interest	10,000
Long-term capital gains	15,000
Commissions and miscellaneous expenses allocable to corpus	7,000

The Murphy Trust's distributable net income is: (IRS 97 3C-52)

   a. $70,000
   b. $63,000
   c. $60,000
   d. $53,000

____ 11. Trust D, a complex trust, is required to distribute $20,000 to its beneficiary under the terms of the trust instrument. The trust's distributable net income is $40,000. The $20,000 is deemed to have been paid from the following items of income (all expenses have been allocated):

Rent	$ 2,000
Taxable interest	14,000
Dividends	16,000
Tax-exempt interest	8,000
Total	40,000

What is the trust's distribution deduction? (IRS 97 3C-53)

   a. $15,000
   b. $16,000
   c. $19,000
   d. $20,000

SOLUTIONS

True or False
1. F (p. 19-14)
2. F (p. 19-26)
3. F (p. 19-23)
4. T (p. 19-26)
5. T (p. 19-5)

Fill in the Blanks
1. grantor; trustee; beneficiary (p. 19-4)
2. grantor (p. 19-4)
3. income; principal; income (p. 19-4)
4. fourth (p. 19-7)
5. distributable net income (p. 19-18)
6. first-tier (p. 19-23)
7. distributable; first and second-tier; income tax (p.19-28)
8. gift (p. 19-30)
9. life tenant (p. 19-4)

Multiple Choice
1. c
2. a (p. 19-7)
3. c (500 + 700 + 4,000; the life insurance proceeds are not taxable)
4. d (the trust can claim a distribution deduction and would not be taxed on prior year accumulations)
5. b (p. 19-5)
6. c (p. 19-5, 8)
7. c (p. 19-28)
8. b (p. 19-22; apportioned ratably)
9. c (50%(8,000)taxable interest + 50%(12,000)tax-exempt interest)
10. b (p. 19-18; DNI is reduced by expenses allocated to corpus)
11. b (p. 19-19; tax-exempt interest is removed from DNI to calculate the deduction)